Awakening Power *in the* Yoga Sutra

Books in This Series

The Secret of the Yoga Sutra: Samadhi Pada
The Practice of the Yoga Sutra: Sadhana Pada
Awakening Power in the Yoga Sutra: Vibhuti Pada

Upcoming Books in This Series

The Promise of the Yoga Sutra: Kaivalya Pada

Also by Pandit Rajmani Tigunait, PhD

Sri Sukta: Tantra of Inner Prosperity
Vishoka Meditation: The Yoga of Inner Radiance
The Pursuit of Power and Freedom: Katha Upanishad
Touched by Fire: The Ongoing Journey of a Spiritual Seeker
Lighting the Flame of Compassion
Inner Quest: Yoga's Answers to Life's Questions
The Himalayan Masters: A Living Tradition
Why We Fight: Practices for Lasting Peace
At the Eleventh Hour: The Biography of Swami Rama
Swami Rama of the Himalayas: His Life and Mission
Tantra Unveiled: Seducing the Forces of Matter and Spirit
Shakti: The Power in Tantra (A Scholarly Approach)
From Death to Birth: Understanding Karma and Reincarnation
The Power of Mantra and the Mystery of Initiation
Shakti Sadhana: Steps to Samadhi
Seven Systems of Indian Philosophy

Awakening Power *in the* Yoga Sutra

VIBHUTI PADA

PANDIT RAJMANI TIGUNAIT, PhD

HIMALAYAN INSTITUTE®

HONESDALE, PENNSYLVANIA USA

Himalayan Institute, Honesdale, PA 18431
HimalayanInstitute.org

Printed in the United States of America

25 24 23 22 1 2 3 4 5

ISBN-13: 978-0-89389-282-1

Cover design by Meera Tigunait

∞ This paper meets the requirements of ANSI/NISO Z39-48-1992 (Permanence of Paper).

Contents

Preface

I'm grateful to the masters who walked into my life and instilled my heart with the conviction that the greatest reward comes from within and lasts forever.

From early childhood I was drawn to esoteric practices. The conducive environment my parents provided put me on the path without any effort on my part. But the masters knew that, like anyone else, I had weaknesses to overcome and my quest needed to be guided and nurtured by direct experience.

As a child, I was afraid of ghosts. When an adept gave me a potent mantra that dispelled my fear of ghosts, it strengthened my faith in the mystical power of mantra. My mother lost her eyesight a few years later, and the doctors told her nothing could be done. Another adept guided me to recite a set of mantras dedicated to the sun god; my mother's eyesight returned full force on the twelfth day of the recitation. This gave me a firsthand experience of the healing power that eludes medical science. During my college years, that same adept taught me an esoteric practice, *chhaya purusha*, a special method of concentrating on one's own shadow. This practice breathes life into the shadow, infusing it with the capacity to know the future or to foretell impending death. From this I gained a new understanding of death and rebirth.

Later I had the good fortune to sit at the feet of two adepts for three days and three nights in one of New Delhi's five-star hotels. They discussed *kundalini shakti,* the power of consciousness lying dormant in the human body; *prana shakti,* the pulsation of the life force; and how the combined forces of mind and prana shakti are directed to the fontanelle and beyond. These two adepts also discussed the method of casting off the body voluntarily, transporting the knowing power of the mind into a self-created locus, and descending into a new body without being born—a yogic feat known as *parakaya pravesha.* A short while later, one of the adepts cast off his body voluntarily and effortlessly.

Today, while narrating these stories, I find myself transported to those times and places. And I realize yet again how mysterious divine providence is—how subtly and perfectly it makes its plans and employs us to execute them. Divine providence gave me birth in a family where the study and practice of spirituality and mysticism were mandatory. It guided me to study at academic institutions in both India and the United States known for these subjects. It brought adepts into my life who normally live in the safety and comfort of solitude. It has planted me in the sheltered environment of the Himalayan Institute, where I do not need to teach and write as a means of earning my livelihood. And it is divine providence that inspired me to write a commentary on the third chapter of the *Yoga Sutra,* which is all about extraordinary, extrasensory powers.

This volume is a treasury of practices leading to myriad extraordinary experiences. Whether or not I have mastered any of these practices is irrelevant. What is relevant is that I have sat at the feet of masters who have demonstrated some of these practices and embodied the power they impart. I have studied the source texts and drawn on them to expound on the practices Patanjali documents here. Deep in my heart, I know this volume was guided and nourished by Sri Vidya, the presiding divinity of the Himalayan masters. Therefore, this work is dedicated to the masters who have preserved this knowledge and to those who through their own study and practice will learn from it and preserve it.

Introduction

Yoga is therapeutic and powerfully transformative. Yet it is not these aspects but the mystique surrounding *siddhis*—extraordinary yogic powers—that has been drawing spiritual seekers to yoga throughout the ages. This enduring mystique is the subject of "Vibhuti Pada," the third chapter of the *Yoga Sutra.*

Vibhuti means "extraordinary power or grandeur"; *pada* means "leg or pillar." The first fifteen sutras in this chapter lay the groundwork for mastering the fundamentals of yoga sadhana required to effectively study and practice what is presented in the rest of the text. The last forty sutras unlock the extraordinary power of nature hidden deep within different quarters of our mind and consciousness. Hence the title "Vibhuti Pada."

Magic and mysticism have captured our imagination throughout history. With the advent of modern science and technology, magical feats such as walking on water, fire breathing, and levitating have lost some of their allure. But clairvoyance, the power to disappear and rematerialize somewhere else, the ability to reverse aging and elude death, the ability to move at the speed of the mind, and the ability to destroy and reconstitute a physical object using only mental power remain as fascinating as ever. Some of us believe in such things because we wish to believe. Some of us believe because we have a hunch such things are possible, and we leave it at that. But a few of us go a step further—we wish to know the dynamic principles involved in the unfoldment of these extraordinary powers. This chapter explains these principles in full and delineates the steps for gaining access to a range of extraordinary abilities.

As we have seen in the two previous chapters, Patanjali and the commentator Vyasa never tire of reminding us of the limitless power of the human mind. But these masters have never conveyed this message as boldly as they do here: the mind is the biggest reservoir of powers and possibilities imaginable. The mind can see the source of the beginning at a glance, as well as where the end comes to an end. With no outside aid, the mind can see itself—how it came into being, how it operates, how it constructs and deconstructs its creations, how stubbornly it defends its turf from its own creator, and how effortlessly it drops its defenses and becomes reabsorbed in its primordial source.

"Vibhuti Pada" is a textbook for understanding this most mysterious of all forces—the human mind. It delineates the principles and practices we need to enter the deeper dimension of our mind and awaken the extraordinary powers lying dormant there. In short, this chapter is the doorway to siddhis, extraordinary yogic accomplishments. What has been taught in the first two chapters—"Samadhi Pada" and "Sadhana Pada"—lays the foundation for the study and practice of "Vibhuti Pada."

"Vibhuti Pada" opens with *dharana*, *dhyana,* and *samadhi*, the last three limbs of *ashtanga yoga* described in the previous chapter. In Patanjali's own words, "In relation to the preceding limbs, the triad of dharana, dhyana, and samadhi is an internal limb" (YS 3:7). With this statement, Patanjali makes it clear that the practice of the first five limbs (*yama, niyama, asana, pranayama,* and *pratyahara*), described in chapter 2, helps us organize and prepare our personal and interpersonal life so the mind can use all its resources to discover its infinitely vast and rich inner world. In the truest sense, yoga as an inner quest begins with the practice of dharana and concludes with samadhi. During this quest, the highly trained, perceptive mind of the yogi passes through numberless terrains of consciousness characterized by unique powers and privileges. "Vibhuti Pada" is both a comprehensive map of those varied terrains and a textbook of practices for awakening those powers and privileges.

The most important practice presented in "Vibhuti Pada" is one without which none of the other practices described here are possible. That practice, presented in sutra 3:34, is meditation on the lotus of the heart. This unique practice leads to the awakening of the knowing power of the mind. When this power is awakened, the mind is capable of knowing itself, the subtle mysteries of the phenomenal world, and the dimensions of the reality that transcends the phenomenal world. Until this power is awakened and the mind is guided by it, the techniques described in this chapter bear little or no fruit.

For this reason, in my commentary on sutra 3:34 I have elaborated on doctrinal intricacies to support the practice, divided the practice into steps, and referenced ancient texts where further elaborations of these steps can be found. The instructions I have provided here are not complete; they must be augmented by experienced teachers who are familiar with the ancillary practices integral to this unique system of meditation.

It is important to understand at the outset that the practice related to the lotus of the heart is the cardinal practice of yoga vidya. All advanced practices of yoga and tantra require the highly enlightened and empowered mind that this system of meditation grants to a practitioner. Further, the degree of accomplishment in the practice introduced in sutra 3:34 determines the degree to which the siddhis introduced in the rest of the chapter will awaken.

The technical term for a fully enlightened mind is *chitta samvit. Chitta* means "mind"; *samvit* means "the knowing power of the knower." *Chitta samvit* is the mind's knowing power—the mind's intrinsic ability to know itself, its relationship with its creator, and its relationship with the phenomenal world. Chitta samvit pervades and permeates all our mental faculties: the faculty of discernment, the faculty of thought, the faculty of self-identification, and the faculty imbued with the power to store experiences as memory. This completely independent knowing power trains our mental faculties and impels them to action. The mind's capacity to train and guide our sense organs, nervous system, and vital organs flows from this independent power. In yoga sadhana, as in any other endeavor, the mind's decision to undertake a practice and carry it through comes from and is sustained by chitta samvit.

The practice of meditation on the lotus of the heart described in sutra 3:34 takes us all the way to chitta samvit. Once we are receiving guidance and nourishment from chitta samvit, all practices—including those that sound impossible or highly esoteric—are within the range of our comprehension and accomplishment.

This powerful practice is a continuation of what is described in sutra 1:36 and augmented in sutras 2:49 through 2:54. The method described in those sutras leads to the awakening of the intrinsic capacity of one of our mental faculties—*buddhi*, the faculty of discernment. Buddhi is the decision-making faculty. It is imbued with clarity and has the capacity to pull us out of doubt and indecisiveness. Its self-knowing power is *buddhi samvit.* The awakening of buddhi samvit brings stability to our mind and illuminates the pathways leading to even deeper dimensions of chitta.

The awakening of buddhi samvit transforms us into *buddhi sattva* (in the Pali language, *bodhisattva*), and the awakening of chitta samvit transforms us into Buddha. Bodhisattva is a necessary step toward finding the Buddha within.

The meditation on the lotus of the heart described in sutra 1:36 gives us limited access to the vast powers and privileges of our mind, whereas the higher stage of the same practice, described here in sutra 3:34, gives us unlimited access to the universe of siddhis residing in our mind and in primordial nature. The formal term for the meditation described in sutra 1:36 is *vishoka* or *jyotishmati*. I have elaborated on this system of meditation in *Vishoka Meditation: The Yoga of Inner Radiance*. The meditation on the lotus of the heart described in sutra 3:34 builds on the system of meditation detailed in that volume. Vishoka meditation and meditation on the lotus of the heart are parts of a single system and should be regarded as the first and second stages of the same practice.

Upon perfecting the first stage, we gain the clarity, stability, and one-pointedness of mind needed to penetrate nature's treasure trove, where extraordinary powers of lesser importance are deposited. For an ordinary mind, even these lesser powers are quite startling. Gaining knowledge of the past and future, clairvoyance, immobilizing an object or person at will, disappearing and rematerializing somewhere else, moving through a solid wall, intuitively diagnosing an imperceptible disease, and communicating with disembodied celestial beings are some of the siddhis lying at the outskirts of yogic attainment. To casual seekers and spiritual enthusiasts, these siddhis are impressive. But to those familiar with yoga philosophy and aspiring to life's twofold purpose—lasting fulfillment and ultimate freedom—these siddhis are understood to be ordinary occurrences on the path.

The natural unfoldment of these so-called extraordinary powers is a sign of maturity in the first stage of meditation on the lotus of the heart. If we are not distracted by the allure of these siddhis, the body's pranic pathways present themselves as passageways to the lotus of the heart. It is here that the second stage of meditation on the lotus of the heart begins.

This crucial stage of meditation opens the door to siddhis par excellence. One of the most fascinating and highly coveted of these siddhis is *parakaya pravesha*, casting off the body consciously and entering a new body without being born. Nothing is more mystical and extraordinary than eluding death and reincarnating with or without the aid of parents. With the practice of parakaya pravesha (YS 3:38), Patanjali brings this most mystical and extraordinary feat into the realm of possibility—a possibility completely dependent on awakening chitta samvit, the knowing power of the mind. This is what provided the impetus for me to deviate from my standard style of commentary and to provide enough detail to inspire practitioners to prepare themselves to undertake the practice leading to this exalted state.

It is important not to be intimidated by the loftiness of the goal or the intricacies of the practice. The goal of the practice and the intricacies for reaching it may seem overwhelming today, but as soon as we take the first step, the way will open before us.

Long before the knowing power of our mind awakens fully, we will undergo numerous waves of inner awakening. Each of these waves will add to our inner purity, perfection, and empowerment. They will open our inner eye, enabling us to see that we are custodians of the treasure trove of providence. With this revelation, our quest becomes unstoppable.

Acquisition of extraordinary powers is not an option—it is the natural outcome of the practice. Succeeding waves of inner awakening will continue sharpening our faculty of discernment, leading us to know which extraordinary powers we should use and which we should conceal. The desire for extraordinary powers is in perfect compliance with the inherent call of the soul to experience the creator's limitless grandeur. Fulfillment of this desire will one day culminate in experiencing ourselves as our creator's grandeur. Put simply, acquiring siddhis means recognizing and reclaiming our innate capacities, using them purposefully, and offering them back to the one who gave them to us. This is the message of "Vibhuti Pada"—Patanjali's gift to all seekers.

VIBHUTI PADA

SUTRA 3:1

देशबन्धश्चित्तस्य धारणा ॥ १ ॥

deśabandhaścittasya dhāraṇā ॥ 1 ॥

deśa, field, place, domain, land; *bandhaḥ*, confinement, process of confining; *cittasya*, of the mind; *dhāraṇā*, concentration, holding

Confining the mind to an [assigned] field is *dharana*, concentration.

The title of this chapter, "Vibhuti Pada," establishes the context for the first sutra and all those that follow. *Vibhuti* means "grandeur." The practices described in this chapter (*pada*) aim at discovering the mind's limitless grandeur and acquiring the ability to access it.

The process of discovery and acquisition begins with the overarching practice of *dharana*. *Dharana* is derived from the verb root *dha* (more precisely, *ḍudhāñ*), which has two sets of meanings: "to hold, to wield, to contain, to retain, to nourish"; and "to heal, to rejuvenate, to sustain." Thus, *dharana* encapsulates the process of holding, anchoring, and containing the mind and its intrinsic attributes, as well as nourishing, healing, and sustaining them. Because it is used to define and describe the sixth limb of yoga, here *dharana* means yoga sadhana for accessing the limitless grandeur of our mind and using it to materialize life's twofold purpose: lasting fulfillment and ultimate freedom.

A cursory survey of the mind's grandeur and the vast scope of its domain will shed light on the role of dharana in yoga sadhana. As the mantras of Shiva Sankalpa Sukta tell us, the mind is the brightest and fastest of all lights in the universe. When we are awake, it travels far and wide—one-pointedly or in a scattered manner. It contacts the object of its experience joyfully or painfully. It may become entangled in a complex situation and fail to extricate itself. It may find itself totally disempowered yet retain the capacity to return to a sleeping state and be free from the pleasures and pains it embraced in the waking state. The mind has the capacity to operate in an orderly manner or to run recklessly. It has the capacity to get lost and return safely. It has the capacity to bind itself and free itself. This is the grandeur of the mind.

The mind is the ruler of the body and senses. It envisions its course of action and executes it. No aspect of creation is as powerful as the mind. For all intents and purposes, things begin to exist only after the mind envisions them. The mind is the creator of the phenomenal world. The perceived value of worldly objects is the mind's creation.

Without the mind, time and space are empty. The mind fills the void with its own content, then splits this content into numberless parts and arranges them at its pleasure. Thus, the mind is the father and mother of form. It assigns names to each form and transfers its reality to all the names and forms it creates, thereby making the names and forms as real as itself. The mind is also the repository of an infinite variety of distinct characteristics, which it uses to make every name and form distinct. The distinctive nature of each object gives rise to the concept of number. The mind has the capacity to remember the numberless contents that exist in time and space and can recall them both linearly and non-linearly. Thus, the mind is the locus of retentive power. This is the grandeur of the mind.

The mind is the light of inner awareness. It is the undecaying and undying elixir in all living beings. The body is able to function and the senses to perceive only in the presence of this immortal reality. It envelops the entire range of time—past, present, and future—and so has the capacity to selectively unearth contents buried in the past, pull them into the domain of the present, and arrange them in a manner that will create a desirable future. This remarkable retentive and discerning power makes the mind the creator of destiny. This is the grandeur of the mind.

Kama, passion for life, is the mind's defining attribute. The desire for pleasure and fulfillment, the drive for success and eminence, the will to live, and the trust in one's ability to conquer old age, disease, and death are a few manifestations of this defining attribute. Since the dawn of creation, the mind has been offering these attributes into the fire of consciousness. This is what makes creation vibrant, desirable, and full of courage, enthusiasm, and creativity.

In the case of our body, the mind is constantly offering these attributes into seven chakras, the centers of sacred fire. Thus, the seers address the mind as *sapta hota*, one who makes the sevenfold offering into seven fires. As long as the mind keeps the fire of consciousness fully nourished through these offerings, we are alive and fulfilled, but the slightest disruption in these offerings renders us weak and frail. The mind is both the source of ambition and the feeder of it. Our capacity to rule over an empire comes from and is fed by the mind's intrinsic passion to be the ruler of both our inner and outer worlds. This is the grandeur of the mind.

Just as all the spokes of a wheel are anchored to a hub, the entire range of knowledge—all forms of science, art, vocation, and creative expression—is anchored in the mind. The mind has the ability to intuit what previous generations knew, what the present generation knows, and what future generations will come to know. Interest in the unknown and the capacity to make it known are the mind's intrinsic attributes. It has the capacity to know itself as well as the minds of others. This is the grandeur of the mind.

Like a well-trained and experienced chariot driver with full command of his horses, the mind sets our course and guides us in reaching our destination. This ageless, swift, and powerful mind is seated in the depths of our heart. It is our inner guide, controller, enabler, and nurturer. The mind captures all-pervading pure consciousness and ties it to the stake of time and space, thus giving form to formless reality. By lending its power of self-identity, it gives form to ever-present consciousness. The mind also has the power to release consciousness from the stake of time and space. By using its self-revealing power, it can free consciousness from the cycle of birth and death. Being creator of both bondage and liberation is the grandeur of the mind.

Summarizing this grandeur, the legendary yogi Gorakhnatha says, "The mind is Shiva and the mind is Shakti. Anchoring itself in the body, the mind is Jiva, the living being. One who transcends the mind by using the mind penetrates the mystery of the three worlds."

This powerful and penetrating mind can become crippled by disease, inertia, doubt, and carelessness, however. At times, it becomes confused and delusional. It runs recklessly after sensory objects and fails to slow down and return to its pure and pristine state. It exhausts itself chasing ambition and often ends up with disappointment. In some cases, it realizes its ambition but fails to hold it for long. All these debilitating conditions cause pain, fuel negativity, shake the mind's belief in itself and in its relationship with the body and senses, and—worst of all—disrupt the harmonious functions of inhalation and exhalation. The longer these conditions last, the weaker the mind becomes. Its self-revealing and healing powers decline. A sense of hopelessness sets in. The mind becomes increasingly dependent on the material world. At this juncture, the law of mind over matter no longer applies. This is how the mind—the mighty ruler of our body and the circumstances surrounding it—becomes subservient to what it is designed to command. The guiding light of the objective world begins to seek guidance from what it is designed to guide. In this way, a seemingly unending chain of suffering is forged.

The mind's lack of trust in its ability to transcend suffering gives birth to fear. We become afraid of losing our dearest possessions—our body and mind. The desire not to lose them and our inability to prevent losing them makes us sad and angry. We begin questioning the abilities of our body and mind. We question whether divine providence exists, and if it does, whether it has any concern for us. This is how doubt is born. Fear, anger, sadness, and doubt lead to confusion. We become irrational. Our power of discernment plummets. These conditions further tarnish the pure and pristine mind. If this process is not checked promptly, the mind continues manufacturing such impurities.

To arrest this process, Patanjali prescribes *abhyasa* and *vairagya* (YS 1:12–22). Abhyasa is the ardent effort to retain the peaceful flow of mind, free of roaming tendencies. Vairagya involves voluntarily detaching the mind from its pleasant and unpleasant experiences. The practices of abhyasa and vairagya, laid out in the first chapter of the *Yoga Sutra*, are demanding and fully comprehensible only to a highly disciplined mind. In other words, these practices are for those who have already cultivated a one-pointed mind and have gained mastery over it. They are not for those whose minds are disturbed, distracted, and stupefied—mental states that are bound to be present as long as the mind is operating under the influences of its deep-rooted impurities.

To assist aspiring yogis in cultivating abhyasa and vairagya and reclaiming a pure and pristine mind, Patanjali prescribes a fourfold formula for ridding the mind of impurities: cultivating the attitudes of friendliness, compassion, happiness, and non-judgment toward people who are happy, miserable, virtuous, and non-virtuous, respectively (YS 1:33). Next, Patanjali introduces an advanced pranayama practice known as *pracchardana vidharana* (YS 1:34). This pranayama burns deeply buried layers of contaminants while infusing the mind with vitality, clarity, and one-pointedness.

Practicing the four attitudes protects the mind from forming new contaminants arising from animosity, cruelty, jealousy, and self-righteousness. Even though these practices are less demanding and somewhat easier to practice than abhyasa and vairagya, they still require a fairly sharp, determined mind and a robust body. Knowing that many practitioners lack these prerequisites, in the second chapter of the *Yoga Sutra* Patanjali introduces *ashtanga yoga*, the eight limbs of yoga (YS 2:29). Dharana, the subject of the current sutra, is the sixth of those limbs.

According to both Patanjali and Vyasa, the realization of the full grandeur of the mind and its relationship to absolute reality dawns in direct proportion to its degree of freedom from mental impurities. All forms and shades of mental impurity are ultimately rooted in and propelled by the fivefold affliction: *avidya*, ignorance; *asmita*, false sense of self-identity; *raga*, attachment; *dvesha*, aversion; and *abhinivesha*, fear of death (YS 2:3). These impurities block the mind's radiance and prevent the mind from knowing itself and its vast powers. Practicing the eight limbs of yoga systematically attenuates and eventually destroys both the impurities and the afflictions that feed and propel them.

As the attenuation and destruction of impurities progresses, the brilliance of the mind begins to radiate unobstructed. When this process reaches its climax, the mind is able to see itself, its powers and privileges, and its relationship with both the immutable ultimate reality and the ever-changing objective world. This state of realization is *viveka khyati*, unshakable discerning knowledge, which nullifies the misery resulting from the ignorance-driven comingling of pure consciousness and the world of cognitions and notions. Viveka khyati is the ultimate goal of ashtanga yoga.

Yama and niyama, the first two limbs of ashtanga yoga, are designed to bring a qualitative change in our thought, speech, and action. The practice of yama (non-violence, truthfulness, non-stealing, continence, and non-possessiveness) and the practice of niyama (purity, contentment, austerity, self-study, and trustful surrender) help us build an internal and external environment conducive to cultivating a clear and joyful mind. The third limb, *asana*, is for building a robust and energetic body and preparing it to assist the mind in reclaiming its clear radiance.

The fourth limb of ashtanga yoga, *pranayama*, is for providing vitality and nourishment to both the body and mind and, most importantly, helping the mind to rediscover its relationship with *prana*, the life force. The most remarkable function of pranayama is to help the mind cultivate the power of concentration and use that power to gain mastery over the senses, which otherwise throw the mind into a state of disturbance, stupefaction, and distraction.

The second chapter closes with *pratyahara*, the fifth limb of ashtanga yoga. Pratyahara is an extension of the practice of pranayama, with special emphasis on voluntarily disengaging the mind from pleasant and unpleasant experiences and their corresponding objects, and allowing it to rest in the body. Pratyahara collects all the mind's scattered forces and faculties and prepares it to focus fully on its exclusive domain—its limitless grandeur. According to Vyasa, the first five limbs of ashtanga yoga are the means for practicing the sixth limb, *dharana*, and the two limbs that follow—*dhyana* (meditation) and *samadhi* (perfect mental stillness).

Before examining the subtle dimensions of dharana and delineating its inner anatomy, it is useful to highlight two important points Vyasa makes in his commentary on sutra 3:1. He divides the eight limbs of ashtanga yoga into two major categories, external and internal, stating that the first five are external limbs and the last three—dharana, dhyana, and samadhi—are internal. He further states that the first five limbs serve as a means for reaching the internal limbs. What is the reason for these statements?

By definition, yoga is a system of practice that enables a practitioner to attain mastery over the roaming tendencies of the mind (YS 1:2) and restore the mind's intuitive power, which is so pure and laser-focused that the mind is able to see the seer without any distortion (YS 1:3). In the absence of this pure and focused intuitive power, the mind relies heavily on the senses. Preconceived notions, prejudices, habit patterns, and deeply rooted attachments and aversions force the senses to put their own spin on the information they gather; thus, they relay flawed information to the mind. The goal of practicing the first five limbs before venturing into dharana, dhyana, and samadhi is to cleanse our body, mind, and senses so the impurities stored in them do not derail our inner quest.

In sutras 2:41 and 2:43, Patanjali explains how eliminating impurities leads to *kaya siddhi*, bodily perfection; *indriya siddhi*, perfection of the senses; and *sankalpa siddhi*, perfection of will and determination. Earlier, in sutra 2:18, Vyasa and Patanjali describe how nature has deposited in our body and senses everything the mind needs to discover its intrinsic radiance. Nature has also deposited everything the mind needs to discover the essential nature of pure consciousness. The process of unveiling the mind's own hidden wealth and employing it to discover the essential nature of pure consciousness is the goal of the last three limbs of ashtanga yoga. However, the mind is able to embark on the path of dharana, dhyana, and samadhi only after it has attained a high degree of freedom from the impurities that hide the tools and means contained in our body and senses. Removal of these impurities and access to the tools residing in the body and senses come from practicing the five external limbs of ashtanga yoga.

When practiced with perfection and precision, these five limbs lead to kaya siddhi, bodily perfection. Bodily perfection is measured by the manifestation of natural beauty, charm, vitality, and self-healing power (YS 3:45–46). These qualities are *kaya sampat*, the body's intrinsic wealth. In the absence of impurities, the body's healing and nourishing powers awaken on their own. Vital organs function harmoniously. Sense organs are revitalized and their capacity to comprehend their corresponding objects is awakened. We become acutely aware of subtle changes in our body and their meaning. Thus, we have a natural and spontaneous instinct to refrain from eating, sleeping, and breathing in an unhealthy manner. The law of similar attracting similar is triggered, and we no longer have a taste for living an unhealthy life.

Perfection in this process automatically leads to indriya siddhi, perfection of the senses. Perfection of the senses is measured by the manifestation of three extraordinary powers: the ability to move at the speed of mind, the ability to comprehend without relying on the sense organs, and the ability to enter and explore primordial prakriti (YS 3:48). Bodily perfection and perfection of the senses prepare the foundation for sankalpa siddhi, perfection of will and determination. Sankalpa siddhi keeps our decisions and resolutions in the forefront of our mind. We maintain constant awareness of our goals and objectives. Perfection of will and determination enables us to employ all the tools and means available in our body, senses, and mind to discover that which in normal circumstances appears to be beyond the reach of the mind. That is why Vyasa considers the first five limbs of yoga to be the means for reaching the last three. And because we use the tools and means available both in the objective world and in our physical body to practice these five limbs, they are external. That is the focus of the second chapter. Here, in the first sutra of the third chapter, Patanjali introduces the practice of dharana, the first of the three internal limbs of yoga.

Dharana means "concentration." In this sutra, Patanjali describes the subtle anatomy of concentration—what to concentrate on, the process of concentration, and the experience arising from the process of concentrating. Relying on the literal meaning of this sutra, we understand that dharana, concentration, is the process of confining the mind to an assigned field. But a deeper analysis of *chitta* (*chittasya*) gives us a clue about what aspect of the mind is to be confined and where, and why that mental confinement leads to concentration.

The ordinary meaning of *chitta* is "mind." Among the several Sanskrit words for mind, the most prominent are *manas* and *chitta*. *Manas* refers to the faculty of thinking, brooding, perceiving, comprehending, and imagining. It is the part of the mind that is curious. It works in collaboration with our cortex, employing the senses to collect experiences from the objective world. It processes those sensory experiences with the active engagement of the cortex. The weaker and more sluggish or agitated the cortex, the more poorly it processes and perceives the content of sensory experiences. Similarly, the more disturbed, stupefied, distracted, and confused this thinking faculty of the mind, the more poorly it engages the cortex. Manas is operational when we are awake. In modern psychology, this particular faculty of the mind is known as the conscious mind. Yogis call it *antahkarana*, the internal instrument for cognition.

As long as we are awake, this aspect of the mind manufactures cognitions and goes on attributing its own notions of good and bad, right and wrong, positive and negative, constructive and destructive to these cognitions. This so-called conscious mind is constantly engaged in either revisiting its self-created cognitions or creating new ones. This process is exhausting for the mind as well as for the body, brain, and senses. But the mind does not know how to slow itself down, let alone how to stop manufacturing the train of cognitions, because it has fallen into the habit of constantly attending one thought after another.

As long as we are awake, the senses of seeing, tasting, touching, smelling, and hearing continually present the experiences of the objective world to the mind, and the mind continually analyzes and associates itself with them. When exhausted, it helplessly falls asleep. When it fails to detach itself from those sensory experiences even during sleep, dreams ensue. The less disciplined the mind and the more strongly entangled it is with sensory experiences during the waking state, the more complex and tiring the dreams. Such a mind is the victim of sensory onslaught and is incapable of guiding, protecting, and nourishing the body.

The five external limbs of yoga are designed to calm and control the behavior of this so-called conscious aspect of the mind, whereas the first of the internal limbs—dharana—tackles the behavior of a deeper aspect of the mind and the highly potent and extremely subtle afflicting contents stored there. This deeper aspect of the mind is known as *chitta*, the term Patanjali employs in this sutra.

Chitta is derived from the verb root *chiti*, meaning "to comprehend completely, to become aware of the total range of the objects of experience." Chitta refers to the totality of the mind, particularly the aspect of the mind that serves as the locus for the entire range of our past experiences. It is the repository of the subtle impressions of all actions—physical, mental, or verbal—we have ever performed. It is the locus of memory. It is the seat of our subtlest and most potent afflictions—ignorance, distorted sense of self-identity, attachment, aversion, and fear of death. It is also the seat of the revealing and liberating knowledge and experiences that nullify those afflictions. This is the seat of our soul and its eternal companion, the divine being. By using the term *chitta* here in this sutra, Patanjali is conveying a message: we concentrate our own essence—our soul and the divine in us—by confining the deepest and all-pervading aspect of the mind to an assigned space.

It is important for the practitioner to understand that Patanjali is not describing how to practice dharana, but simply defining it. He introduced the process of practicing concentration in the previous chapter in the context of pranayama, more precisely *chaturtha pranayama* (YS 2:51). There we saw how pranayama engenders a highly captivating energy field, which pulls the mind toward itself like a magnet. This gives the thinking mind a taste of how it feels to be quiet and anchored within.

By entering this highly charged pranic field and resting there, the mind begins to soak in the revitalizing and illuminating properties of prana shakti. This revitalizing effect gives the thinking mind the strength to withstand sensory storms; this illuminating effect infuses it with discerning power. With the help of this discerning power, the mind is able to decide how to engage itself with sensory experiences wisely, when to withdraw from the pleasant and unpleasant experiences, and when to turn inward to rest and rejuvenate. Even though technically this process and the experience emerging from it fall in the domain of pranayama, this is where the practice of dharana begins. This subject is detailed in sutras 2:51 through 2:54.

When the mind is united with prana for the duration of 12 breaths (approximately 48 seconds), such a state of practice constitutes pranayama. When mind and prana remain united for the duration of 144 breaths (approximately 9.6 minutes) such a state of practice constitutes pratyahara. By the virtue of this long union with prana, the thinking mind is freed from all disturbances and intrusive thoughts and is strong enough to deflect sensory pressures and demands, as well as clear enough to see the deeper causes of disturbance arising from chitta, the vast mental field within. At this stage, Patanjali prescribes focusing the combined forces of prana and mind on specific spots in the body, either to overcome a particular obstacle or to realize an aspect of the extraordinary grandeur of the mind; he defines this practice as dharana.

Pranayama introduces the twin forces of mind and prana to each other. With pranayama practice, the mind enhances its sensitivity to pranic movement, and prana enhances the mind's sensitivity to the flow of intelligence. As the practice becomes more refined, especially with chaturtha pranayama, mind and prana merge. This merger fills the mind with confidence that it can attend the objects of its thoughts voluntarily and masterfully and can also disconnect itself from those objects at will. As this confidence matures, the mind's willpower and determination manifest and can then be reinvested in a prolonged union with prana. This prolonged union is pratyahara, the ability to withdraw the mind from the objective world, rest it in the body, and rejuvenate it with the healing and nourishing power of prana.

In the practice of dharana, this fully rested, healed, rejuvenated, and illumined mind is employed to concentrate itself in a well-defined space. The selection of the space is based on the objective of practicing dharana. For example, if the purpose of practicing dharana is to sharpen the mind precisely for learning the subtle anatomy of the pranic body, we are told to concentrate the mind at the navel center, the gateway to the inner body. The navel center is also the source of enthusiasm, courage, self-confidence, and indomitable will. Furthermore, the space at the navel center is naturally infused with the highly concentrated fire called *vaishvanara agni*. This type of fire is responsible for all forms of change occurring in the body.

If, on the other hand, we are interested in discovering the dynamics of the fivefold affliction (YS 2:3–15) and are determined to annihilate the karmic impressions stored in our chitta, we are guided to concentrate at the heart center. Similarly, concentration at the crown center, the light above the crown center, the opening of the nostrils, and the tip of the tongue all lead to different results.

The purpose of practicing dharana on these and other precise fields inside or outside the body is not to develop mental concentration nor is it to overcome disturbed, distracted, or agitated states of mind. Nor is the practice of dharana described in this sutra, and elaborated on with precision and prerequisites in the upcoming sutras, for cultivating a clear, calm, and one-pointed mind.

Patanjali assumes we have completed the practice of the first five limbs of yoga as described in the previous chapters. As a result, we have adopted a healthy lifestyle and have assimilated the spiritual values of the yamas and niyamas in our daily life. We have freed our body of toxins with the practice of asana. By practicing pranayama we have cultivated a fully alert and energized nervous system, which is so harmonious that sensory interaction with the objective world does not affect the natural rhythm and functions of our vital organs. Through the practice of pratyahara we have gained the ability to engage our mind with the objects of the senses voluntarily and withdraw it at will. The practice of these five external limbs of yoga has granted us a clear, calm, one-pointed mind with the ability to turn inward with little effort. Furthermore, the mind has learned the art of uniting itself with the breath and receiving nourishment from this union. Thus, we have acquired a highly nourished, energetic, perceptive, and stable mind.

Now, in the practice of dharana, we employ our one-pointed, well-trained, highly motivated, and penetrating mind to concentrate itself on a precisely defined space infused with the power unique to that space. With consistent repetition of the practice of dharana, the mind has the opportunity to soak in the power unique to the space where it is concentrating. Eventually, this process matures into a state where the mind and the unique power of the space become one. The mind begins to experience that power from inside the space rather than viewing the space from outside. The power intrinsic to that space becomes the mind's own power. This is how the mind realizes its limitless grandeur.

In practice, however, there is a gap between the external limbs of yoga and the internal limbs. If we are to practice the internal limbs of yoga successfully, we must close that gap. We do this in two steps.

The first step involves intensifying the practice of chaturtha pranayama as described in sutras 2:51 through 2:53. The stand-alone practice of chaturtha pranayama gives the mind an opportunity to discover its relationship with the breath and gain a firsthand experience of the tranquility and joy emitted by the union of the mind and breath. Chaturtha pranayama also gives the mind a taste of the psychoenergetic experience unique to four specific spots: the opening of the nostrils, the inner corners of the eyes, the center between the eyebrows, and the center of the forehead. This helps the mind conclude that there may well be other spots in the body as energetically sensitive as these particular spots.

We intensify the practice of chaturtha pranayama and the experience resulting from it by applying two specific practices—*aharana pranayama* and *samikarana pranayama*. Aharana pranayama helps the mind comprehend the existence of a deeper and more subtle dimension of our body. This practice involves withdrawing the mind from its train of thoughts and guiding it systematically from one spot in the body to another. The second practice, samikarana pranayama, restores the harmonious balance of the functions of the body, mind, brain, nervous system, and vital organs. It involves selecting ten spots in the body—the perineum, pelvic center, navel center, bottom of the sternum, heart center, throat center, the nostrils, eyebrow center, center of the forehead, and the crown center—and allowing the united forces of breath and mind to sweep through these spots, from the crown center to the perineum and back again.

The second step in closing the gap between the external and internal limbs of yoga is practicing *prana dharana*, which is the key to mastering any of the practices presented in this chapter. Prana dharana takes the practice of chaturtha pranayama and the experience it engenders to a point that marks the beginning of the practice of dharana as defined by Patanjali in this sutra.

Prana dharana has seven steps. The first is *prana anusandhana*, a process of isolating pranic movement from the physiological movement of the breath. Here we learn the art of distinguishing the force that makes us breathe from the breath itself. The second step is *prana samvedana*, cultivating sensitivity to the subtle pranic current and allowing the mind to follow it. The third step is *prana jagarana*, awakening or lighting prana, thereby shaking off inertia. The fourth step is *prana manthana*, churning prana to isolate it from karmic clutter. The fifth step is *prana sanchaya*, gathering and storing pranic elixir. The sixth step is *prana prasara*, expanding the domain of prana. The seventh and final step of prana dharana is *prana samyama*, restraining prana in a well-defined space.

Prana dharana, especially the last three steps—prana sanchaya, prana prasara, and prana samyama—condenses the pranic force in the region corresponding to the center of the forehead so intensely that the space of awareness in that region begins to glow. With sustained practice of prana dharana, this self-illumined space of awareness acquires its own self-identity. *Yoga Sutra* 1:36 calls this luminous space *jyotishmati*. Because this luminous space is free from all forms of *shoka*—suffering arising from fear, doubt, anger, grief, and regret—sutra 1:36 also calls it *vishoka*, that which is devoid of shoka. The longer the mind stays in this state of jyotishmati and vishoka, the more it is transformed. This transformation emerges from an internal process called *samapatti*, complete mental absorption (YS 1:41). At this stage, the mind has fully absorbed the intrinsic qualities of prana and is energetic, fresh, enthused, and charged with the energy to breathe life into anything it wishes. Most importantly, it has acquired a self-identity identical to prana shakti in every regard. The mind is now capable of reaching, illuminating, and rejuvenating any point within the range of pranic pulsation. Acquisition of this kind of mind fills the gap between pratyahara and dharana.

The dharana presented here in this first sutra entails holding the mind in a defined field and nurturing it with the shakti unique to that field. This is traditionally understood to be the field physiologically corresponding to the region of the forehead. In yogic literature this field is called the *ajna chakra*, the command center. This space in the forehead is the seat of the mental faculty that works in collaboration with the senses and cortical brain. It is the center of our thoughts and cognitive activities. When this center is lit, nourished, protected, and guided by prana—the life-giving stream of consciousness—the mind is crystal clear and fully centered. When this center is poorly lit by pranic effulgence, the mind is subject to disturbing, distracting, and confusing thoughts. It roams aimlessly. Its decisions are faulty.

The experience of chaturtha pranayama, further intensified by prana dharana, lights up the ajna chakra. Holding the mind in this field for more than 9.6 minutes is dharana. Because in this particular practice of dharana the mind has no object other than itself, this dharana is technically known as *chitta dharana*, the concentration of the mind on the mind itself. Chitta dharana leads the mind to discover itself in its fullness and infuses it with the capacity to reign over itself. Because of its absolute union with prana, the mind is able to pierce the object on which it is focusing and gain access to its inherent properties.

Chitta dharana is a logical and natural outgrowth of pratyahara, which is engendered and fed by the protracted union of prana and mind at the ajna chakra. There is a clear sign that distinguishes dharana from pratyahara. In pratyahara, the mind is brought back to its home base, the ajna chakra, and is in the process of settling there. It is still riding the wave of pranic pulsation and is cognizant of moving up and down in the space of awareness corresponding to the region of the forehead. As it drops the effort involved in riding the pranic wave, the process of becoming still accelerates. This stillness allows the mind to become effortlessly absorbed in the prana shakti filling that space. The mind begins to experience itself as a pranically lit space. It begins to witness that space as a ball of light. Initially, this ball of light may not be particularly discrete. It may fade and reappear, but eventually it becomes stable. *Svacchanda Tantra* 1:38 describes this light as being as golden and round as the kadamba flower (*Neolamarckia cadamba*). Complete absorption in this ball of light is chitta dharana.

Chitta dharana is preceded by the practice of pratyahara, which is itself preceded by pranayama, particularly chaturtha pranayama. And the practices leading to chitta dharana are intensified and enlivened by the practice of prana dharana. The tradition insists that we first employ this highly stable, energized, and penetrating mind to pierce the ball of light at the center of the forehead before we venture to undertake practices designed to unleash *vibhutis*, extraordinary powers. The scriptures call piercing that light *bindu bhedana*.

There are several methods of bindu bhedana. Some are propelled by the power of mantras, others by the power of alchemy. In the context of the *Yoga Sutra*, bindu bhedana is propelled by *pranava*, the sacred sound *om*—a process technically known as *pranava anusandhana*. In this practice, the mind is employed to hear the unique sound *om* reverberating from each and every cell of the body, and to experience its pulsation moving up and down with the inhalation and exhalation. Finally, the mind is instructed to feel the pranic pulsation between the opening of the nostrils and the center of the forehead. In the last phase of the practice, the ball of light spontaneously rises and fills the space in the region of the forehead. At this juncture, the mind is led to release all effort and allow prana to further condense itself and make the space brighter. Eventually, the mind loses the cognitions of time, space, size, and form, transcends the physicality of the body, and is fully immersed in the space of consciousness unconfined by the linearity of time.

According to *Yoga Sutra* 3:54, this experience contains *taraka*, liberating knowledge. This knowledge is a locus for the entire range of objective cognitions and yet is itself not an object of cognition. In other words, bindu bhedana allows a yogi to transcend the mind with the help of the mind. The mind charged with this extraordinary ability can be employed to explore the vast range of siddhis described here in this third chapter of the *Yoga Sutra*.

Bindu bhedana gives the mind complete access to the forces unique to the ajna chakra. It gives the mind mastery over its roaming tendencies. The mind is no longer subject to disturbing, distracting, and confusing thoughts. It is free from sloth, inertia, and doubt. Bindu bhedana gives the mind a firsthand taste of its pure essence. The mind realizes how it feels to be here and now. This experience fills the mind with the enduring motivation to explore and reclaim its domain all the way to the furthest frontier. In the truest sense, the journey toward lasting fulfillment and ultimate freedom begins here and ends here. In the absence of a firsthand taste of the mind's pure essence, our inner quest is normally propelled by our desire to overcome sorrow or by mere curiosity. But once we have had this firsthand taste, our quest is propelled by the thrill of experiencing our unlimited grandeur. Gaining this taste and being filled with the thrill of experiencing the vast scope of our unlimited grandeur is the outcome of practicing dharana, particularly the chitta dharana of this sutra.

The greatest among all forms and shades of grandeur is the mind's ability to know itself and its relationship with the phenomenal world and with the higher reality that creates the phenomenal world, and most importantly, to transcend all of its self-created limitations. The mind reclaims its grandeur as soon as it becomes established in the state of dharana. This highly stable and penetrating mind can then dissect the domain of time and enter *kshana*, the distinct unit of time bridging past and present or present and future. The mind's capacity to identify and enter that distinct unit of time comes from chitta dharana. It is this capacity that allows the mind to gain the extraordinary knowledge of past and future as described in sutra 3:16. Similarly, by undertaking the practice described in sutra 3:18, such a highly stable and penetrating mind can have direct realization of the subtle impressions of the past and thus can have a clear understanding of previous lives. These and many other practices mentioned in this chapter are possible only for a mind that has perfected chitta dharana.

If dharana holds the key to this vast capacity, what then is the role of the two remaining limbs of yoga, dhyana and samadhi? To answer this question, Patanjali introduces the next sutra.

SUTRA 3:2

तत्र प्रत्ययैकतानता ध्यानम् ॥२॥

tatra pratyayaikatānatā dhyānam ॥ 2 ॥

tatra, there; *pratyayaika-tānatā*, the continuous flow of a single cognition; *dhyānam*, meditation

There the continuous flow of a single cognition is *dhyana*, meditation.

D*hyana*, meditation, is an advanced stage of *dharana*, concentration. Dhyana emerges when the mind attends the object of concentration for a prolonged period with little or no effort and—this is the key—without attending any other thought. Furthermore, dhyana occurs in the same field designated for dharana. Thus, in its advanced stage, dharana itself is dhyana and, by implication, refers to a more profound and more transforming experience than what is normally defined as dharana.

According to Vyasa, dhyana is distinguished from dharana by the state of concentration in which the mind is one-pointedly engaged in attending the flow of cognitions of a single object. These cognitions are nearly identical and so seem like one long cognition, but they are actually a stream of cognitions. In dhyana, the mind is constantly aware of one cognition—the pranic pulsation in the pranically charged space in the region of the forehead. It is so one-pointedly involved in witnessing the pranic pulsation that it pays no attention to the details of pulsation—where the pulsation begins, where it ends, the size of the pranically lit space in the forehead, what distinguishes that space from the space outside its boundaries, and so on. The awareness of each detail constitutes a totally independent cognition. In dhyana, none of these details come to the forefront of the mind. Thus, neither the mind nor its central cognition is touched by any other cognition.

In dharana, the mind is still somewhat diffused. In an absolute sense, its union with pranic pulsation is not perfect. Even though the mind is constantly engaged in observing the pranic pulsation in the uniquely lit ball of light, its attention is divided among observing the beginning and ending points of the pulsation, the pranically lit space itself, and the presence of the space parallel to the face and the forehead. In dhyana, the mind is withdrawn from all these details and their cognitions and is aware only of the pranic pulsation. The flow of a single cognition pertaining to the pranic pulsation is so uninterrupted that the mind is not aware of anything other than the cognition pertaining to pranic pulsation. This is dhyana.

The secret of transitioning from dharana to dhyana lies in attending the practice of dharana without making an effort. As soon as we make an effort to go deeper into the practice of dharana, we become aware of the effort. That awareness is itself a cognition, one which poses an obstruction to entering the deeper state of meditation.

A meditative state emerges when, due to its intrinsic force, the object of cognition pulls the mind toward itself. The mind is effortlessly drawn to the locus of cognition, and this pull is so strong and so absorbing that the mind is oblivious of everything else. Because focusing the mind on the pranic pulsation in the well-defined space corresponding to the region of the forehead is the essence of dharana, the intensity of pranic pulsation is the determining factor in reaching the state of dhyana. The stronger the pranic pulsation and the more well-formed and intense its pranic field, the more strongly and effortlessly the mind will be drawn to it. Therefore, yogis place greater emphasis on refining the practice of dharana than on reaching the state of dhyana.

There are several practices to intensify and condense the pranic field, thereby accelerating mental absorption in the pranic pulsation. Chief among such practices described by Patanjali is *pracchardana vidharana* pranayama. It is divided into two parts: *pracchardana* and *vidharana*. Pracchardana is characterized by rapid and forceful inhalation and exhalation through both nostrils. Vidharana consists of breath retention right after the last exhalation of pracchardana. Both parts of this pranayama are detailed in the commentary on sutra 1:34 in *The Secret of the Yoga Sutra: Samadhi Pada*.

Pracchardana vidharana intensifies the pranic field and accelerates mental absorption due to its direct impact on the *talu chakra*. In yogic literature, the talu chakra is subsumed in the ajna chakra. However, in the tantric tradition, particularly the Trika and Sri Vidya traditions of tantra, the talu chakra is highly significant in its own right. Physiologically, it is located in the general area of the soft palate. However, it is important to understand that all chakras are located in the energetic correlate of a physical spot in the body. Therefore, the talu chakra is more precisely associated with the pranic field that serves as a cushion for the portion of the brain that sits right above the region of the soft palate.

The forceful and rapid inhalations and exhalations that characterize pracchardana vidharana are pushed through the region of the soft palate before the air enters the trachea during inhalation, and pushed into the soft palate during exhalation before the air is expelled through the nostrils. Each time we inhale and exhale in this manner, we stimulate, and in advanced stages churn, the prana shakti unique to the talu chakra. With sustained practice, we can cultivate the capacity to inhale and exhale comfortably 100 times a minute. Only then—at the end of the last exhalation, while keeping the mind fully engaged in this highly energized space of the talu chakra—do we apply breath retention. This practice simultaneously energizes and intensifies the shakti unique to the inner corners of the eyes, the center between the eyebrows, and the center of the forehead.

Pracchardana vidharana is not integral to the practice of dharana and dhyana. However, it is a perfect practice for intensifying the pranic field of the ajna chakra and all the "minor" chakras in its orbit. It is particularly suited for those who have an established practice of hatha yoga and are reasonably well grounded in their body and nervous system. A similar effect is induced by specific mantras or by the application of alchemy, both of which are highly specialized. All of these practices are significant in refining the practice of dharana, which, in its advanced stages, evolves into dhyana. When the state of meditation emerges, we find ourselves pulled into it. Just as it was difficult to withdraw our mental faculties from the objective world in the earlier stages of dharana, now, in the deeper states of dhyana, our mind is so well centered that it is difficult for the mind to reassociate itself with the external world.

As we have seen, dharana is marked by the manifestation of a uniquely lit ball of light in the center of the forehead. Dhyana is marked by the experience of the mind's deep absorption in the pranic pulsation effortlessly rising and subsiding in this ball of light. The ball of light itself is so vivid to the eye of the mind that its physical counterparts, such as the head, forehead, and face, are no longer in the mind's view. Furthermore, the mind is so well absorbed in the pranic pulsation that it does not see any difference between itself and the pranic pulsation. All have merged. All mental imagery has vanished. Experientially, cognition pertaining to the existence of our body is replaced by cognition of pranic pulsation.

During inhalation, the mind follows the almost-motionless upward movement, and during exhalation, it follows the almost-motionless downward movement. The experiences of upward and downward movement in this pranically lit field are cognitions. These cognitions, which are absolutely uninterrupted by other cognitions, are so alike that it is as if they are one long cognition, but they are actually a stream of cognitions. Both Patanjali and Vyasa call this profound experience dhyana.

In the state of dhyana, cognitions pertaining to the details of the object of cognition have faded, but the mind is still aware of itself as the meditator. It is also aware of the object of meditation and the process of meditation. The streams of these three unique cognitions are flowing incessantly. Sometimes they are totally intermingled and appear to be a single cognition, but a tiny sliver of memory—"I am meditating and am experiencing this peaceful flow of cognition"—pulls these three intermingled cognitions apart. Immediately, we become aware of ourselves as the meditator, the object of meditation, and the process of meditation. Absorption in the object of dharana—without any interruption caused by cognitions pertaining to the object of dharana—while retaining the awareness of ourselves as the meditator and the process of meditation is dhyana, meditation.

Only when even this threefold awareness comes to an end, and the mind begins to melt into the uninterrupted flow of cognitions pertaining to the single object of dharana, do we transition from dhyana to samadhi. This transition is propelled primarily by grace rather than by our effort. When we have invested ourselves in the practice of pranayama, more precisely chaturtha pranayama, and in the practice of pratyahara, dharana, and dhyana, the domain of self-effort comes to an end. Now the fruits of our practice fall into our lap. The only practice needed at this stage is to allow the deeper state of meditation to rise and not to stand in its way.

How this state arises—how the mind transcends the triple cognitions of ourselves as the meditator, the process of meditation, and the object of meditation—is the subject of the next sutra.

SUTRA 3:3

तदेवार्थमात्रनिर्भासं स्वरूपशून्यमिव समाधिः ॥३॥

tadevārthamātranirbhāsaṁ svarūpaśūnyamiva samādhiḥ ॥ 3 ॥

tat, that; *eva*, only; *artha-mātra-nirbhāsaṁ*, expressive of just its meaning; *svarūpa*, defining feature; *śūnyam*, devoid; *iva*, as if; *samādhiḥ*, completely established state of mind

When that [object of dharana and dhyana] seems to have lost its defining features and is expressive only of its meaning, it is *samadhi*.

As we have seen, dhyana rises out of dharana when the mind is so fully absorbed in the experience pertaining to the central point of concentration (in this case, pranic pulsation) that it is completely disengaged from observing the details of the object. This marks the evolution of dharana into dhyana. In the state of dhyana, we are still aware of ourselves as the meditator, the object of meditation, and the process of meditating on that object. Experientially, we are cognizant of these three streams of awareness, so our focus is divided. The secret to restoring an undivided mind, the ground for samadhi, is practicing dharana and dhyana consistently and sincerely for an extended time.

As we continue our practice, the mind becomes increasingly

still. The more the mind basks in the luminosity of the pranic field, the more it is drenched in the intrinsic joy of that luminosity. It is spontaneously and effortlessly drawn to the center of this self-luminous pranic field—the central pranic pulsation. The more deeply the mind is pulled into the pranic pulsation, the weaker is its awareness regarding the process of meditation and itself as the meditator. Eventually, there comes a time when the mind is no longer aware of the process of meditation and itself as the meditator—the object of meditation alone is in the full view of the mind. No other cognition stands between the mind and the object of meditation. This is samadhi.

As this state matures, the mind transcends even the cognition pertaining to the details of the object. The mind is aware only of the sheer presence of the object. Not only has the mind transcended all awareness pertaining to the size and shape of the object, but the qualifying factors of time and space—past, present, future, here, there, somewhere, and so on—have also vanished. The mind has also transcended the awareness of its own existence. Experientially speaking, the mind no longer exists. Vyasa defines this state as *chitta vimukti*, freedom from mind (YS 2:27). The mind is dissolved in the self-luminous pranic field. The central pulsation of prana has become the mind's locus. The mind sees itself as pure pulsation through the eye of pulsation itself. The purity of the mind in the state of samadhi is identical to the purity of the self-luminous prana shakti and its primordial source, Ishvara.

In other words, the mind is no longer the mind that set out on this yogic quest, but has once again become the mind that began as an outward flow of divine will. This is the mind the highest reality uses to measure its boundless grandeur. In this state, there is no trace of the fivefold affliction: ignorance, false sense of self-identity, attachment, aversion, and fear of death. With the disappearance of these afflictions, the mind's wandering tendencies have also vanished. The mind is free to see reality as it is and free to abide in its essential nature.

For a logical mind residing outside this experience, samadhi and the mind engrossed in samadhi seem devoid of all defining features. However, by using the word *iva* (as if), Patanjali is warning students not to be fooled by the lack of defining features. In samadhi, what has disappeared are the mental attributes, qualities, characteristics, cognitions, and thought processes that block the intuitive capacity of the mind to see and experience reality as it is. What has disappeared is the mind's conviction in the validity of the objective world and the sensory experiences associated with it. What has disappeared is the mind's unwillingness to consider the validity of the reality beyond the sensory domain. Most importantly, what has disappeared is the mind's fear of letting itself become an integral part of the reality that it once vested with the power to discover its own grandeur. The loss of these limitations is the mind's achievement in the state of samadhi. With the loss of these limitations, the mind has become *artha matra nirbhasam*, capable of expressing the pure content and intent of the reality in which it is absorbed.

The literal meaning of *artha matra nirbhasam* is "that which illuminates, reveals, or reflects the sheer meaning of the object of concentration and meditation." Here the object of meditation is the uniquely lit pranic field and the pranic pulsation that continuously arises and subsides in it. According to this sutra, the state of samadhi illuminates or reveals the meaning of this luminous field and the pranic pulsation continuously arising and subsiding in it. Had this phrase been used in casual conversation, we would assume that in the state of samadhi we would spontaneously comprehend the meaning of the words "luminosity" and "pranic pulsation." But because here this phrase is precisely employed to describe the dynamics of samadhi, the words "luminosity" and "pranic pulsation" warrant careful examination.

As described in my commentary on the two previous chapters (specifically, YS 1:13, 1:24, 1:31, 1:34 and 2:49, 2:51–52), prana is ever-pulsating divine will. It is as omniscient, omnipresent, and omnipotent as Ishvara, the primordial divine being. It is beginningless, middleless, and endless. The outward flow of pranic pulsation is in response to the intention of the divine being to breathe life into matter so that it becomes a living being. A discrete body of matter becomes animate as soon as it comes in touch with prana. In other words, prana is the life force and is not dependent on matter for its existence.

In the state of samadhi, the mind is so pure and still and so completely absorbed in the luminosity of the pranic field that it does not feel itself as different from that luminosity. In this state of mental absorption, it is as cognizant of the intrinsic attributes of the pranic luminosity as prana is. It is as close to Ishvara as prana is. It is as identical to Ishvara as prana. It is as cognizant of Ishvara's intention as prana. Complete understanding of the place and role of Ishvara and her intention for our life is the meaning saturating the mind in the state of samadhi. The spontaneous joy that arises from being drenched in this meaning is described as *vishoka*, absolute sorrowless joy (YS 1:36).

It is important to acknowledge that the emergence of samadhi is not static. It is not an event. It is a process of dhyana moving toward samadhi, touching it, and returning to a state of dhyana and sometimes to dharana, and then moving again toward samadhi. During each such wave in this process, the mind becomes clearer and calmer. Spiritually speaking, it becomes sharper and, after each backward slide, has the ability to move forward more quickly. Eventually, the mind is able—in less time and with less effort—to become so absorbed in the self-luminous pranic field that it passes the threshold of dhyana and spontaneously begins to experience samadhi. To describe this process, Patanjali introduces the next sutra.

SUTRA 3:4

त्रयमेकत्र संयमः ॥४॥

trayamekatra saṁyamaḥ ॥ 4 ॥

trayam, group of three; *ekatra*, together, *saṁyamaḥ*, technical term for dharana, dhyana, and samadhi

Together [these] three are called *samyama*.

This sutra tells us that the process of moving from dharana to samadhi is a continuum. The precise term for this continuum is *samyama*. The terms *dharana*, *dhyana*, and *samadhi* are employed only for the sake of study and philosophical discussion. In actuality, they are practiced together.

According to Vyasa, *yoga* means *samadhi*, and samadhi is a universal attribute of the mind (YS 1:1). But this universal attribute is obscured by the kind of mind most of us have. The mind we possess vacillates among states of disturbance, stupefaction, distraction, one-pointedness, and complete stillness. Vyasa also states that the practice of yoga leading to samadhi begins with a one-pointed mind.

The first three states of mind—disturbed, stupefied, and distracted—are not fit for the practice of yoga. The first five limbs of ashtanga yoga—yama, niyama, asana, pranayama, and pratyahara—are designed to help us transcend these three states and cultivate a one-pointed mind. These five limbs infuse the mind with the capacity to identify the object of concentration clearly and grip it tightly. Because in our current discussion of dharana, dhyana, and samadhi, pranic pulsation is the object of concentration, the practice of the first five limbs infuses the mind with the ability to perceive pranic pulsation as distinct from the breath. By the time we are practicing the fifth limb, pratyahara, the mind is sharp enough to sense pranic pulsation and is also acutely aware of the pranic field lit by it. The capacity to comprehend and concentrate on pranic pulsation and the uniquely lit field around it is both inseparable from the practice of dharana, dhyana, and samadhi and necessary for practicing them successfully.

Patanjali encapsulates the process leading to the triad of dharana, dhyana, and samadhi in one word, *samyama*. The literal meaning of *samyama* is "well-rounded discipline." By using this term, Patanjali is also emphasizing the essence of sadhana. Success in sadhana depends partly on assessing our physical capacity, emotional maturity, and intellectual comprehension and partly on assessing our earnestness and the degree of willpower and determination that supports it. This twofold assessment helps us build the course of discipline needed for prolonged and uninterrupted sadhana.

Elaborating on the deeper intent and content of the term, Vyasa writes, "*Samyama* is tantric terminology for this triad." With this phrase, according to the tradition in which I am trained, Vyasa pulls in a vast range of supporting practices documented in tantric literature. The tantric approach to sadhana stands on the foundation of the yogic insight set forth in the second chapter of the *Yoga Sutra*, "The objective world, composed of elements and senses and having the inherent properties of illumination, action, and stability, has a twofold purpose: fulfillment and freedom" (YS 2:18). According to this sutra, all objects—living or non-living—are endowed with the properties of illumination, action, and stability and have the inherent capacity to help us find fulfillment and freedom.

This unalterable fact led tantric yogis to discover how to accelerate their spiritual quest by using the objects of the world in various ways. It enabled them to discover the extraordinary power of the breath, mind, and senses and the dimension of the body that transcends its physical counterpart. This is how the techniques of asana, pranayama, bandha, mudra, and the techniques for awakening the chakras and kundalini came into being. Chief among the discoveries of the tantric masters are the sciences of mantra and alchemy.

These masters, particularly those belonging to the Sri Vidya, Shaiva Agama, Natha, and Siddha traditions, adopted a highly comprehensive and integrative approach to sadhana. The word *samyama* in this sutra refers to that approach. Tantric application of ayurvedic alchemy, particularly *rasayana*, which is used exclusively for *kaya siddhi*, bodily perfection, and *indriya siddhi*, perfection of the senses, is an example of this approach (YS 2:43).

In the ayurvedic system of medicine, rasayana refers to the application of herbal and metallic formulas leading to the rejuvenation of the body in general and the vital organs in particular. In yoga sadhana, the science of rasayana and its application is far more refined. In general, yogis use rasayana-centered formulas to restore and retain the vitality, strength, and stamina of the body, freeing the mind from the obstacles that seed themselves in a weak and frail body. But those aspiring to higher yogic achievements apply advanced formulas of rasayana to awaken the dormant forces of their nervous and endocrine systems, thus boosting their pranic sensitivity and power of memory. Whenever appropriate, yogis further combine the application of alchemy with select mantras, making the practice of dharana, dhyana, and samadhi more complete, inclusive, and effective. According to the yogis of the Sri Vidya tradition of tantra, this is what is captured by the term *samyama*, well-rounded discipline.

Where this well-rounded discipline leads us is the subject of the next sutra.

SUTRA 3:5

तज्जयात्प्रज्ञालोकः ॥५॥

tajjayātprajñālokaḥ ॥ 5 ॥

tajjayāt, mastery over that [samyama]; *prajñā*, intuitive wisdom; *ālokaḥ*, light

From mastery over that [samyama], the light of intuitive wisdom [arises].

Commenting on this sutra, Vyasa says that as the practice of samyama progresses, the light of intuitive wisdom, intrinsic to samadhi, begins to shine. It is important to point out that the light mentioned here is not the light of the physical world. It refers to inner illumination, which infuses our mind with a higher degree of clarity and understanding. It also refers to the retentive power capable of firmly holding the memories of past experiences and retrieving them with little or no effort.

Inner illumination is referred to here by the term *prajna* because of its self-revealing power and its ability to shed light on the mind and the vast karmic contents stored there. Furthermore, prajna is infused with a high degree of stability and tranquility, enabling it to remain unperturbed by the positive and negative, meaningful and meaningless content illuminated by it. Prajna is the intrinsic property of a pure and pristine mind, which no longer perceives its existence apart from the highest reality, Ishvara.

Simply put, prajna is the ever-shining light of the highest reality, which has enveloped the mind from every direction and from every vantage point so fully that the mind is transformed into this light. The emergence of prajna is the outcome of immersion in the practice of samyama.

The emergence of prajna is an ongoing process. While its full manifestation occurs right before we are fully immersed in *nirbija samadhi*, which is marked by supreme spiritual absorption, preliminary waves of prajna begin to emerge even during the initial stages of the practice of samyama.

In fact, by the time we are grounded in the practices of pranayama and pratyahara, which precede dharana, the innate wisdom of our body and senses is illuminated by prajna to a considerable extent. Our endocrine and nervous systems, for example, become acutely cognizant of their powers, privileges, and functions. In the light of intuition, these systems spontaneously know when and how to react to their environment and when and how to refrain from reacting. The light of prajna at this stage empowers the body and nervous system to remain alert, responsive, and at the same time, relaxed.

As practice continues, we enter the domain of samyama. This domain is marked by three distinct, yet interlinked, stages: the manifestation of the uniquely lit pranic field at the center of the forehead, immersion in pranic pulsation, and transcendence of the threefold cognition described in the previous sutras. In addition to the experience of absolute sorrowless joy, the emergence of prajna through the practice of samyama is marked by the revelation of seven levels of intuitive understanding (YS 2:27).

In the light of prajna, we begin to see the true nature of the phenomenal world. We realize that everything in the world has a beginning and an end. Nothing is stable. This law applies to our body and all pleasant and unpleasant experiences. In the final analysis, what has value is not the obtaining of objects, nor our achievements and failures, but rather the lessons learned from them. This realization is so clear and firm that we feel no urge to verify its validity. We also know that this realization is an unalterable truth, not an outcome of intellectual analysis. In the light of this realization, we come to know the causes of our numberless shades of anguish and remorse. We also know that we have the tools and means to destroy those causes and free ourselves from afflicting thoughts. This marks the first level of intuitive understanding.

At the second level, we are certain that the deeper causes of afflicting thoughts are being attenuated and that the process of attenuation has gained momentum. At the third level, we begin to see the signs and symptoms of afflicting thoughts and experiences coming to a complete halt. At the fourth level, we begin to see the light of prajna so clearly that we have no doubt regarding the power and function of our discernment. At this level, we are certain that the impressions of the past no longer have the capacity to smear our judgment. We have complete trust in our willpower and determination. This frees the mind from all doubt and fear. We are no longer concerned about the subtle traces of our previous actions influencing our present and future. Together, these four levels of the manifestation of prajna lead to *karya vimukti*, freedom from karmic consequences.

The remaining three levels of the manifestation of prajna lead to *chitta vimukti*, freedom from the mind and its deep-rooted contents. Here the light of prajna is so bright that not only are we able to see our subtle karmic impressions, but we are also able to confront and conquer them. This is due to a high degree of mental absorption in prajna. For all intents and purposes, we no longer have a mind. Our old mind has been replaced by a mind untouched by all previous samskaras (YS 1:45–49 and 2:25–27). This highly refined mind is spontaneously drawn to its source: the pure and pristine prakriti of Ishvara. This pure and pristine prakriti of Ishvara is the final resting ground of our individuated consciousness and all good and bad, right and wrong, liberating and binding forces associated with it.

From the standpoint of sadhana, the most important effect of prajna on the mind is that from this point onward the mind remains free of the subtle impressions associated with any action it performs. The light of prajna nullifies the samskaras of our current and future actions, including samskaras created by the practice of samyama (YS 1:50). This is how the highly immersive and illuminating light of prajna opens the door to the highest state of samadhi, technically known as *nirbija samadhi.*

How to minimize and eventually eliminate the pitfalls illuminated by the light of prajna and accelerate the practice of samyama is the subject of the next sutra.

SUTRA 3:6

तस्य भूमिषु विनियोगः ॥६॥

tasya bhūmiṣu viniyogaḥ ॥ 6 ॥

tasya, of that; *bhūmiṣu*, contexts; *viniyogaḥ*, application

In different contexts and circumstances, the application of that [samyama] differs.

The practice of samyama is an ongoing process. Each step of the process is marked by a unique experience. As the steps mature through prolonged and uninterrupted practice, the experiences also mature. The more mature a step, the more firmly it forms the basis for the next step. Though there is no airtight demarcation distinguishing one step from another, there are signs that indicate whether or not the previous steps in the practice of samyama are fully mature.

For the sake of clarity, we will slice the continuum of samyama into segments: dharana, dhyana, and samadhi. For example, during a ten-minute practice of dharana, on most days, we are able to focus our mind on the uniquely lit pranic field at the center of the forehead for a few minutes before we are distracted by random thoughts. On other days, we are able to focus for ten minutes with a few fleeting thoughts distracting our mind. On rare occasions, we are totally focused on the pranic field with no intervening distractions for the entire ten minutes. Then, a month later, we find ourselves in such a disturbed and distracted state of mind that the practice of dharana eludes us. According to Vyasa, in this situation, the practice of the dhyana segment of samyama is not possible—when the practice of dharana is blocked, we have no access to dhyana. Similarly, due to the successful practice of dharana, we climb the ladder of dhyana and thus, for the most part, the mind seems to be fairly absorbed in the pranic pulsation at the center of the forehead. Then we may suddenly find ourselves in a phase in which maintaining the awareness of the pranic field becomes difficult, so reaching and maintaining the state of dhyana is impossible. These are common experiences.

To clear such hurdles and reach and maintain the deeper states of samyama, Patanjali advises that in different contexts and circumstances we should apply different components of samyama, particularly the practices that support the main body of the practice of samyama, such as asana, pranayama, alchemy, and mantra. For example, if we find our distractions are mainly caused by a poor meditation posture, it is better to make asana our main practice for a while and consider the practice of dharana, dhyana, and samadhi to be secondary. This will allow us to free the mind of distractions caused by physical discomfort.

Similarly, if inability to reach and maintain a deeper level of samyama seems to be caused by lethargy, stupor, or difficulty in breathing, we can adopt specialized pranayama techniques and augment them with the application of alchemy. Or, if we notice our practice of samyama is being hijacked by emotional turmoil arising from the unlit corners of the mind, we can adopt the practice of specific mantras, such as *gayatri* and *maha mrityunjaya*. If lack of will seems to be the major obstacle, we should undertake a time-bound practice known as a *purashcharana*. The intensity of these supportive practices determines how quickly we overcome the hurdles blocking our access to the deeper dimensions of samyama. The intensity of these practices is further determined by the intensity of our desire to reach the goal (YS 1:20–22).

Commenting on this sutra, Vyasa reminds us that even though the perfection and precision needed in practice, and the sincere effort we put into carrying it out, enable us to reach samadhi, we must not forget the importance of *Ishvara pranidhana*, trustful surrender to Ishvara, in this process. Patanjali has addressed Ishvara pranidhana in sutras 1:23–29, 2:1, and 2:44–45. From these sutras and Vyasa's commentaries on them, we draw four conclusions. First, that Ishvara is an ever-present, all-pervading omniscient reality with no anthropomorphic trappings. Second, only Ishvara fully comprehends the mystery of the mind and its infinitely vast contents. Third, upon attaining the state of samadhi, the adepts are fully absorbed in the boundless radiance of Ishvara (YS 1:19, 1:47–51, and 2:22–27). These adepts are as unlimited as Ishvara. Like Ishvara, they do not have a discrete body. Experientially, they are the sheer radiance of Ishvara. In response to the unconditional will of Ishvara, their guiding grace descends in our mind. Fourth, correct understanding of Ishvara and the adepts absorbed in Ishvara is enlightenment. Commitment to attaining this understanding is Ishvara pranidhana.

According to Vyasa, trustful surrender to Ishvara is a force without parallel. Riding the wave of Ishvara pranidhana, we can reach the higher states of samyama without perfecting the lower stages. The grace of Ishvara and the adepts absorbed in Ishvara is not bound by the rules of yoga practice. However, Vyasa is adamant that only through sincere and methodical practice do we comprehend the profound concept of divine grace and prepare ourselves to receive and absorb it.

The standard rule of yoga sadhana is to identify the steps of practice, follow them carefully, and make sure the foundation has been well laid. Patanjali introduces the next sutra to reinforce this idea.

SUTRA 3:7

त्रयमन्तरङ्गं पूर्वेभ्यः ॥७॥

trayamantaraṅgaṁ pūrvebhyaḥ ॥ 7 ॥

trayam, group of three; *antar*, internal; *aṅgaṁ*, limb; *pūrvebhyaḥ*, in relation to the preceding

In relation to the preceding [limbs], the triad [of dharana, dhyana, and samadhi] is an internal limb.

If this were not a sutra text written by Patanjali, an adept and scholar known for his measured and precise use of words, we could easily dismiss this sutra as redundant. After all, from the six preceding sutras it is clear that the last three limbs of ashtanga yoga (the triad of dharana, dhyana, and samadhi) are internal and the first five limbs (yama, niyama, asana, pranayama, and pratyahara) are external. What is Patanjali trying to convey by restating this?

The purpose of yoga is to train and transform the mind (YS 1:2). Training that leads to transformation requires practice. Success in practice depends on discipline (YS 2:1). A set of disciplines arranged in the right order (YS 3:15) ensures that our practice is not derailed or misdirected. A carefully regulated practice eventually enables us to discover the mysterious power of the mind. This discovery empowers us to uncover the mystery of everything in the world that falls within the range of our comprehension.

Vyasa divides the entire range of the mind's power and function into two broad categories: completely perceptible and completely imperceptible (YS 3:15). Mental cognitions are perceptible. The mind is cognizant of the thought process and the object of thought. It can be cognizant of what has triggered that thought; it can also be cognizant of how far that thought has already reached. The mind can clearly see whether or not it has any control over that thought. The mind can assess and be fully cognizant of the strength of its roaming tendencies. It can also assess whether or not it has enough willpower to change the direction of its roaming tendencies. All of these are examples of the perceptible dimension of the mind's power and function. And, according to Vyasa, they are intrinsic to the mind.

The completely imperceptible abilities and functions of the mind are sevenfold. It has the ability to bring its roaming tendencies to a complete halt (*nirodha*). It has the ability to become fully cognizant of its intrinsic properties (*dharma*). It has the capacity to create, store, retain, and destroy all impressions (*samskara*). Continuous transformation (*parinama*) is its essential nature. And finally, the capacity to feel the pulsation of consciousness (*jivanam*), volition (*chesta*), and the capacity to be and become (*shakti*) are also intrinsic to the mind.

Practically speaking, the mind's perceptible attributes, properties, functions, and behaviors are external layers. The seven imperceptible abilities the mind embodies are the internal layers. The first five limbs of yoga help us train and transform the external layers of the mind, whereas the last three limbs give us access to the mind's internal dimension. At maturity, the practice of the external limbs frees us from obstacles arising from our body, senses, and surroundings. The practice of the internal limbs provides the opportunity to discover our inner world, which is beyond the reach of our senses. That is why what is found there is defined as *siddhi*, extraordinary accomplishment.

The external limbs of yoga deal with our body, senses, the mind's external layers, and the phenomenal world. For example, the practice of yama, the first limb of yoga, helps us formulate a philosophy of life conducive to living in the world peacefully. By observing the principles of non-violence, truthfulness, non-stealing, self-discipline, and non-possessiveness, we eliminate room for distractions and complications to a great extent. Similarly, the observances of niyama—purity, contentment, austerity, self-study, and trustful surrender to Ishvara—help us cultivate inner strength and stay focused on life's higher purpose. The practice of asana enables us to maintain our body's resilience and keep it pain-free. The practice of pranayama expands the field of our vitality, whereas pratyahara protects our body and mind from draining our inner buoyancy. Even though these five limbs are characterized as external, from a practical standpoint they are no less important than the last three limbs, which are characterized as internal.

The placement of this sutra in relation to what has come just before gives a clear instruction that, in different contexts and circumstances, focusing on one of the external limbs is as important as practicing samyama itself. If, for example, the practice of the seventh limb, dhyana, is frequently disrupted by fear and worry, it is important to incorporate the practice of contentment, one of the components of the second limb. In other words, in an attempt to practice the deeper dimensions of yoga, we must not disconnect ourselves from its external aspects.

Within the range of samyama, samadhi is more internal than dhyana, and dhyana is more internal than dharana; in an attempt to practice the deeper aspects of samyama, we must not disconnect ourselves from its more external aspects. In fact, wisdom lies in filling the cracks between two limbs and even within a limb.

This is what is indicated by the placement of this sutra. In the preceding sutra, Patanjali emphasizes the importance of incorporating unique techniques for allowing our experiences to flow seamlessly from the more external levels of consciousness to the deeper levels.

One such technique that bears mentioning here is *pranava anusandhana*. *Pranava anusandhana* means "shooting the target with pranava." Practically speaking, it is a technique to awaken pranic sensitivity and guide the pranic flow methodically throughout the body. Pranic sensitivity accelerates when the combined forces of prana and mind are further combined with pranava (*Svacchanda Tantra* 1:38–40). *Pranava* is a technical term for *om*, which is indicative of Ishvara and lies beyond the framework of the mind.

According to Patanjali, meditation on pranava accelerates the inward flow of consciousness and eliminates obstacles to samadhi (YS 1:27–29). In the beginning stages, this practice is done in *shavasana*, the corpse pose, and later, in a meditative pose. In order to enhance the pranic sensitivity at the center of the forehead, the combined forces of prana, mind, and pranava are directed there. The emergence of a ball of light in the mental space corresponding to the center of the forehead is the hallmark of perfection in this practice. On the firm foundation of pranava anusandhana, yogis build a sophisticated structure of yoga sadhana, including practices such as *prapancha vyapti* and *maha vyapti anusandhana* (*Svacchanda Tantra* 3:49–97). According to the tradition, these are the practices which, in different contexts and circumstances, we can use to fill the cracks in our sadhana and reach the furthest frontier of samadhi.

The furthest frontier of samadhi and the process of reaching there is the subject of the next sutra.

SUTRA 3:8

तदपि बहिरङ्गं निर्बीजस्य ॥८॥

tadapi bahiraṅgaṁ nirbījasya ॥ 8 ॥

tat, that; *api*, even; *bahiḥ*, external; *aṅgaṁ*, limb; *nirbījasya*, of seedless samadhi

Even that [samyama] is an external limb of nirbija samadhi.

In "Samadhi Pada," Patanjali and Vyasa divide the range of samadhi into two broad categories: *sabija* and *nirbija* (YS 1:42–51). *Sabija* means "samadhi with seeds," while *nirbija* means "samadhi without seeds." In casual discussion, *sabija* is described as "lower samadhi" and nirbija as "higher samadhi." However, the terms *sabija* and *nirbija* describe two distinct experiences of yoga sadhana.

From the standpoint of experience, the practice of yoga—which according to Vyasa is samadhi (YS 1:1)—begins as soon as we decide to curb the roaming tendencies of our mind (YS 1:13). When we apply the principles of yama and niyama in our daily life and begin practicing asana, pranayama, and pratyahara, the journey toward samadhi is underway. The practice of pranayama and pratyahara evolves naturally into samyama.

There is a sense of ownership of the practice from the decision to curb the roaming tendencies of our mind all the way to the practice of samyama. This sense of ownership is a seed. We know we are engaged in our practice and we know the intensity of our engagement. We know whether or not we are progressing satisfactorily. We are aware of how the deep-seated contents of our mind—love, lust, attachment, dispassion, cruelty, kindness, ambition, despondency, fear, courage, clarity, confusion, ego, and humility—are influencing our practice. We are cognizant of the gradual attenuation of these mental contents and aware that the stream of cognitions, which distracts our mind from being anchored in the object of samyama, is fading.

Cognizance of this process is the seed that invariably accompanies our practice. Therefore, as long we are aware of ourselves as the practitioner, aware of the object of our samyama, and aware of the process of focusing on it, we are operating within the range of sabija samadhi. Sabija samadhi is characterized by the presence of seeds—mental tendencies and their subtle causes.

The practice of samyama—the triad of dharana, dhyana, and samadhi described in the previous sutras—is the practice of sabija samadhi. It is important to note that success in the practice of sabija samadhi is largely dependent on the quality of the object of concentration. If the object of concentration is inherently illuminating, the practice will engender an illuminating experience. Because pranic pulsation is the direct manifestation of the divine will of Ishvara, it is inherently illuminating. Because pranic pulsation is the direct manifestation of Ishvara's unalterable intention to grant us lasting fulfillment and ultimate freedom, it creates an internal atmosphere conducive to experiencing fulfillment and freedom. Concentration on pranic pulsation, therefore, naturally results in the experience of extraordinary luminosity imbued with fulfillment and freedom. In the light of this experience, mental cognitions and the objects associated with them begin to lose their luster.

With sustained practice, the mind becomes calmer, clearer, sharper, and more penetrating. It becomes increasingly cognizant of both its superficial and its deeper tendencies. Due to its union with the pranic force, the mind has the strength and insight to recognize the causes of inner instability and agitation. It also gains the capacity to rise above its agitating tendencies and remain focused on the pranic illumination.

This is how the practice of sabija samadhi undergoes the process of gradual refinement. This refinement culminates in recognizing the most subtle contents of the mind, which define our self-identity. We clearly see that our unwillingness to let go of our *asmita*, our self-identity, is preventing us from experiencing our oneness with all-pervading, eternal, omniscient reality. We also see that this unwillingness is grounded in sheer *avidya*, ignorance. With further practice and the refinement engendered by it, the seeds of avidya, asmita, and the numberless tendencies fed by them are rendered inert. The only seed that exists at this stage is the subtle impression created by the practice of sabija samadhi itself. When even this seed is destroyed, we enter nirbija samadhi (YS 1:51).

Before we entertain the discussion on how the subtle impressions of practicing sabija samadhi are destroyed and how the absence of those impressions results in nirbija samadhi, it is helpful to explore how sabija samadhi nullifies our deep-rooted afflictions and the mental tendencies arising from them. In sutra 1:47, Patanjali tells us that the furthest frontier of sabija samadhi is marked by spiritual transparency and joy. "Spiritual transparency" is another term for *jyotishmati*, inner luminosity. For "joy," Patanjali uses *vishoka*, a blissful state untouched by anguish and remorse. As the mind becomes more and more absorbed in pranic pulsation, the experience of spiritual transparency and joy expressed by the terms *jyotishmati* and *vishoka* becomes increasingly refined and potent. This leads to the rise of *prajna*, intuitive wisdom.

Prajna is non-sensory knowledge. It transcends the domain of the ordinary mind, which always works in collaboration with the sense organs and the cortical brain. Prajna is a unique faculty of knowledge that comprehends itself and the objective world both linearly and non-linearly. Its comprehension is neither regulated nor blocked by the forces of time, space, and causation. It simultaneously comprehends the whole and its minutest parts. It illuminates the entire range of time—past, present, and future—and has the ability to identify any experience deposited in any niche of time. Most importantly, the function of prajna is not dependent on our normal channels of understanding: sensory perception, inference, comparison, postulation, and scriptural authority. The most distinctive attribute of prajna is that it is infused with *ritam* (YS 1:48), the unalterable law of nature.

Prajna is intrinsically imbued with the power of comprehending the subtle dynamics of ritam. When we are established in the fully mature state of sabija samadhi, the landscape of our mind and consciousness is fully lit by prajna. With this illumination, we spontaneously comprehend the dynamics of ritam. We become cognizant of the natural laws responsible for creating and maintaining the bond between body, breath, mind, and consciousness. We intuitively realize that by conforming to the law of ritam, we can discover and materialize our full potential and thus become connected to the inexhaustible pool of inner elixir, *amritam*.

As the *Yajur Veda* tells us, the discovery of inner elixir prevents us from developing conditions that drain our vitality, *ayakshmam*. We attain freedom from disease, *anamayam*. We are filled with the passion for life, *jivatum*, which in turn ensures our longevity, *dirghayutvam*. The prospect of a fully secured, long life nullifies our feeling of animosity toward those who pose a threat to us, *anamitram*. This leads to complete fearlessness, *abhayam*. Freedom from fear leads to comfort, *sukham*, a condition necessary for restful sleep, *shayanam*. Restful sleep makes night a good night, *susha*; that leads to a good day, *sudinam* (*Yajur Veda* 18:6). All twelve of these qualities, beginning with ritam and ending with sudinam, are intrinsic to prajna.

In the light of prajna, we see our true guide, protector, and provider. We see the source of all goodness and auspiciousness. Life's day-to-day issues, unsettling memories of the past, and insecurity about the future lose their grip on our mind. A mind illuminated by the waves of joy radiating from the self-luminous field of prajna fills us with an unconditional love for meditation. At this stage, we meditate not because we want something from meditation but because we cannot live without meditation. We are drawn to our practice as a honeybee is drawn to a flower filled with nectar. The samskara created by this stage of practice nullifies all previous samskaras (YS 1:50). At this stage, the samskara of practice that arises from the mind and subsides in it is described as *dharma megha*, cloud of virtues, and the experience of it is *dharma megha samadhi* (YS 4:29).

Dharma megha samadhi is the transitional stage between sabija and nirbija samadhi. From the standpoint of sabija samadhi, it is a transcendental state, but from the standpoint of nirbija samadhi, it is a lower stage. Dharma megha samadhi emerges when the triad of dharana, dhyana, and samadhi has become one undivided continuum of experience, and this experience is no longer intercepted by the cognition of the process of meditation (*dhyana*), the object of meditation (*dhyeya*), and the cognition of ourselves as the meditator (*dhyata*). The feeling of ourselves as the meditator and the process of meditation have dissolved into the object of meditation, in this case, pranic pulsation. The mind and asmita, the awareness that claims ownership of the mind, are totally absorbed into pranic pulsation.

According to Patanjali, this level of absorption is *samapatti* (YS 1:41). It transforms our mind and our individuated sense of I-am-ness into pranic pulsation. We no longer experience ourselves as separate from prana; rather, we experience ourselves as prana. We see prana with the eye of prana. We are aware of unborn and undying prana shakti as the core of our being. We see our core being, prana, as a beginningless and endless pulsation of divine will. The power packed in this realization frees us from even the most subtle desire—freedom from the cycle of death and birth. This is the highest form of dispassion. Dharma megha, the cloud of virtues, is made of this degree of dispassion. When this cloud rains, every aspect of our being becomes saturated with the guiding and nourishing shakti of divine grace. We are fully enlightened, nourished, and protected.

Dharma megha samadhi is beyond the range of our practice. Practicing dharma megha samadhi simply means enjoying being there (YS 1:18). It is the realm of consciousness in which the high-caliber yogis reside (YS 1:19 and 2:44). This realm of consciousness is characterized by *para vairagya*, absolute dispassion, and constant awareness of pranic pulsation as a manifestation of divine will. Dispassion and constant awareness of divine will are the locus of these yogis. They are not yet one with Ishvara's prakriti, yet they are not part of the objective world. They are not bound by the forces of time, space, and causation, nor are they yet one with the absolute reality, who creates the forces of time, space, and causation and rules over them.

In other words, dharma megha samadhi transcends sabija samadhi, yet is somewhat below nirbija samadhi. From the standpoint of yogis who have reached and tasted dharma megha samadhi, the entire range of sabija samadhi is external. They use sabija samadhi as a springboard to reach nirbija, the highest state of samadhi, which is devoid of even the most subtle samskara—the samskara of duality.

How to block the cognitions that defuse our concentration during the practice of sabija samadhi and how to facilitate the commencement of cessation of cognition so we can transition from sabija to nirbija samadhi is the subject of the next sutra.

SUTRA 3:9

व्युत्थाननिरोधसंस्कारयोरभिभवप्रादुर्भावौ
निरोधक्षणचित्तान्वयो निरोधपरिणामः ॥९॥

vyutthānanirodhasaṁskārayorabhibhavaprādurbhāvau
nirodhakṣaṇacittānvayo nirodhapariṇāmaḥ ॥ 9 ॥

vyutthāna-nirodha-saṁskārayoḥ, subtle impressions of an agitated and of a well-contained mind; *abhibha-vaprādur-bhāvau*, decline and rise; *nirodha*, confinement; *kṣaṇa*, moment; *citta*, mind; *anvayaḥ*, yoking; *nirodha*, confinement; *pariṇāmaḥ*, result

The decline of samskaras that cause mental agitation and the rise of samskaras that impel the mind to confine itself to the object of concentration introduce a brief moment of time filled with the essence of self-restraint. Yoking the mind to that moment results in mastery over its roaming tendencies.

Up to this point, Patanjali and Vyasa have been addressing the role of mental tendencies in the practice of sabija samadhi, particularly their role in slowing or blocking our progress to nirbija samadhi. Here these masters are addressing the deeper causes of the roaming tendencies and how to uproot them once and for all.

Commenting on this sutra, Vyasa makes an illuminating statement: "Samskaras of mental agitation and distraction are defining attributes of chitta. These are different from agitating and distracting cognitions and thoughts. Upon restraining these distracting cognitions, the samskaras that churn up agitation and distraction are not restrained." With this statement, Vyasa is emphatically stating that to attain a lasting victory over the roaming tendencies of the mind we must attenuate the potent force of samskaras that churn up mental tendencies from deep within. In other words, trying to stop the roaming tendencies of the mind is of little or no use.

Vyasa then makes an even more illuminating statement: "Samskaras of restraint are defining attributes of chitta. These are different from the process of restraining the mind from distracting cognitions and thoughts." Here Vyasa is telling us that samskaras of restraint are buried in our mind. When they awaken and arise, we are naturally impelled to disassociate ourselves from both distracting thoughts and the subtle samskaras that churn up those thoughts. Therefore, according to Vyasa, awakening and actively supporting the rise of the samskaras of restraint is as important as the effort we put into attenuating the samskaras that churn up the mental tendencies.

There are two sources of disturbance—external and internal. External disturbance originates in the objective world and is carried by the senses. When we disconnect our senses from their corresponding objects, this form of disturbance vanishes and the mind is free. But internal disturbance originates in the world of our memories, and that disturbance is not carried by the senses. Furthermore, this form of disturbance courses through the mind uninvited. Disconnecting the mind from this form of disturbance is difficult.

The phenomenon of restraining the mind from embracing disturbing thoughts is also of two kinds—external and internal. When we try to restrain the mind from disturbing thoughts by engaging it elsewhere, it is external restraint. This is a passive form of restraint, which entails diverting our attention instead of actively arresting the disturbing thoughts, and its effect is short-lived. But internal restraint originates in the world of our memories and by its intrinsic virtue arrests the disturbing thoughts. This form of restraint courses through the mind spontaneously, forcing it to confine itself to the object of its focus.

Essentially, Patanjali and Vyasa are advising us that in order to enter and successfully pass through the deeper stages of samyama or sabija samadhi, we have to attenuate and eventually eliminate samskaras that agitate our mind and replace them with samskaras that impel the mind to confine itself to the object of its focus. To comprehend the import of this advice, we first have to understand samskaras—what they are, how they are created, where they are stored, and how they influence our thought, speech, and action.

Samskaras are the subtle impressions of our actions. Each time we perform an action—physical, verbal, or mental—the subtle impression of that action is imprinted in the mind and stored there in the form of memory. When we perform the same action repeatedly, the memory pertaining to that action becomes stronger. Its inherent strength impels us to repeat that action more easily and more effortlessly until that subtle impression turns into a habit. When we perform our actions driven by habit, we further reinforce the subtle impressions. At this point, the impressions are transformed into samskaras. They are now powerful enough to demand that the mind perform similar actions. This sets the cycle from actions to samskaras and from samskaras to actions in motion. Slowing this cycle and eventually bringing it to a halt is essential to the practice of samyama.

Every disturbing, stupefying, and distracting thought emerges from and is fed by corresponding samskaras buried deep in our mind field. Slowing such thoughts is easier than weakening their corresponding samskaras, but unless those samskaras are weakened and eventually erased, we will not be successful in curbing the roaming tendencies of our mind. Decline in the potency of the samskaras that churn up disturbing and distracting thoughts comes from the practice of vairagya, non-attachment (YS 1:12 and 1:15–16).

Vairagya is more than simply letting go. It is an active process of cultivating the power of discernment and the inner strength to disassociate ourselves from thoughts and feelings that distract our mind from the object of samyama. As described in sutra 1:15, the practice of vairagya entails making a decision to discover the inner dimension of our mind, *yatamana*, and isolating prominent currents of distracting and disturbing thoughts from the less significant ones, *vyatireka*. It entails identifying the most stubborn disturbing behavior, *ekendriya*, and, by using the power of will and determination, resolving to discard it once and for all. Finally, the practice of vairagya entails cultivating a state of desirelessness toward all religious and spiritual temptations, *vashikara*. These four components of the practice of vairagya weaken the samskara of *vyutthana*, mental agitation. However, this is only half of the practice. The remaining half requires actively creating the samskaras of *nirodha*, subtle impressions that impel the mind to remain confined to its object of focus.

The samskaras of nirodha are created through a consistent, sustained practice of abhyasa (YS 1:12–14). Abhyasa is an earnest attempt to anchor the mind in an object. In the practice of abhyasa, it is important to remember that no matter how subtle and intangible the object, it is always associated with time and space. Whenever an object comes into the mind's view, the time and space that give room to that object are automatically drawn into the mind's focus.

In other words, the object exists in the field of time and space. The object is bordered by a well-defined time and space.

Practicing abhyasa means not allowing the mind to slip out of the time and space that surround the object of our mental focus. Abhyasa entails remaining so fully focused on the object of our concentration that the mind is not aware of any other thoughts or mental tendencies. As soon as we realize that the mind has begun noticing a non-meditative thought, we immediately make an effort to bring the mind back to the object of concentration and the time and space that surround it.

According to Patanjali, making this effort sincerely for a prolonged period and with reverence for the practice is abhyasa. This engenders nirodha samskaras, subtle impressions imbued with the power to restrain the mind in a well-defined time and space. These samskaras were created through the action of meditation when the mind was alert and aware of the importance of meditation. Thus, quality of alertness and the cognizance of the importance of meditation are intrinsic to these samskaras. Due to their intrinsic qualities, these nirodha samskaras fill the mind with a distaste for roaming tendencies. When coupled with the decline of vyutthana samskaras, the subtle impressions that churn up roaming tendencies, the rise of nirodha samskaras leads the mind to a higher level of stability.

In a living tradition, adepts help aspirants identify major obstacles to curbing the samskaras that churn up the roaming tendencies and to accelerating the formation of samskaras that fill the mind with a distaste for roaming tendencies. There are hundreds of techniques yogis apply to overcome a particular obstacle or group of obstacles. In the Sri Vidya tradition of tantra, masters employ one or more of three main tools to overcome such obstacles—mantra, alchemy, and a precise method of meditating on the chakras in the body. The application of these tools yields a twofold result: first, they cleanse the body, breath, senses, and mind and restore their natural ecology; and second, they fill the body and mind with the vitality and resilience needed to assimilate the inner radiance generated by the practice of samyama.

As with any experience, the experience pertaining to the cessation of the mind's roaming tendencies emerges in a particular moment in time. In this sutra, Patanjali tells us that in order to progress and finally reach the furthest frontier of samyama, we must identify the instant when all cognitions except the cognition pertaining to the object of concentration have come to a halt. In yogic literature, this particular instant is described as *nirodha-kshana*, a minute segment of time marked by the absence of non-meditative cognitions. Cognizance of this moment allows the mind to register the experience unique to this moment. The conscious registration of this experience is then purposefully stored in the mind field. The technical term that describes this process is *nirodha-kshana-chitta-anvaya*, yoking the mind to the segment of time marked by nirodha.

For example, if the breath is the object of focus, we then pay attention to the exact moment when the incoming breath is first felt touching the general region of the opening of the nostrils. The more clearly and acutely we become aware of this particular moment, the greater our success in uniting our mind with the experience that fills that moment. Furthermore, the clearer our cognizance of this moment, the firmer the memory of the experience filling that moment. The experience of being here and now is a unique quality of the space corresponding to the general region of the opening of the nostrils. Paying attention to the exact moment inhalation touches that space empowers the mind to become cognizant of the experience of being here and now.

When this experience is repeated through consistent practice, the subtle impressions of this experience become potent.

As our practice matures, this experience rises from the depths of our mind of its own accord. Creating the subtle impressions of nirodha initially requires effort. When they arise spontaneously at the merest hint of our intention, we have reached the advanced stage of sabija samadhi. Thus, in the advanced stage of sabija samadhi, self-effort comes to an end and we are led to the final state, nirbija samadhi.

Why the subtle impressions of nirodha are not intercepted by the roaming tendencies of the mind is the subject of the next sutra.

SUTRA 3:10

तस्य प्रशान्तवाहिता संस्कारात् ॥१०॥

tasya praśāntavāhitā saṁskārāt ॥ 10 ॥

tasya, that; *praśāntavāhitā*, peaceful flow; *saṁskārāt*, due to the subtle impression

The peaceful flow of that [the result engendered by nirodha] is due to the samskaras.

Samskaras, the subtle impressions stored in our mind field, are as alive as we are. Their defining qualities are as vibrant as the life force in us. Samkaras seek the manifestation of their grandeur, just as we seek ours. Commenting on sutra 2:3, Vyasa explains how samskaras bring about karmic fruition. He describes this entire process in four steps: first, the self-propelled pulsations of the samskaras solidify and provide nourishment to the distinctive attributes of the samskaras; second, they lay the foundation for change; third, they connect the currents of cause and effect; and fourth, they incentivize cause and effect to inspire and feed each other, thus creating an environment conducive to the manifestation of the distinctive qualities of the samskaras. Let us examine how these four steps operate in the context of our current discussion on the peaceful flow of the samskaras of nirodha.

In the daily course of life, our mind is tossed by positive and negative tendencies. These tendencies originate from and are nourished by the deep-rooted subtle impressions corresponding to them. External circumstances simply provide the spark. Each samskara is pulsating with its inherent craving for fulfillment. The potential for fear and anger, for example, is buried in the deeper niches of our mind. The samskaras of fear and anger are pulsating with the desire to manifest. This desire is the keeper, protector, and nurturer of fear and anger. This vibrant force of desire is constantly engaged in laying the foundation for change by churning up the emotions of fear and anger from the depths of their corresponding samskaras.

The intrinsic intelligence of the desire for fulfillment subtly pulls the currents of the causes from inside and connects them with the currents of the effects in the external world. The same intelligent force of desire incentivizes these currents of cause and effect to further feed each other. This process culminates in the full-blown manifestation of agitation infused with fear and anger. This entire process is described as *vyutthana-samskara*, a subtle impression causing mental agitation. In the previous sutra, Patanjali explained how to attenuate and finally eliminate the potency of these samskaras.

Nirodha samskaras lead the mind to lose its taste for vyutthana samskaras and impel it to confine itself to the object of its focus. These samskaras also function in accordance with the four-step process described above. Through consistent and sustained abhyasa we confine our mind to the object of our focus. Confining the mind to its object of focus is an action. This action creates an impression in the mind. The perfection and precision of the methodology we use to focus the mind empowers it to remain free from distracting thoughts. Because the process of confining the mind to its object of focus inherently carries the energy of restraint, the impression created by this action is saturated with the impression of restraint. With sustained practice, these nirodha samskaras eventually mature and become an integral part of our mind. They pulsate from deep within the mind field.

Like other samskaras, the samskaras of nirodha seek fulfillment. The intrinsic qualities of nirodha samskaras are constantly engaged in laying the foundation for change by churning up the feelings of distaste and disinterestedness in non-meditative objects. These intrinsic qualities subtly pull the currents of the true causes of restraint from inside and connect them with the currents of effect in the external world. The same qualities incentivize these currents of cause and effect to feed each other further. This process culminates in the full-blown manifestation of restraint regarding all thoughts and cognitions except that of our object of focus.

As explained in the previous sutra, cessation of the mind's roaming tendencies is a cognition. It is both a process and a state of experience. This experience emerges in a particular moment of time. The precise term for this moment is *nirodha-kshana*. This moment is imbued with the intrinsic qualities of nirodha. Because time is a force that flows incessantly, the instant imbued with the samskaras of nirodha also flows incessantly. In the case of immature and imperfect samskaras of nirodha, the instant imbued with these nirodha samskaras is intermittently disrupted by distracting thoughts. But in the case of fully mature and perfect nirodha samskaras, nirodha-kshana flows uninterruptedly. This uninterrupted flow of nirodha-kshana further enhances the power of the nirodha samskaras.

In the practice of samyama, a state eventually arises where nirodha-kshana, the instant imbued with the intrinsic qualities of nirodha, is succeeded by similar instants. The quality of this state is described as *prashanta vahita*, peaceful flow. This peaceful flow is an effortless process, one driven by the essential attributes of nirodha samskaras.

How the peaceful flow of nirodha samskaras leads to samadhi is the subject of the next sutra.

SUTRA 3:11

सर्वार्थतैकाग्रतयोः क्षयोदयौ चित्तस्य
समाधिपरिणामः ॥११॥

sarvārthataikāgratayoḥ kṣayodayau cittasya
samādhipariṇāmaḥ ‖ 11 ‖

sarvārthatā, all cognitions; *ekāgratayoḥ*, one-pointedness; *kṣayodayau*, elimination and rise; *cittasya*, of mind; *samādhi-pariṇāmaḥ*, transformation characterized by all-consuming focus

The elimination of all cognitions and the rise of one-pointedness lead to the transformation characterized by a completely still, pristine state of mind.

Samadhi is all-consuming awareness, including awareness of the mind's absorption in the object of samyama. As long as the mind is aware of itself and its effort to meditate on the object of its focus, its focus is split in a minimum of three parts: awareness of itself, the effort of meditating, and the object of meditation. While this threefold cognition persists, the mind cannot reach the all-consuming awareness that defines samadhi. This threefold cognition forces the mind to remain diffuse. This diffusion not only prevents the mind from attending one cognition wholeheartedly, it also creates an atmosphere of perceiving numerous cognitions—directly or indirectly, clearly or vaguely—associated with the threefold cognition of oneself as the meditator, the effort of meditating, and the object of meditation. Patanjali describes this cognition in one word: *sarvarthata*, awareness of numerous objects.

The mind is one and indivisible. In order to bring numerous objects into its view, it has to spread itself thin. As a result, it will not have a laser focus on a single object. It is aware of numerous objects but not fully cognizant of any. This diffused awareness prevents it from being fully absorbed in its main object.

The awareness of numerous objects is distraction. When the mind is distracted and moves in rapid succession from one object to the next, accompanied by agitation, it is disturbed. When the mind is depleted and tired of being tossed by distracting and disturbing thoughts, it succumbs to sloth, inertia, and stupor. A distracted, disturbed, and stupefied mind is not fit for samadhi (Vyasa on YS 1:1). When, due to the peaceful flow of nirodha samskaras, the awareness of numerous objects comes to an end and one-pointedness begins to flow incessantly, the state of samadhi emerges.

In samadhi we acquire a one-pointed mind. Through continuous reinforcement of the practice of vairagya as described in sutras 1:12, 1:15–16, and particularly 3:9, we attenuate and eventually eliminate the subtle impressions that churn up disturbing, distracting, and stupefying tendencies. That automatically supports the conditions conducive to cultivating a one-pointed mind. However, the rise of one-pointedness with a lasting effect comes from abhyasa, ardent and methodical practice that promotes and further intensifies the peaceful flow of nirodha samskaras, the subtle impressions that impel the mind to confine itself to a single object. In other words, the practice of samyama, consisting of mutually supportive abhyasa and vairagya, curbs the mental tendency to attend numerous thoughts while training the mind to confine itself to a single object. This leads us to experience *samadhi parinama*, change characterized by samadhi, the well-settled state of an unperturbed mind.

How the mutually supportive practices of abhyasa and vairagya curb disturbing thoughts and impel the mind to confine itself to a single object, leading to a completely still, unperturbed state of mind, is the subject of the next sutra.

SUTRA 3:12

ततः पुनः शान्तोदितौ तुल्यप्रत्ययौ
चित्तस्यैकाग्रतापरिणामः ॥१२॥

tataḥ punaḥ śāntoditau tulyapratyayau
cittasyaikāgratāpariṇāmaḥ ॥ 12 ॥

tataḥ punaḥ, thereafter; *śāntoditau*, that which has disappeared and that which is appearing; *tulyapratyayau*, two identical cognitions; *cittasya*; of mind; *ekāgratāpariṇāmaḥ*, transformation emerging as one-pointedness

Thereafter, the cognitions that have passed and those that are arising become identical. This results in a transformation characterized by one-pointedness of mind.

Here Patanjali distills the essence of the three preceding sutras. In sutra 3:9, he tells us that curbing samskaras that churn up agitating thoughts and creating samskaras that impel the mind to confine itself to the object of its focus result in the emergence of a moment filled with samskaras of restraint. Yoking the mind to that moment leads to mental transformation characterized by restraint. Thereafter, the peaceful flow of this mental transformation is sustained by the inherent power of these samskaras (YS 3:10). With continued practice, this transformation destroys the mind's tendency to run after non-meditative objects and empowers it to remain anchored in meditative thoughts. This engenders the next level of transformation, which is characterized by a completely still, unperturbed mind (YS 3:11). According to sutra 3:12, as the practice deepens further, the mind is led to *ekagrata parinama*, a higher level of transformation characterized by one-pointedness.

This level of mental transformation is unique in that it is self-propelled and the cognition of the object in the mind's view is identical to the previous cognition. Due to the lack of intervening thoughts, the present cognition is replaced by an identical cognition before vanishing into the past. This is how a series of cognitions that have slipped into the past and the cognition occupying a brief moment in the present are perceived by the mind as a single object. This meditative phenomenon makes a completely still, unperturbed mind fully one-pointed.

Experientially, the process of cultivating a one-pointed mind begins with choosing an object of concentration. Selecting the right kind of object is more important than focusing on it. The inherent property of the object not only accelerates or slows the process of cultivating one-pointedness but also determines the development of the unique capacities that accompany a one-pointed mind. For example, by using the image of a donkey as an object of concentration, we may succeed in cultivating a one-pointed mind, but this image will not infuse the mind with the power of self-illumination and self-understanding because the image of a donkey does not possess those qualities.

Equally important is holding the object in a well-defined space corresponding to the most suitable region of the body. This suitability is determined by the inherent quality of the space corresponding to a particular region in the body. For example, we choose a highly illuminating mantra but we hold the sound of the mantra in the space corresponding to the general region of our kidney. The mantra as an object of concentration is correct, the process of concentration is correct, but the inherent property of the space corresponding to the region of the kidney is not suitable to the manifestation of the illuminative properties of the mantra. The wrong object will not yield the right result, nor will focusing on the right object in the wrong place. That is why Patanjali and the masters before and after him are so particular about choosing an object of concentration and holding that object in the most suitable, well-defined space.

Based on what has been said in the previous eleven sutras and what is about to come, it is easy to ascertain what kind of one-pointed mind Patanjali expects us to cultivate. He expects us to have a mind that is not merely one-pointed but also radiant, sharp, and penetrating. He expects us to have a mind strong enough to renounce its karmic possessions and charged with the desire to restore its pure and pristine nature. For this reason, as we have seen in sutras 2:49–55 and 3:1–11, Patanjali chooses the breath as an object and chooses a specific point, such as the region of the forehead, as the space in which to hold our focus on the breath and, more precisely, on pranic pulsation, the subtle counterpart of the breath.

The breath is the most vivid manifestation of the life force. Pranic pulsation is the subtle counterpart of the breath. Pranic pulsation contains everything contained in primordial prakriti. Yogic metaphysics describes the vast range of the intrinsic capacities of prakriti in eight categories: *dharma*, unalterable essential attributes (sattva, rajas, and tamas); *jnana*, knowledge; *vairagya*, unsmearability; *aishvarya*, absolute power to command; *adharma*, essential attributes in flux; *ajnana*, veiled or limited knowledge; *avairagya*, smearability; and *anaishvarya*, limited or no power to command. Prana contains all these capacities.

In simple language, the fourth capacity, *aishvarya*, is divine will. It is the unrestricted and self-governed absolute power of intention. From the standpoint of the phenomenal world and the disembodied soul seeking an opportunity to enter this world, this power of intention manifests as pranic pulsation. Pranic pulsation is the living body of primordial prakriti's power of intention. As soon as pranic pulsation unites itself with matter, matter comes to life. Pranic pulsation also takes the lead in awakening the seven other categories of prakriti's intrinsic capacities. Pranic pulsation determines the relative excellence of our knowledge, vitality, and motivation for action.

In other words, pranic pulsation is the fundamental force behind our actions and inactions, our upward or downward journey. Interest in spiritual unfoldment and worldly achievements is governed by this fundamental force. Cultivating sensitivity to pranic pulsation is cultivating sensitivity to divine will. Establishing a conscious connection with pranic pulsation is establishing a connection with divine will. Absorption in pranic pulsation and the pranically charged space of consciousness that surrounds it is bathing in unconditional, infallible divine grace. In the tradition, this is known as *prana samapatti*, the mind's absorption in prana.

Prana samapatti infuses the mind with all the intrinsic properties of prana, particularly aishvarya, the absolute power to command. This pranic immersion puts our karmic impressions to sleep. The subtle impressions that once churned up the mental tendencies from deep inside are rendered inert and thus have no power to stir up the mind field. The new samskaras created by concentration on pranic pulsation are free from adverse karmic impressions. This allows meditative samskaras to pass their quietude on to the cognitions emerging in the present, thus enabling the mind to experience the cognitions of both past and present as identical. This experience also frees the mind from the cognitions of past, present, and future. As the stream of instants continues to flow uninterruptedly, the mind is able to experience constancy in flux. This leads the mind to a new level of one-pointedness.

This newfound one-pointedness empowers the mind to precisely track the transformation occurring both in the mind itself and in the phenomenal world. The exact nature of this transformation and the ways to measure it is the subject of the next sutra.

SUTRA 3:13

एतेन भूतेन्द्रियेषु धर्मलक्षणावस्थापरिणामा व्याख्याताः ॥१३॥

etena bhūtendriyeṣu dharmalakṣaṇāvasthāpariṇāmā vyākhyātāḥ ॥ 13 ॥

etena, with this; *bhūtendriyeṣu*, in the individuals and senses; *dharmalakṣaṇāvasthāpariṇāmāḥ*, transformation of defining qualities, symptoms, and conditions; *vyākhyātāḥ*, scrutinized and comprehended

With this [degree of mental concentration], transformation of defining qualities, symptoms, and conditions occurring in individuals [or elements] and in tools of cognition can be scrutinized and comprehended.

Mental concentration evolving from pranic immersion makes the mind as clear, strong, determined, radiant, confident, and self-trusting as prana shakti itself. This high degree of mental transformation is due to the mind's absorption in the pranic force. This absorption enables the mind to acquire all the qualities, properties, and capacities of prana.

Prana manifests before even the minutest living organism comes into existence. Pranic pulsation breathes life into matter. This self-guided, intelligent life force knows why and how it breathed life into us. With *prana samapatti*, absorption in prana, we become cognizant of where we come from, who keeps us alive, what we are anchored in, and who leads us through the lanes of joy and sorrow. This pranically charged, concentrated mind is capable of tracing its journey all the way back to the instant when—at the tender touch of pranic pulsation—it came to life and became a thinking agent. It is capable of pinpointing the circumstances in which it thought, felt, and acted in a particular way and can observe how such thoughts, feelings, and actions led to the formation of subtle impressions and how those subtle impressions impelled the mind to attend similar thoughts, feelings, and actions.

In short, this uniquely concentrated mind can trace back and discover that significant moment when *vritti samskara chakra*, the wheel of cognition to samskara and samskara to cognition, was set in motion. Charged as it is with vairagya, the intrinsic property of unsmearability, the mind has the capacity to disassociate itself from its long-cherished habit of clinging to this wheel. From the standpoint of yoga sadhana, the mind has the ability to scrutinize and comprehend all forms of change occurring in its vast landscape and so is able to recalibrate the practice to expedite the journey to nirbija samadhi.

Transformation is complex. In this sutra, Patanjali describes the dynamics of transformation both as a process and as a phenomenon. He divides the range of transformation into three broad categories: *dharma parinama*, transformation in defining attributes; *lakshana parinama*, transformation in symptoms; and *avastha parinama*, transformation in conditions. Because the goal of yoga sadhana is to gain mastery over the mind's roaming tendencies, make the mind one-pointed, and then use that laser-focused mind to discover its limitless grandeur and eventually reach nirbija samadhi, Patanjali confines his discussion on transformation to the body and mind.

Dharma parinama is the most subtle and significant of the three categories of transformation. *Dharma* means "defining qualities of a substance." The mind is the substance, and its distinctive qualities and properties are its dharma. Both the subtle impressions that churn up agitating thoughts and cognitions and the subtle impressions that impel the mind to confine itself to a single object are the mind's dharma (Vyasa on sutra 3:9). Being cognizant of numerous fleeting objects and being one-pointed are also the mind's dharma (Vyasa on sutra 3:11). When, with the practice of samyama or sabija samadhi, the mind loses its taste for paying attention to the subtle impressions and the agitating thoughts and cognitions arising from them, it has a greater ability to confine itself to its object of focus.

As the practice matures, we gain the experience of *samadhi parinama*, complete stillness of mind. Upon further maturation, samadhi parinama leads to complete one-pointedness (YS 3:12). This degree of one-pointedness infuses the mind with the capacity to observe the fundamental transformations occurring in the most subtle realm of its dharma.

This one-pointed mind now has the ability to pinpoint the exact strand of samskara or group of samskaras that churned up agitating thoughts and cognitions in earlier stages of sadhana. It has the ability to see how, with practice, those samskaras were transformed from very strong to less strong, from less strong to weak, and eventually to quiescent. It has the ability to see when deep-rooted afflicting impressions rose to the surface in an almost uncontrolled manner. It can see how, with practice, there came a time when their strength declined. Then there came a time when there was a tug-of-war between old afflicting samskaras and newly created meditative samskaras. The mind is able to see that at this stage there was a significant transformation in afflicting samskaras even though the meditative samskaras were not yet strong enough to nullify the non-meditative afflicting ones.

In other words, this highly concentrated mind is capable of making an accurate assessment of the changes in its deepest constituents. This capacity gives it confidence that the transformations occurring in the realm of its deepest constituents are real. And because it knows how those changes occurred, it has confidence in the efficacy of the practice and is confident that a more subtle and more potent transformation is on its way. Such a clear understanding of the transformation in its dharma—the subtle samskaric constituents that make up its body—empowers the mind to comprehend the next category of transformation, lakshana parinama.

Lakshana means "symptom, sign, indication." A highly concentrated mind has the ability to detect and examine the signs and symptoms that validate the changes occurring in its fundamental constituents. It also has the capacity to observe the changes occurring in the signs and symptoms themselves. These might be vivid and easily perceived or too subtle to be easily perceived.

A yogi with a highly concentrated mind can perceive both vivid and subtle signs and symptoms. For example, violent speech and actions are vivid signs of anger. By observing these signs, anyone can deduce the existence of anger in the mind. But the exact cause of anger, what feeds it, what keeps it hidden, and what makes it erupt are subtle dimensions of anger. A yogi with a highly concentrated mind can detect these subtle dimensions and devise a plan to eradicate anger and its cause once and for all. He can also perceive and scrutinize the signs and symptoms that indicate to what extent that plan has been effective.

The third category of transformation is avastha parinama. *Avastha* means "condition or state." A highly concentrated mind has the ability to observe and examine changes occurring in both physical and mental conditions. These conditions are also twofold: vivid and subtle. For example, childhood, adolescence, adulthood, and old age are vivid conditions of the body. Anyone can see and comprehend these conditions. Aging is regarded as a normal condition of the body. But a yogi with a highly concentrated mind is able to detect the subtle conditions that accelerate or retard aging—a subject that is elaborated on in sutras 3:45 and 3:46.

In the context of the practice of samyama, a highly concentrated mind is able to assess the changes that have already occurred in its disturbed, stupefied, and distracted states. Because it is also able to assess the changes that have taken place in the state of nirodha, the yogi can predict his own ability to confine the mind to a well-defined space. In other words, he has the ability to observe and examine the changes occurring in deeply rooted subtle impressions (*dharma*), the changes occurring in the signs and symptoms that verify the changes in dharma (*lakshana*), and the changes that have evolved into the current condition (*avastha*). The ability to observe and comprehend the inner dynamics of this threefold change empowers the yogi to recalibrate and fine-tune the course of sadhana in its advanced stages and thus avoid the subtle and potent pitfalls unique to each individual.

How this threefold transformation brings about the complete transformation in our core being is the subject of the next sutra.

SUTRA 3:14

शान्तोदिताव्यपदेश्यधर्मानुपाती धर्मी ॥१४॥

śāntoditāvyapadeśyadharmānupātī dharmī ॥ 14 ॥

śānta, past; *udita*, present; *avyapadeśya*, future; *dharma*, attribute; *ānupātī*, that which conforms to; *dharmī*, substratum, locus

The substratum conforms to [the changes occurring in its] past, present, and future attributes.

The practical application of this sutra rests on a clear understanding of the relationship between *dharma* and *dharmi* (*dharmin*). *Dharma* means "quality, characteristic, intrinsic property." *Dharmi* means "substratum serving as a locus for dharma."

To illustrate, all forms of energy originating in the sun and radiating from it are the dharma of the sun. The sun is the dharmi and serves as the locus for all forms of energy known and unknown. The power of gravity inherent in the sun is its dharma, its attribute, and the sun is the dharmi, the substratum. The size of the sun and the density engendered by its humongous mass are its attributes and the sun is their substratum. The extraordinary scale of the nuclear reaction at the sun's core and the flames flaring half a million miles into space are the sun's dharma; the sun is the dharmi, the locus of all those attributes.

Philosophers have long been debating the relationship between dharma and dharmi. Using the sun and its numberless forms of energy as an example, philosophers attempt to describe the nature of God and her relationship with her defining attributes. This has led to the development of dualism, non-dualism, qualified dualism, purely non-qualified dualism, and so on, to the point where the hairsplitting logic defies reason. Patanjali, however, draws on the concepts of dharma and dharmi only to show the relationship between the mind and its defining attributes. His purpose in introducing these concepts here is to demonstrate how the mind conforms to the changes occurring in its defining attributes.

The mind's ability to think, perceive, comprehend, discern, identify, and decide is its dharma; in relation to these abilities, the mind is the dharmi, the substratum. The mind has the power to transform these actions and the experiences they generate into memory. It has the power to transform short-term memories into long-term memories and store them as samskaras, subtle impressions. This power is the mind's dharma, and the mind itself is the dharmi.

The mind has the capacity to quiet the manifesting properties of the impressions or to awaken them. In other words, the subtle impressions sitting quietly in the mind field are the mind's dharma, and so are the subtle impressions pulsating there restlessly. The subtle impressions eager to merge with the divine essence of our creator are the mind's dharma. The subtle impressions intent on expanding their domain in the phenomenal world are the mind's dharma. Maintaining and losing the awareness of its dharma is also the mind's dharma. The mind itself is the dharmi, the substratum for all its known and unknown mysteries.

The mind is the finest evolute of primordial prakriti. It is as pure and pristine as prakriti. The mind's luminosity mirrors the luminosity of prakriti. The essential self-luminous nature of the mind is known as *buddhi sattva*, the pure and pristine essence of *buddhi*, our self-illuminating faculty. In the highest sense, buddhi sattva is dharma and the mind is dharmi. However, this degree of relationship between dharma and dharmi is applicable only to the highest-caliber yogis—*brahma rishis*, *siddhas*, *devas*, *prakritilayas*, and *videhas*—and clearly most of the practices described in the *Yoga Sutra* are not relevant to them.

From the standpoint of our sadhana, samskaras are the building blocks of our mind. They are the mind's inherent attributes, and the mind conforms to the changes occurring in them. Patanjali divides the entire range of the mind's attributes into three major categories: past, present, and future. The majority of our samskaras are lying dormant in the deeper niches of our mind. The mind is not aware of their existence—they are far removed from memory. However, their existence can be inferred, so our common sense puts them in the category of "past." For the sake of simplicity, we will call them inactive or silent samskaras.

The second category of samskaras consists of those that lie in a climatic zone of the mind conducive to their awakening. They have already been touched by the pranic breeze and are eager to manifest. They are in the mind's view and the mind is cognizant of their existence. Such samskaras fall into the domain of the present. Most of the time, the mind is engaged in cognitions pertaining to these samskaras; these cognitions are validated by direct perception.

Then there are samskaras with the potential to manifest in the future. The mind has the capacity to comprehend them, but that comprehension is beyond the range of inference and direct perception. Without relying on full knowledge of the silent samskaras or even on the samskaras currently in view, the mind has the capacity to intuit and bring forward its indescribable potential to envision and create a future. By using this capacity, the mind makes a map of the future and designs a plan to turn it into reality. This unique dharma, the mind's attribute, enables the mind to selectively choose the silent or active samskaras or avoid them altogether. By using this unique dharma, the mind generates the excitement and enthusiasm to do something which has never been done before and to create something which has never been created. Reclaiming this dharma and employing it is the objective of this entire chapter. In order to better comprehend what is presented in sutra 3:16 onward, a further study of the mind, its attributes, and the relationship between the two is warranted.

The concept of the mind in the *Yoga Sutra* is markedly different from the scholarly view of the mind. For thousands of years, scholars have been using the model of Sankhya philosophy to describe the dynamics of the mind. In so doing, they use the *Sankhya Karika* of Ishvara Krishna as their source text, which, according to our tradition, is incomplete and full of interpolations and thus does not represent Sankhya as understood by Patanjali.

According to the *Sankhya Karika*, there are two distinct entities: *purusha* and *prakriti*. Purusha is the conscious entity and is numberless. Prakriti is unconscious, one, unintelligent, and the cause of the objective world. The world and life in the world are full of sorrow. The world evolves from the comingling of purusha and prakriti. The complete disunion of these two entities is the way to end sorrow.

The first and foremost entity evolving from prakriti is the mind—technically known as *buddhi*. The term *buddhi* represents our individual faculty of comprehension. Parallel to buddhi is *mahat*, the collective faculty of comprehension. All other faculties of the mind—the essence of the physical elements, the senses, the five gross elements, and the phenomenal world made of these elements—evolve from the mind. According to the conventional view of Sankhya philosophy, we achieve liberation by isolating consciousness from the mind and everything evolving from it.

By contrast, yogis view prakriti as Ishvara's inherent attribute. Prakriti is the dharma of Ishvara and Ishvara is prakriti's substratum. To illustrate, Ishvara is the sun and prakriti is the sun's glow. The first principle evolving from this glow is the power of comprehension, buddhi. From buddhi evolves the power of identification, *asmita* or *ahamkara*. From this comes the power of thought, *manas*. Together, these three and the infinitely large variety of powers and privileges contained in them constitute chitta. When we use the term "mind" in the context of samyama or sabija samadhi, it refers to chitta. The purpose of the *Yoga Sutra* is to enable us to understand the dynamics of the mind and its intrinsic attributes.

The essence of Ishvara is the intrinsic attribute of the mind. The mind is the locus of this attribute. Due to this attribute, the mind is able to comprehend the fullness of Ishvara. It is also able to comprehend the fullness of the phenomenal world evolving from prakriti, which is Ishvara's essence.

Experientially, however, this intrinsic attribute of the mind has been mixed with the mind's acquired attributes. The long course of its interactions with sensory experiences and the superimposition of feelings of right and wrong, good and bad, pleasant and unpleasant on these experiences have made deep and potent impressions in the mind field. These impressions are the mind's acquired attributes and the mind is their locus. In the case of novice practitioners, these attributes churn up mental cognitions, preventing the mind from confining itself to the object of its focus.

As the practice of samyama is refined, these acquired attributes are transformed into sheer memory and absorbed into their locus, the mind. More precisely, they are absorbed in the mind's intrinsic attribute, its illuminating and comprehending power, where they reside as retentive power. In his commentary on sutra 2:4, Vyasa defines these fully transformed acquired attributes as *shakti matra pratishtha*, residing as sheer power. With practice, they are quieted to the point that they no longer demand the mind's attention. In this sutra, Patanjali calls these attributes *shanta*, quiet, another term for "past." This choice of words indicates that past experiences and the subtle impressions created by them are not dead but rather have been transformed into a unique ability, which the mind can use at its discretion.

Patanjali uses *udita*, that which is risen, to indicate present experience. A yogi has the capacity to bring forward fully transformed quiescent memories of the past. They arise from the mind like the sun rises at dawn. The rise of these subtle impressions illuminates the present without creating the slightest agitation. The mind is able to witness the rise of its own attributes without being affected by them.

Patanjali's choice of *avyapadeshya* to indicate the future is particularly significant. *Avyapadeshya* means "that which has not yet begun occupying the mind; that which is not in the mind's view." Knowing what will occur in the future on the basis of past and present experiences is within the capacity of a logical mind, but the highly concentrated mind of an accomplished yogi has the capacity to comprehend a future occurrence which may or may not be associated with what has transpired in the past or is transpiring in the present. This capacity of the mind is due to its intrinsic inner luminosity, which has been passed on to it from primordial prakriti, the essence of Ishvara.

According to this sutra, changes occurring in the building blocks of the mind bring a qualitative change in the mind. Noisy samskaras make the mind noisy, whereas dull ones make it dull. Sattvic, resilient samskaras make the mind cognizant and peacefully alert. In the beginning stages of sadhana, we attenuate and eventually nullify the strength of afflicting samskaras by applying the principle of vairagya. In proportion to the maturity of vairagya, the afflicting samskaras lose their capacity to churn up agitating thoughts and cognitions.

With the help of abhyasa, we create a new set of illuminating and calming samskaras. We do this by confining the mind to a well-defined space intrinsically filled with illuminating and calming energy. Together, vairagya and abhyasa lead us to a state in our inner journey where a disorganized, unstructured, restless past is transformed into shanta—a completely peaceful, still past. It also takes us to a point where our current thoughts and cognitions are rising in a peaceful and illuminating manner. Thus, the thoughts and cognitions in the present flow from one moment to the next without allowing a dissimilar thought to intervene.

When we sustain this practice for a long period of time without interruption, all our samskaras are transformed into sheer shakti. This shakti becomes the mind's attribute. Even though it is an acquired attribute, it is so sattvic, so transparent, and so illuminating that for all intents and purposes it poses no obstruction to the radiance of the primordial intrinsic luminosity of the mind. The acquired attributes of our mind have merged into its self-luminous intrinsic attributes. The self-illuminating property of this state is *prajna* (YS 2:27). Vyasa calls this state *chitta vimukti*, freedom from mind. Experientially, it dawns when our shakti (*sva*), the acquired attributes of our mind, unites with the shakti of our *svami*—Ishvara, the lord of life (YS 2:23).

To reiterate, in the earlier stages of our yoga sadhana, acquired attributes are the dharma of the mind and the mind is their locus, dharmi. As these acquired dharmas are transformed, the mind as their locus is also transformed. The mind's transformation (*anupati*) is always in proportion to the transformation of its defining attributes. This is one level of transformation.

The second level of transformation occurs when this transformed mind fully embraces the inner luminosity of Ishvara. Its fully transformed and purified attributes merge into the luminosity of Ishvara. At this moment, the pure and pristine intrinsic luminosity of Ishvara becomes the mind's intrinsic attribute; the mind becomes its locus. This mind is no longer "our" mind but Ishvara's mind. Its will is Ishvara's will. Actions performed by this mind are Ishvara's actions. As Patanjali clarifies later in sutra 4:6, actions performed by this mind no longer engender new samskaras. A yogi of this caliber is free here and now. This level of freedom is marked by absolute freedom from all desires, including the desire to be free and enlightened.

A yogi of this caliber does not predict the future, but rather sees a future which exists only in the eyes of Ishvara and his intrinsic prakriti. He is capable of projecting his internally conceived vision, and as soon he does, it begins to exist. This is what is indicated by the term *avyapadeshya*. This future is completely different from what is ordinarily understood as the future. This highly refined mind, which is totally immersed in the seeing power of Ishvara, is the mind of a rishi, a seer. What it sees is its own seeing power. Because there is nothing to obstruct what it sees, its inwardly perceived cognition is transformed into a living reality. That is how highly potent mantras come into being. A highly refined mind totally immersed in the seeing power of Ishvara is the dharmi, the locus of the mantra, and the intrinsic potential of the mantra is the dharma.

The entire range of experience pertaining to the least enlightened, the supremely enlightened, and all those in between falls into the threefold category of past, present, and future. Accomplishments in yoga sadhana, particularly those related to the development of the extraordinary powers described in this chapter, are totally dependent on how successful we have been in refining and transforming this threefold category of samskaras. The most crucial component of sadhana in determining our likelihood of success is the subject of the next sutra.

SUTRA 3:15

क्रमान्यत्वं परिणामान्यत्वे हेतुः ॥१५॥

kramānyatvaṁ pariṇāmānyatve hetuḥ ॥ 15 ॥

kramānyatvaṁ, change in sequence; *pariṇāmānyatve*, change in result; *hetuḥ*, cause

Change in the sequence alters the result.

With this sutra, Patanjali is stating a fact and highlighting its importance. *Dharma*, the defining attributes of our mind, changes; this is a fact. As it does, *lakshana*, the signs and symptoms pertaining to the change in the mind's attributes, also changes. This two-fold change leads to a change in *avastha*, the condition of the mind. The purpose of yoga sadhana is to understand the dynamics of this process and maneuver it in our favor. Maneuvering the process of change requires understanding how every step of change is linked with every other step. The sequence (*krama*) in which various steps of the process are arranged greatly influences the outcome of the process—change in the sequence alters the result.

The mind is the locus of its attributes and conforms to the changes occurring in them. Attributes are the locus of the sequence in which they are arranged, and they conform to the changes in the sequence. Similarly, a system of meditation is the locus of its various parts, and that system conforms to the changes occurring in those parts. The parts of the practice are the locus of the sequence in which they are arranged, and they conform to the changes in the sequence. This is the formula on which the entire process of transformation rests.

The practice leading to the furthest frontier of sabija samadhi, and eventually to nirbija samadhi, begins with dharana. In sutra 3:1, Patanjali tells us that confining the mind to an assigned field is dharana. He does not tell us what or where that space is or how to draw a boundary around it. Nor does he tell us that there comes a time in our practice of dharana when we allow our mind to purposefully travel from one assigned space to another. In commenting on that sutra, Vyasa lists a few spaces—the navel center, the lotus of the heart, the fontanelle, the region corresponding to the opening of the nostrils, and the tip of the tongue—as examples. Neither of these masters provide prerequisites or supporting practices. They leave these details to the living tradition with a warning: change in the sequence alters the result.

A system of practice has a set of identifiable components, which are carefully arranged in a particular sequence. Learning a system of practice involves understanding each of its components individually as well as in relation to each other. It also entails understanding the inherent value of the placement of each component and how that inherent value is suppressed or enhanced when the placement of those components is altered. Change in the sequence can come about in three different ways: *krama viccheda*, disrupting the sequence; *krama vyatyaya*, altering the order; and *krama sankarya*, adulterating the components, thereby adulterating the sequence.

One system of practicing dharana begins with uniting the mind with the breath. The ultimate goal is to lead the united forces of mind and breath to the center of the forehead and anchor them there. This sequence consists of sitting in an upright position, removing shallowness and noise from the breath, withdrawing the mind from sensory objects, taking the mind on a tour of the body following a precise route, and finally, bringing the mind to the opening of the nostrils and uniting it with the breath. This constitutes a practice preparatory to the main body of dharana. The different components of this preparatory practice are carefully arranged in a particular sequence. Disrupting, altering, or adulterating this sequence will lead to an unintended result. Similarly, the main body of the practice of dharana consists of bringing the region of the opening of the nostrils, inner corners of the eyes, eyebrow center, and center of the forehead into conscious awareness. Changing this sequence also leads to an unintended result.

The advanced practices of yoga, many of which are about to be introduced, are highly sequence sensitive. Hereafter, every practice described in the *Yoga Sutra* requires precision in a sequence verified by a living tradition. For example, there are two ways of approaching the center of the heart and meditating there—*aroha krama*, ascending order, and *avaroha krama*, descending order. We can begin our mental journey from the perineum and move upward to the heart, or we can start from the crown and move downward to the heart. These two sequences are a specialty of the Kaula and Samaya schools of Sri Vidya. There are two subspecialities within these schools: Sri Krama and Kali Krama. Disrupting, altering, or adulterating the sequence of each of these practices by mixing the techniques of these two different systems will change the result.

Maintaining the purity and precision of the sequence of different components of the practice becomes even more crucial when we are involved in a laser-focused practice of samyama meant to awaken the extraordinary powers of our mind and explore reality beyond the phenomenal world. Awakening these extraordinary powers is the subject of the rest of the chapter.

SUTRA 3:16

परिणामत्रयसंयमाद् अतीतानागतज्ञानम्
॥१६॥

pariṇāmatrayasaṁyamād atītānāgatajñānam ॥ 16 ॥

pariṇāmatrayasaṁyamād, from samyama on the threefold transformation; *atītānāgatajñānam*, knowledge of the past and future

From samyama on the threefold transformation, knowledge of the past and future.

In sutras 3:1 through 3:12, Patanjali and Vyasa explain how to cultivate a highly concentrated mind by practicing samyama. This yogically evolved mind is perceptive, stable, and still. It has little or no taste for associating with samskaras that churn up agitating thoughts and cognitions. It is disciplined enough to remain focused on the object of samyama without being distracted by sensory experiences. Its deep interest in attending the object of samyama, coupled with the power of contentment, frees it from anxiety and curiosity about the future. This leaves the mind with ample capacity to identify a particular cluster of samskaras. This highly perceptive mind is able to analyze the significant strands in that cluster and to separate the principal strand from the secondary ones.

As part of the practice referred to in this sutra, the mind is directed to observe and register the process of change that has occurred in the principal strand in a cluster of samskaras and, more importantly, the influence of the secondary strands on this process. The mind is primarily engaged in comprehending the change in the samskaras rather than in analyzing their merits and demerits. It is focused on observing the change in the secondary strands and the way this change has disrupted or supported the change in the principal strand. In this first step, the mind registers the changes that have occurred in *dharma*, the defining properties of both the central and secondary samskaras.

The next step is to pay attention to the signs and symptoms of the changes, *lakshana*. Here the mind is focused on observing the events or processes that supported or suppressed the manifestation of signs and symptoms. The intention behind this step is to determine why the mind, the locus of the samskaras, was fully able, partially able, or totally unable to see the change in the central strand of the samskaras. When the change occurring in the realm of samskaras manifests fully but the signs and symptoms are suppressed and thus invisible, the mind is overpowered. The mind is then run by the result of this change, which becomes an inescapable reality. The term for this reality is *avastha*, the condition of the mind. The mind is also guided to focus on how the condition could have been altered if the signs and symptoms were not suppressed and preventive measures had been applied in a timely manner.

The third step of the practice is to pay attention to the changes occurring in the conditions associated with both the principal and secondary strands under scrutiny. The mind is focused on observing how long a condition lasted, what caused it to last that long, and what kind of changes took place both in the cluster of samskaras and in the signs and symptoms that weakened, nullified, or enhanced the condition.

The fourth step of the practice is to pay attention to what is occurring in the present—to notice whether or not it is a continuation of the changes that have occurred in the past and, most importantly, whether the changes occurring in the present are inherently capable of weakening, nullifying, or enhancing the current conditions.

The result of this four-step practice is a clear understanding of what happened in the past and what is going to happen in the future. How correct this understanding will be hinges on how successfully we have applied the practice of samyama in quieting our fivefold affliction: ignorance, distorted sense of self-identity, attachment, aversion, and fear. We need a highly concentrated mind to observe the threefold transformation identified in this sutra: the changes occurring in dharma, the building blocks of our mind; the changes in lakshana, the signs and symptoms of transformation; and avastha, the condition these changes create.

Equally important, however, is a purified and inwardly turned mind with the capacity to remain untouched by what it touches. It must have the capacity not to be overwhelmed by what it sees. It must have mastered the art of witnessing without becoming involved in what it witnesses. Only a non-judgmental, highly concentrated mind interested in discovering facts and arranging them in the correct sequence allows us to comprehend the past accurately. Thereafter, by drawing on the lessons of the past, we can accurately predict the future.

With this practice, we can gain a good understanding of our past, but we cannot change it. Yet there is a value in knowing the future, provided we apply the lessons learned from practicing samyama on the threefold change. After all, the primary objective of yoga sadhana is to avert the possibility of sorrow manifesting in the future.

In advanced stages, we can apply the outcome of this practice to observe and analyze changes that have occurred in the dharma, lakshana, and avastha of a particular society, community, or nation. This allows us to see its past accurately and predict the future. The prediction will be borne out only if that society or community passively watches, takes no action, and lets the threefold change run its course. But in any case, such prophecies have no spiritual value.

SUTRA 3:17

शब्दार्थप्रत्ययानामितरेतराध्यासात्
सङ्करस्तत्प्रविभागसंयमात्सर्वभूतरुतज्ञानम् ॥१७॥

śabdārthapratyayānāmitaretarādhyāsāt
saṅkarastatpravibhāgasaṁyamātsarvabhūtarutajñānam ‖ 17 ‖

śabdārthapratyayānām, of word, meaning, and cognition; *itaretara*, one or the other; *adhyāsāt*, from superimposition; *saṅkaraḥ*, fully conflated, completely mingled; *tatpravibhāgasaṁyamāt*, from samyama on their distinct parts; *sarvabhūtarutajñānam*, the understanding of the sounds [produced by] all creatures

The superimposition of word, meaning, and cognition engenders a fully conflated perception of them. From samyama on their distinct parts, comprehension of what creatures are saying.

A look at how babies express themselves and how they comprehend the meaning and intent of conversations long before they learn a language will help us understand the practice described in this sutra and the basis of the extraordinary accomplishment engendered by it.

According to Sankhya philosophy, we are born with eight natural capacities. The first three are particularly germane here. They are *uha*, intuitive comprehension; *shabda*, the capacity to associate the meaning with the word; and *adhyayana*, the capacity to dissect the content of words and sentences and arrive at a conclusion (*Sankhya Karika* 51).

As babies, we are aware of our immediate surroundings even before our sense organs are fully developed and trained and before bidirectional communication is fully established between our sense organs and cortex. We are instantly aware of our mother's presence, and within a matter of days we become aware of those who frequently share our space and of the pleasant and unpleasant vibrations that fill that space. We do all this without any apparent assistance from others. The actual guide, trainer, and enabler in the early stages of our childhood is uha, the flash of intuition.

While lying in a crib or sitting in our mother's lap, we are bombarded with a variety of sounds: the television is on, family members are talking, and siblings are banging pots and pans. We comprehend everything going on around us at some level but are unable to express what we understand and feel because we lack a fully trained nervous system and vocal organs. However, the power of intuition is putting pressure on the mind and brain to train the nervous system so that we will be able to communicate with those around us.

Initially, the process of comprehension is totally intuitive. As infants, we do not rely on distinct words or the sentences they form but intuitively understand the meaning behind clusters of sounds. Without knowing the distinct words or their distinctive meanings, we comprehend the essence of a sentence as well as a cluster of sentences. *Pratibha*, intuition, is the locus of this understanding. Thus, according to the distinguished yogi and grammarian Bhartrihari, intuition is the meaning of the sentence. Intuitive understanding is the meaning of the cluster of sentences that comprise a conversation.

By the time the second word in a sentence begins, the first word has vanished into space. By the time the second sentence has begun, the first sentence has vanished. By the time a statement is complete, all the sentences have vanished, yet the essence of the statement remains. This is what a baby comprehends, and it responds on the basis of that comprehension. It responds not to what was said but to what was meant. This intuitive understanding is the basis of comprehension.

Our second innate capacity is shabda, the ability to associate word and meaning. Our innate power of intuitive wisdom is guiding the current of our comprehension, but we observe that those around us rely mainly on words to express their feelings and intentions. This observation puts pressure on our intuition to discover the precise meaning they have superimposed on words.

The body of a word is made of a distinct set of sounds. We have the capacity to comprehend the smallest unit of sound, the smallest gap between units of sound, and the difference these small units of sound make in the formation of a word when their sequence is changed.

Furthermore, we have the capacity to decipher the subtle anatomy of sounds. We intuitively sense which part of the vocal organ produces a sound and whether the sound is soft or hard, aspirate or non-aspirate. We have the capacity to intuit the origin of a sound—whether it is nasal, short, long, or a diphthong—and whether it is produced by letting the air of exhalation touch two spots in the vocal cords simultaneously or consecutively. We can sense further variations of the sound produced by accents, high pitches, low pitches, and a variety of pitches in between. By using this power, we can reproduce the sounds of the words we hear.

By using our first innate ability, intuitive comprehension, we superimpose the same meaning on the words that the people in our surroundings have superimposed on them. That is how language is born. Language is an auditory tool for communicating our feelings and intentions. Constructing a word by superimposing a meaning on a body of sound is artificial and arbitrary. We have done this from time immemorial, and it has been acknowledged and approved by the innate wisdom of our intuition. In this way, language has created an unalterable reality.

Our third innate capacity is adhyayana, the ability to dissect both a word and its meaning and arrive at a conclusive understanding. This ability enables us to comprehend what is conveyed by subtle intonations of words and their inflections in a particular portion of a sentence. This ability allows us to comprehend both the explicit and implicit meaning of a word or series of words. It enables us to apprehend the messages hidden between sentences, words, and even between syllables and phonemes.

Our second and third innate capacities are extensions of the first innate capacity—intuition. The cognizance of a cluster of sounds and the meaning associated with them is a function of intuition. We identify a set of sounds as words only when they become associated with a meaning. What is conveyed by a word is actually not contained in the word itself but is in the field of our intuition. Both the sound and the meaning conveyed by it reside in intuition in the form of memory. As soon as we hear a sound or a set of sounds, the memory pertaining to them springs forth from the intuitive field, transforming the sounds into words and sentences laced with meaning.

Tracing the evolution of words and sounds is at the crux of sutra 3:17. Describing the practical application of this sutra, Vyasa states, "What we hear through our ears is simply a sound. Comprehension of sound as a word is due to what has been drawn from nada, the intelligent force that propels the sound and presents it to our mental faculty as an object of comprehension. Segments of sound recognized as phonemes cannot be uttered simultaneously. Only one phoneme can be uttered at a time. Two segments of sound are distinct from each other only because there is a gap between them. Consequently, two phonemes never touch each other; yet, without touching, they appear and disappear. And yet, for our faculty of comprehension, the continuity of those segments of sound is maintained."

Cognition of the continuity of the segments of sound that form the body of a word is due to the ever-stable, unbroken flow of intuition. All segments of sound, words, and the sentences constructed by them find their meaning—convey their essence—only when empowered by intuition. In reality, every phoneme disappears before the next phoneme is born and thus has no ability to form a word. Yet it does so due to the power of intuition.

When seen from the vantage point of intuition, the soul of the words and sentences inheres in every syllable and phoneme. Every phoneme is infused with the power to convey all possible meanings and their contents. This happens because the previous phoneme is connected to space, which is followed by the next phoneme, and so on. All these segments of sound along with the minute spaces between them, as well as the sequence in which they are arranged and the meaning that has been superimposed on them, are always present as memories in the field of intuition. It is intuition's presentation of those memories to our faculty of comprehension that manifests as the cognition of words and sentences and their explicit and implicit meanings. This is the dynamic of the sounds, words, sentences, and comprehension of their meanings within the context of the human species.

The same dynamic applies in comprehending the meanings of sounds made by other creatures. Cultivating the capacity to comprehend what a creature is saying is mainly dependent on how one-pointed our mind is and to what extent it is free from the fivefold affliction. Freedom from the fivefold affliction opens the door to the field of intuition. Using the power of intuition, we concentrate on the sounds made by a creature. And just as a baby intuitively discerns a cluster of sounds, breaks it down into small units, comprehends those units in sequence, attributes a meaning to that cluster of sounds, and thus learns the language, we focus our highly concentrated mind on the sounds made by that creature. Success in this practice hinges first on our ability to discern the smallest parts of the sounds the creature produced. Second, it involves invoking a vast range of memories preserved in the field of intuition and identifying those that are related to the behaviors of that creature.

The practice of dharana as described in sutra 3:1 gives the mind the ability to unearth the memories pertaining not only to its own experiences but also to those of others. From time immemorial, in the cyclical journey of life, we have lived and interacted with all forms of life and, at a deep level, memories pertaining to all those interactions are fully preserved. By practicing samyama on minute segments of a sound, the gap between those segments, the sequence of those segments, and the feelings the creature expresses through those sounds in that particular order, we can decipher its intention in making that sound. By observing a wider range of that creature's behavior and the range of sound the creature produces to express those behaviors, we can map out the "language" of that creature fairly accurately.

It is important to note that this practice gives us access to understanding the language only of non-human species. The range of consciousness and expressions of humans is infinitely vast. Understanding the meaning of all spoken and unspoken words of humans is not within the scope of this sutra but is a theme Patanjali picks up in sutra 3:33.

SUTRA 3:18

संस्कारसाक्षात्करणात्पूर्वजातिज्ञानम् ॥१८॥

saṁskārasākṣātkaraṇātpūrvajātijñānam ॥ 18 ॥

saṁskārasākṣātkaraṇāt, from direct realization of samskaras; *pūrvajātijñānam*, knowledge of previous birth[s]

From direct realization of samskaras, knowledge of previous births.

In introducing this sutra, both Patanjali and Vyasa assume we are fully familiar with the concepts of karma and *karmashaya* and their role in the process of rebirth. Karmas are the physical, verbal, and mental actions we perform. Samskaras are the subtle impressions of those actions. Subtle impressions are stored in our mind in the form of memory; thus, the mind is a karmashaya, a sack of karmic impressions. This subject is elaborated on in sutras 2:12 through 2:15. As we repeat our actions, the samskaras related to them become stronger and are transformed into habits. Once habits are formed, we are no longer in charge. Our habits—powerful karmic impressions—now control our actions. We are compelled to perform actions that conform to the inherent quality of our samskaras. Vyasa calls this *vritti samskara chakra*, the cycle of mental action to samskara and samskara to mental action (YS 1:5). This simple-sounding concept is the ground for the cycle of birth to death and death to birth.

Samskaras are products of our actions, and our actions are products of our samskaras. Both are born in the mind and live there. Due to their long-cherished association with the mind, samskaras and the actions they inspire have become inherent attributes (*dharma*) of the mind; the mind is their locus (*dharmi*). These attributes are the building blocks of our personality.

Samskaras and the actions propelled by them fall into two broad categories: *klishta*, afflicting, and *aklishta*, non-afflicting. Afflicting samskaras churn up afflicting thoughts and feelings. They embody the qualities of lack of understanding, distorted sense of self-identity, attachment, aversion, and fear. They are created by actions smeared with desire, anger, hatred, jealousy, greed, and fear, and they churn up tendencies that match these negative qualities. Non-afflicting samskaras embody the qualities of self-understanding, discernment, non-attachment, concern for others, and trust in divine providence. They are created by actions enlivened by discrimination, love, selflessness, compassion, non-possessiveness, patience, and most importantly, the desire to find a connection with the life force. These samskaras churn up tendencies that match their positive qualities. We are a blend of afflicting and non-afflicting samskaras.

Our samskaras are our most valued possessions. We have assimilated them so thoroughly that we fail to see any difference between them and the mind. Because they have become one with the mind, the defining attributes of the samskaras define the mind's qualities and characteristics. Thus, the inherent properties of the samskaras become the mind's motivating force.

Samskaras are subtle impressions of our past actions, yet they remain forever alive and vibrant in the form of memory. The most potent quality of our samskaras is the desire that motivated us to perform actions in the first place. As long as samskaras exist, the seeds of desire persist. At the earliest opportunity, the seeds of our desires stir the domain of samskaras, and in response, samskaras churn up matching thoughts and feelings. Because of its strong identification with its samskaras, the mind conforms to these samskaric pulsations, forcing us to commit ourselves to actions that hold the prospect of fulfilling our desires. This further reinforces the samskaras.

When we do not succeed in fulfilling our desires, disappointment, anger, and sadness result. We begin to doubt our judgment and lose trust and confidence in ourselves. Subtle impressions of these negative feelings are added to the original stock of samskaras. In this way, the world consisting of samskaras and superimposed on our mind becomes complex, confusing, and impenetrable. This complex, confusing, and indiscernible reality becomes our most valued possession. We are compelled to invest all of life's resources in protecting and expanding this possession. For a mind stained by samskaras, fulfillment comes from protecting and expanding them.

According to Patanjali and Vyasa, the cycle of birth and death is propelled by samskaras. Samskaras shape our personality. They determine our tastes and interests, our likes and dislikes. They guide our ambitions and motivations. Samskaras subtly awaken the talents conducive to fulfilling the desires lying dormant in their bosom. They also awaken feelings of hatred and dislike toward the objects and activities that oppose their inherent quality. For all these reasons, each of us chooses our unique path and strives to achieve our goals in a unique way. Our idea of freedom and fulfillment is designed and orchestrated by our samskaras. For all intents and purposes, samskaras are the creators of our destiny. That is why a clear and accurate understanding of our most compelling samskaras allows us to gain knowledge of our previous births.

Our most compelling samskaras originate in a deep, highly

potent pool of numberless samskaras. Some of these are quite strong, while others are relatively weak. For the sake of discussion, these two categories are called primary samskaras and secondary samskaras.

External circumstances are simply instigating factors (*nimitta karana*). Instigating factors awaken primary samskaras, which in turn stir up secondary samskaras. In this way, our powerful primary samskaras, assisted by secondary samskaras, determine where and how we are to be born, how long we will live in that body, how our personality traits will develop, how our unique habits and behaviors will propel the major course of our actions, and how those actions will serve as a gateway for our destiny (YS 2:12–14).

How our primary samskaras play out during the last phase of our life gives us a clue to how they determine the course of our rebirth. By the time most of us reach the end of our life, our body has become frail. The capacity of our lungs and heart has declined. Cortical function is no longer sharp. At this stage, the thinking and discriminating mind has little capacity to ward off the powerful current of thoughts, feelings, and sentiments arising from the most powerful and potent pool of samskaras. Thoughts originating from these samskaras hover in the mind and we are overpowered by them. When divine providence again puts us in the current of transmigration, the awareness with which we departed begins to pulsate in that powerful pool of samskaras. This pulsation takes the leading role in our rebirth and sets the ground for the manifestation of our unique personality traits, tastes, interests, and the major characteristics of our behaviors.

We are born with no memory of our past. We do not know the connection between our current and previous lives. Tracing our past requires understanding the factors that give an abstract sensory experience a perceivable body. Those factors are time, space, and the efficient cause that impels the senses to come into contact with their respective objects.

The mind comprehends an experience along with its context. The context is always associated with time, space, and the efficient cause. Experience is preceded by an action; an action takes place in a particular time and space. The memory of an action and of the experience brought by that action is drenched in the memory of the time when the action and the experience took place, as well as the memory of the place. Furthermore, this memory is fastened to the mind's own unique sense of time and space. In other words, neither an action nor its associated experience can be comprehended in isolation from time and space.

Further, actions are always facilitated by an efficient cause. For example, making a clay pot requires clay, tools, and a potter. Clay is the material cause, the tools are the secondary cause, and the potter is the efficient cause. In the case of an action, samskaras and the desires originating from the samskaras are the material causes. The mind as a conscious entity and the locus of the samskaras is the efficient cause. The memory of the action and of the experience emerging from it are therefore always accompanied by the memory of the mind's involvement in carrying out the action.

An action consists of a minimum of two components: subject and object—the one carrying out the action and the other directly or indirectly affected by it. Therefore, the memory pertaining to an action and the resulting experience is drenched in the memory of the efficient cause—the mind's involvement in carrying out the action—in addition to the memory of time and space. In tracing our past life, the greater the skill we have cultivated in breaking down these minute details of memory, the more successful we will be.

Primary samskaras are extremely subtle and highly potent. The external causes that awaken them are equally subtle and potent. The external causes present an environment conducive to the awakening of the main strand of primary samskaras. The inherent urge of the primary samskaras then awakens the secondary samskaras. For anyone other than a fully accomplished yogi, the awakening of primary and secondary samskaras is imperceptible and inconceivable.

In sutra 2:3, Vyasa tells us that the awakening of our samskaras is self-propelled, and he explains how this awakening leads to karmic fruition. As he states, when the intrinsic force of the primary samskaras begins to pulsate, the secondary samskaras pulsate in response. The pulsation of secondary samskaras manifests in the form of attracting external conditions conducive to fulfilling the innate urge of the primary samskaras. In this way, consciousness—which serves as a locus for our mind and its samskaric contents—and the conditions required for our rebirth are drawn toward each other. That is how we are born at a particular place, in a particular time, and in a particular species. This is what leads us to develop our unique personality traits and our unique shades of tastes and interests.

The most compelling patterns in our behavior influence, and to some extent even block, our faculty of discernment, thus setting the stage for an unavoidable future. These patterns have their source in our primary samskaras. Secondary samskaras arrange the ingredients we need to justify our behaviors. The more methodically and precisely we identify our current compelling patterns and track how secondary samskaras are supporting those patterns, the more successful we will be in understanding how the primary samskaras led us to where we are today.

When we attempt to decipher the role of secondary samskaras in assisting the irresistible cravings of the primary samskaras, we will be met with resistance. The indomitable will emitting from the primary samskaras will compel us to drop the idea of analyzing the dynamics of the secondary samskaras. However, if we remain firm in our attempt, this resistance will provide a clue to the circumstances in which both the primary and secondary samskaras were formed. That in turn will pull forward the fine details of the primary and secondary samskaras. Discovery of these fine details is the doorway to understanding our past life or a series of past lives.

Adepts caution that a complete understanding of one's past is the domain of highly accomplished siddhas, devas, and rishis—beings who are simultaneously part of the phenomenal world and the absolute. In sutra 4:18, Patanjali clarifies that the absolute being, the lord of our mind, alone is the knower of all our samskaras and their associated tendencies.

In commenting on this sutra, Vyasa cites a dialogue between two accomplished masters, Avatya and Jaigishavya, to describe the vast nature of the practice pertaining to direct realization of our samskaras:

Avatya: Thousands of lives, during different cycles of creation, and all the experiences pertaining to them are fully known to you. Tell me, what is the summary of all that experience? You also know the future. What is the relevance of knowing the past and the future?

Jaigishavya: From this experience, I conclude that life is full of sorrow for a soul lacking knowledge. As long as there is craving, the soul remains caught in the cycle of birth and death. Life is meaningful when the soul uses it to understand the source of craving and makes an effort to rise above the world enveloped in sorrow.

With this dialogue, Vyasa is telling us that the knowledge of the past and future is relevant only if it helps us accelerate our quest to understand our inner essence.

SUTRA 3:19

प्रत्ययस्य परचित्तज्ञानम् ॥१९॥

pratyayasya paracittajñānam ‖ 19 ‖

pratyayasya, of cognition; *paracittajñānam*, knowledge of the mind of others

Understanding another person's cognition leads to an understanding of that person's mind.

In the previous sutra, Patanjali explains that knowledge of our previous life comes from the direct realization of our samskaras. In this sutra, he tells us that direct realization of another person's cognition opens the door to understanding that person's mind. The practice resulting in this accomplishment requires first understanding how two different faculties of our mind—emotion and intellect—influence our consciousness and impel us to take an action.

Cognitions arising from the emotional faculty of our mind instantly color our consciousness and impel us to action. This coloring of consciousness is experienced as feeling. Feeling influences our brain and nervous system. Continuous emotional tides impel our body to express those feelings through different movements and gestures. For example, facial expressions and changes in tone of voice, breathing patterns, posture, muscular tension, and expression in the eyes are responses to what is occurring in our emotional world.

Cognitions arising from the intellectual faculty impel our body to act only in a purpose-driven manner. The intellectual faculty is cultivated to master a skill. Cognitions arising from it are willfully directed toward achieving a goal. They are often intentional and preplanned, and are brought forward for a purpose—to prove a point, form an alliance, reinforce convictions, and so on. These outward intellectual expressions are not accurate indicators of our internal climate.

The practice referred to in this sutra begins with differentiating a person's emotional currents from their intellectual expressions. Next, we invoke the virtue of sympathy and heighten our sensitivity to that person's feelings. Here, in addition to a highly concentrated mind, we need a mind that has absorbed the virtues of friendship, compassion, cheerfulness, and non-judgment, as elaborated on in sutra 1:33. These virtues help remove the wall of duality between us and the one whose feelings we are trying to sense. By using that person's feelings as a pathway, we allow our highly concentrated mind to enter the subject's emotional domain. Those feelings are the pathway to a large pool of similar emotions. By observing the subtle variations in the feelings and their trigger points, we are able to comprehend the general characteristics of the emotional pool and its magnitude.

It is important to remember that, according to sutra 3:14, the entire range of the mind's attributes falls into three categories: past, present, and future. The samskaras lying dormant deep in the mind field belong to the past. Samskaras rising to the surface belong to the present and are experienced as cognitions. The mind also has the ability to comprehend the samskaras that will manifest in the future. The mind is the locus of all these attributes—past, present, and future. Cognitions, particularly those that have an emotional faculty as their source, are just the tip of the iceberg. By comprehending them and practicing samyama on them, we can allow our mind to have a high degree of absorption in that person's feelings. Using those feelings as a pathway, we can enter the pool from where they are rising. However, this gives us only limited access to that pool, and that limited access does not provide access to the mind itself, which is the locus of all of its attributes—a fact Patanjali clarifies in the next sutra.

SUTRA 3:20

न च तत्सालम्बनं तस्याविषयीभूतत्वात् ॥२०॥

na ca tatsālambanaṁ tasyāviṣayībhūtatvāt ॥ 20 ॥

na, not; *ca*, however; *tat*, that; *sālambanaṁ*, accompanied by an object; *tasya*, of that; *aviṣayībhūtatvāt*, because of not being in the domain [of samyama]

That knowledge, however, does not include the object of cognition, because that [object] is not in the domain of samyama.

Here Patanjali highlights a limitation in the knowledge arising from the practices referred to in sutras 3:18 and 3:19. In sutra 3:18, samskaras are the object of samyama. From practicing samyama—concentration, meditation and samadhi—on our samskaras, we gain a deeper understanding of them, including when, how, and in what circumstances they were created. The understanding of samskaras that arises from this practice of samyama includes knowledge of time, space, and the efficient cause associated with our samskaras. This knowledge enables us to know some of the details of our past life. This practice is directed toward knowing ourselves—our past and the role it plays in our current life.

In sutra 3:19, cognitions rather than samskaras are the object of samyama. Cognitions occur in the present. As they arise, they color our consciousness, and the mind registers them as feelings. Cognitions are associated with their corresponding objects, but the mind's association with objects lasts only for a moment. The mind connects with the objects through the senses. At the instant of this connection, the senses relay the information to the mind. Through its familiarity with the objects and their inherent attributes, the mind perceives that information distinctly. This distinctiveness comes from the mind's ability to color its perceptions, which it does by projecting its deeply ingrained likes, dislikes, preconceived notions, habits, and preoccupations. No sensory experience is perfectly pure or pristine—it is always colored by the dominant qualities of the samskaras embedded in the mind. The mind registers this colored experience as a feeling.

The cognition pertaining to this feeling is the object of samyama. By practicing samyama on another person's cognition, we gain knowledge of a limited aspect of that person's mind. Because the cognition and the distinctive feeling associated with it is a fresh experience, meditation on it reveals only the current condition of that person's mind.

The same practice can be applied to identify and meditate on our own cognitions. That will lead us to know the dimension of our mind that is affected by those cognitions and the feelings associated with them. This is a tricky proposition, however. Yogis, who by definition have highly trained, disciplined, and concentrated minds, can successfully concentrate on someone else's cognitions as well as on their own. But those of us caught up in our own cognitions and associated feelings have no ability to observe them. We have no ability to distance ourselves from our cognitions, let alone discover the dimension of our mind affected by them.

Yogis can meditate on others' cognitions because they have mastered the art of remaining untouched by what they touch. They can use this ability to identify a particular cognition or a group of cognitions from the immediate past and use it as an object of the practice of samyama. The purpose of such a practice is solely to discover a deeper aspect of a person's mind. A yogi of this caliber can also use this ability to identify his own cognition or group of cognitions belonging to his more distant past and use it as an object of samyama. In that case, the purpose of the practice is to discover a deeper aspect of his own mind. To that end, he can combine it with the practice described in sutra 3:18.

According to the tradition, the combined practice of sutras 3:18 and 3:19 enables us to peer into the subtler sources of cognitions. As a result, we can know the current condition of our mind as well as the potent samskaras that churn up cognitions. These two distinct yet interconnected practices broaden the field of our knowledge. We become acutely aware of both our superficial and our deeper states. However, as this sutra emphatically states, neither the separate practices described in sutras 3:18 and 3:19 nor the combined practices of the two give us complete knowledge of our mind or anyone else's. This is because what we do not already know cannot be made an object of samyama. The mind is the greatest of all mysteries, and as Patanjali tells us in sutra 4:18, this mystery is known to no one other than purusha, the lord of life.

SUTRA 3:21

कायरूपसंयमात्तद्ग्राह्यशक्तिस्तम्भे
चक्षुःप्रकाशासम्प्रयोगेऽन्तर्धानम् ।।२१।।

kāyarūpasaṁyamāttadgrāhyaśaktistambhe
cakṣuḥprakāśāsaṁprayoge'ntardhānam ॥ 21 ॥

kāyarūpasaṁyamāt, from samyama on the form of the body; *tat*, its; *grāhyaśaktistambhe*, upon immobilization of the power to be perceived; *cakṣuḥprakāśāsaṁprayoge*, upon blocking the light of the eyes; *antardhānam*, disappearance

From samyama on the form of the body, immobilization of its power to be perceived. [In addition to accomplishing that,] upon blocking the light of the eyes, the experience of the disappearance [of the yogi's body].

In this sutra, Patanjali is in effect saying that from samyama on the form of the body comes the immobilization of the body's power to be perceived. In other words, samyama—the practice of concentration, meditation, and samadhi—on the body's form immobilizes or freezes the body's perceptibility. When combined with the next component of the practice, this form of samyama enables the yogi to become invisible to the viewer. This second component includes the technique of blocking the light emitting from the eyes of the viewer.

What does Patanjali mean by the form of the body? Does it mean how the yogi appears? Does the yogi use her own image as an object of samyama? And by doing this, does she inhibit the body's natural quality of being perceptible to others? Furthermore, what does Patanjali mean by the power of perceivability pertaining to the form of the body? Is the perceivability of the form of the body different from the perceivability of the body itself?

The next set of questions is related to blocking the light emitting from the eyes of the viewer. Is Patanjali talking about erecting a wall or drawing a curtain between the viewer and the yogi, thus preventing the viewer from seeing the yogi? Is he referring to the power intrinsic to the sense of sight? Is he referring to some special yogic technique for blocking the sense of sight, or for suppressing the mind's capacity to comprehend the object of sight, or both? Understanding the practices referred to in this sutra and their intended result requires clear answers to these questions.

The question pertaining to the power of perceptibility takes us all the way back to the ultimate source of the phenomenal world—primordial prakriti. It is absolute, formless, untraceable, and thus imperceptible. Pure and pervasive intelligence imbued with the awareness of subjectivity and objectivity is the first step in the evolution of the phenomenal world arising from formless, untraceable, imperceptible prakriti. From the standpoint of its boundless expanse, this stage of evolution is called *mahat*, the grand. From the standpoint of its intrinsic subject-object awareness, it is called *buddhi*, the knowing power. This is the first traceable stage of untraceable prakriti.

Buddhi is the locus of the intelligence that at once embodies *grahaka shakti*, the power to perceive; *grahya shakti*, the power to be perceived; and *grahana shakti*, the power to carry out the process of perception. Together, these three powers are known as *buddhi sattva*, the essence of buddhi. Buddhi alone has the capacity to comprehend the infinitely vast scope of its essence. The faculties of thought, identification, and discrimination; the experiences of sound, touch, form, taste, and smell; the senses of cognition; the senses of action; and the world made of matter and energy all evolve from buddhi. Buddhi knows itself and its essence. It knows it is the perceiver, the object of perception, and the process of perception. Buddhi also knows everything that evolves from it.

All the evolutes of buddhi are imbued with its threefold essence—the power to perceive, the power to be perceived, and the power to carry out the process of perception—yet one of these powers is always more dominant than the others. For example, the mind—the thinking faculty—has the capacity to know everything in the objective world, but can know itself only with the aid of buddhi. *Ahamkara*, the faculty of identification, has the capacity to identify anything in the objective world but can identify itself only with the aid of buddhi. In this regard, the power to perceive inherent in the faculty of thinking and identification is subdued, while the power to be perceived is fully manifest.

The senses have the capacity to apprehend their respective objects but can apprehend themselves only with the aid of the mind. In this regard, the power to perceive inherent in the senses is subdued, while their power to be perceived is fully manifest. However, in comparison to the senses, the mind's power to perceive is very much manifest. Thus, it has the capacity to shed its light on the senses, enabling them to become perceivers.

The aspect of the phenomenal world that has form and size is made of matter and energy. It is visible because it is charged with grahya shakti, the power to be perceived. In material objects, the power to perceive and the power to carry out perception are significantly subdued.

Our body is made of matter and energy. It has form. We perceive the form of our body because it is more than an aggregate of matter and energy. It is an intelligent entity. The physical frame of our body is saturated with the senses and different faculties of our mind. This is what makes our physical frame a living entity. Buddhi is the core of this living entity. The threefold essence of buddhi—the power to perceive, the power to be perceived, and the power to carry out the process of perception—flows unequally in various aspects of our being. The outer shell of our body, which serves as the locus for form, is predominately imbued with the power to be perceived. But at a deeper level, our eyes, the sense organs of sight, are imbued with both the power to perceive and the power to be perceived.

The center of vision in the brain, however, is predominately imbued with the power to perceive. This part of our brain is the recipient of buddhi's power to perceive. Our mental faculties of thinking, discrimination, and identification are directly connected to buddhi sattva. These faculties are the conduits for the flow of buddhi's threefold power. Immobilization of the power to be perceived inherent in the outer shell of the body means reversing the flow of this power, leading it all the way back to buddhi and anchoring it there. This process is dependent solely on our success in practicing the broad range of samyama as described in the first five sutras of this chapter.

The practice described in these five sutras begins with training the mind to follow the flow of the breath. This training enables us to transcend the physical aspect of breathing and become aware of the non-physical pranic counterpart of the breath. Then we unite our mind with this pranic flow and allow our mind to follow the pranic current between the opening of the nostrils and the center of the forehead. When the union between the mind and the breath is firmly established, an effort is made to feel the flow of the outgoing breath beyond the opening of the nostrils, all the way to twelve finger-widths in front of the face.

Next we are guided to feel the beginning of the inhalation from the same point where the exhalation ended and to cultivate a sense of the twelve-finger-width space in front of our face. We are now feeling the fully coordinated flow of our pranic force and the mind between this space and the center of the forehead. The unique points brought into conscious awareness during this practice are the center of the forehead, the center between the eyebrows, the inner corners of the eyes, the opening of the nostrils, and the point in space twelve finger-widths away from the opening of the nostrils. As practice progresses, the mental awareness becomes concentrated in the center of the forehead.

At this stage, as the first five sutras of this chapter explain, there arises the experience of a uniquely lit space corresponding to our forehead. As this experience solidifies, we are able to sense the subtle pulsation of pranic awareness at the center of this self-luminous space. According to sutra 3:1, confining the mind to this space is dharana. The deepening of this practice to the point that we are barely aware of ourselves as the meditator is dhyana. And when we are no longer aware of ourselves as the meditator, the pranic pulsation as an object of meditation, or the process of meditation, but are totally absorbed in the pranic pulsation, that is samadhi. The practice described in this sutra begins from here.

Based on what I have gathered from the living tradition, the siddhi of invisibility mentioned in this sutra and many other siddhis referred to in the rest of the chapter require mastering two specific practices: *prapancha vyapti anusandhana* and *sthana anusandhana* (*Svacchanda Tantra* 1:38–39; 1:59–60; and 3:49–53). Proficiency in these two practices helps us accelerate the flow of buddhi's intrinsic powers.

With prapancha vyapti anusandhana, we are able to mobilize pranic pulsation and the pranic light emitting from it and circulate it in every part of our body with full awareness. With the help of the same practice, we are also able to reverse this process and thus immobilize these powers. With sthana anusandhana, we are able to condense the pranic pulsation and its light and deliberately localize it in specific parts of our body, such as the heart, the navel, the soft palate, the center between the eyebrows, and so on. We are also able to reverse this process and pull these powers from these centers back to their source, the locus of buddhi sattva.

To further refine the efficacy of these two practices, students are led to advanced practices of tantra, such as *Bagalamukhi* and *Jatavedas Agni*. These practices have traditionally been applied to subdue and even completely suppress the body's natural quality of being perceived by others.

The second part of the practice mentioned in this sutra is associated with subduing or completely suppressing the viewer's power to perceive. This requires far greater mastery over the threefold power of buddhi than is required by the previous practice. Commanding one's own body and its intrinsic powers is easier than commanding someone else's.

Furthermore, the practice pertaining to this accomplishment raises an ethical question. What right does a yogi have to manipulate, subdue, or suppress the viewer's natural abilities and functions? In addition to this ethical issue, what if something goes wrong while a well-meaning yogi is playing with the viewer's inherent power to perceive the object of sight? With these complications in mind, the tradition forbids this aspect of the practice. Instead, it substitutes a tantric practice that is safer and milder yet yields the same result—making the practitioner invisible to the viewer. In tantric circles, this practice is known as *tiraskarini vidya*. Tiraskarini vidya is the science of putting a veil on oneself so that one's own identity is obscured. It is ancillary to Sri Vidya practice. Sri Vidya practitioners use it to protect themselves from the limelight (*Saundaryalahari* 41).

However, in rare cases, practitioners are allowed to use the power engendered by this practice to block the perceiving power inherent in the eyes of the viewer. In these cases, as a precaution, the practitioner is required to have mastered a practice known as *chakshusmati vidya*, which ensures the viewer's eyes are infused with the power to perceive (*Parashurama Kalpa Sutra* 10:11). The shakti engendered by this practice is available to the yogi in case the viewer suffers unintended consequences from having his sight blocked.

It is important to remember that this practice and many of those to come may seem thrilling but have no spiritual merit. Patanjali mentions these practices to show something of the underlying metaphysics of yoga, as well as to demonstrate the limitless power of the mind and our ability to awaken it.

SUTRA 3:22

सोपक्रमं निरुपक्रमं च कर्म
तत्संयमादपरान्तज्ञानमरिष्टेभ्यो वा ॥२२॥

sopakramaṁ nirupakramaṁ ca karma
tatsaṁyamādaparāntajñānamariṣṭebhyo vā ॥ 22 ॥

sopakramaṁ, accompanied by consequential factors; *nirupakramaṁ*, without consequential factors; *ca*, and; *karma*, action; *tatsaṁyamād*, from samyama on them; *aparāntajñānam*, knowledge pertaining to the end of the latter part [of life]; *ariṣṭebhyaḥ*, from omens; *vā*, or

Karmas are of two kinds: accompanied by consequential factors and lacking consequential factors. From samyama on them, or from omens, knowledge regarding the latter part [of life].

Drawing from sutras 2:18 and 3:18, as well as from sutras 2:12 through 2:16, we see that our karmas and the samskaras created by them bring us back to the phenomenal world. They determine when and where we are born (*jati*), how long we remain alive (*ayu*), and the major course of our life experiences (*bhoga*) (YS 2:13). These subtle impressions deposited in our mind by our actions are numberless. Some samskaras are extremely significant, others less so. The most significant are those that are qualitatively intense and play a central role in bringing us back to this world. Vyasa calls them *pradhana*, principal samskaras. Those that are less intense but of similar nature he calls *upasarjani bhava*, secondary samskaras. Secondary samskaras coalesce around the most significant ones.

These two sets of samskaras work in tandem. The initial impetus for birth comes from the subtle self-propelled pulsation of the principal samskaras. As that pulsation gains momentum, secondary samskaras become active. These interlinked sets of samskaras thrust us into the torrent of time and transport us to a space conducive to birth. That is how our karmas deliver us to our parents.

The phenomenal world is replete with all we need to find fulfillment. However, what constitutes fulfillment is defined by the desires and cravings inherent in our samskaras and thus is entirely personal. These inherent desires and cravings motivate us to select ingredients from our parents and our surroundings that are compatible with the most subtle and potent urges embedded in our samskaras. That is why, while living in the same household as our siblings, consuming the same food, and exposed to the same influences, we develop our own unique physical, intellectual, and emotional capacities. Our deep-seated samskaras and their underlying urges shape our personality, build a foundation for our likes and dislikes, and define our ideas of pleasure and pain, good and bad, healthy and unhealthy.

The potent urges arising from our samskaras—and the cascade of conditions that ensue—influence our tastes and interests. They influence our power of discernment and accentuate or suppress our innate qualities of tolerance, patience, forbearance, fortitude, forgiveness, love, compassion, and kindness. They elevate or suppress our capacity to let go. They dictate our behavior and set our priorities. In effect, they prepare the ground for us to consume the sap of life wisely or recklessly. Samskaras are thus the most significant factors in determining how long we live.

Karmas and samskaras that drain the sap of life and eventually lead to our demise are of two kinds: *sopakrama* and *nirupakrama*.

Sopakrama means "accompanied by consequential factors." It refers to principal samskaras, which are actively moving forward, fully supported by secondary samskaras. Their *krama*, the sequence in which they will march and their rank, is fully determined. In other words, the law governing their interaction and collaboration in eroding our lifespan is already set.

Because here the discussion of the role of principal samskaras and their ancillaries is in the context of knowing about our death, *sopakrama* refers to samskaras that are inherently afflicting. Ignorance, distorted sense of self-identity, attachment, aversion, and fear are the underlying qualities of these samskaras. The actions that created them were smeared with the properties of attachment, desire, aversion, anger, fear, and confusion. They lacked self-understanding and were fueled by a sense of possessiveness and self-importance. These actions were propelled by the intention of owning the fruits of our actions and removing or obliterating those who posed an obstacle to achieving that goal. Thus, they were smeared with feelings of animosity and violence. The qualities of these actions are passed on to the samskaras engendered by them. When these samskaras are in full swing and are further assisted by secondary samskaras, they grip our consciousness completely.

Health and longevity go hand in hand. Both are highly dependent on our mastery of our body, breath, mind, and senses. Furthermore, this duo is influenced by our unconscious behaviors. The more afflicting and deeply rooted the principal samskaras and the more indiscriminately they deploy secondary samskaras, the more unconsciously and recklessly the systems of our body and mental faculties engage themselves in unhealthy activities. This is why so many of us who know the difference between good and bad, healthy and unhealthy, fail to refrain from harmful behavior. These sopakrama karmas and samskaras embroil us in the torrent of pleasure and pain, drain our vitality, prepare the ground for disease, accelerate aging, and finally result in death.

Describing the dynamism of sopakrama karmas and samskaras, Vyasa gives the example of a wet garment. When a wet garment is wrung out thoroughly, shaken, spread out, and hung in a hot, well-ventilated place, it dries quickly. Similarly, when the forces of disease squeeze the strength and stamina from our vital organs, shake our nervous system, spread our pranic force too thin, and immerse us in a state of fear, doubt, worry, and remorse, our body and mind shrivel, and we helplessly surrender to death.

Nirupakrama means "secondary karmas not in active service." They are lying dormant in the mind field. As soon as they are summoned, they wake up and begin assisting the principal karmas, thus becoming an integral part of sopakrama karmas and samskaras. Vyasa compares them to a garment drenched in water, rolled into a ball, and left in a cool, unventilated space. It will take a long time for the garment to dry unless it is pulled into the domain of sopakrama samskaras, where it will undergo wringing, shaking, and being spread on a line.

A yogi with a highly concentrated mind is able to identify the group of karmas and samskaras that determine life span and nourish or consume the life force. He is able to see which of those samskaras are sopakrama, fully active and accompanied by consequential factors, and which are nirupakrama, not in service but silently waiting to be summoned. By practicing samyama on these sopakrama and nirupakrama samskaras, a yogi is able to see how much longer he will live if his life force continues to be consumed at the current rate. Knowledge pertaining to his approaching death helps him decide whether it is worth living a while longer or whether it is better to prepare to exit in a properly planned, dignified manner.

According to *Srividyarnava* (shvasas 21 and 35), the ability to postpone death or exit the body in a well-planned manner depends on the mastery over *aroha*, the ascending, and *avaroha*, the descending, pranic force. In this regard, the scripture states, "Aroha and avaroha is a central practice of yoga." Upon realizing that the final moments are approaching, a yogi weighs the merit of living in the body or departing from it. If she realizes that having a little more time to withdraw the mind from all worldly concerns and focus it on a single reality will enable her to achieve her most precious goal, she focuses on the power vested in avaroha, the descending current of prana shakti. At the same time, with the help of vairagya, she blocks the sopakrama samskaras from summoning nirupakrama samskaras. This two-part yoga sadhana enables her to live in the body a little longer without suffering from the effects of old age and disease.

If, on the other hand, a yogi sees no merit in prolonging life, she resorts to aroha, the ascending current of prana shakti, and takes it to the *sahasrara chakra*. There, with the help of bhakti, trustful surrender, and yoga shakti, she lifts the united forces of mind and prana all the way to the *dvadashanta*, the space twelve finger-widths above the fontanelle, thus dissolving her individuated consciousness into transcendent consciousness.

The practice described in this sutra up to this point relates only to accomplished yogis. Next, for those unfamiliar with yogic metaphysics and experiences, Patanjali mentions omens—clues that indicate death is approaching. Scriptures, particularly those belonging to the tantric tradition, list myriad omens that forecast death. What follows is a summary of the signs of approaching death as mentioned in the thirty-fifth shvasa of *Srividyarnava*.

If there is a drastic change in the defining characteristic of our personality for no obvious reason, we may meet our fate within a year. If we have healthy eyesight but cannot see Arundhati, a star in the little dipper; Dhruva, the pole star; or the tip of our nose; or if we lose all sensation below the ankles, we may soon die. If we cannot see the head on our shadow, or we begin feeling as if smoke is hanging above our head, death may be near. When we plug our ears and can no longer hear their innate sound, or we cannot see the space between our fingers, or we begin seeing a distorted reflection of ourselves in the mirror, or we see a hole in the sun, our life may soon end.

When for no reason we find ourselves filled with hatred for our mother, father, siblings, or well-wishers, or if we are suddenly consumed with dislike for the sun, the moon, or the name and form of the divinity we have always revered, death may be on the way. Similarly, a strong aversion to our favorite book, our house, or our own bed; or a sudden deformity in our eyes, particularly in the iris and pupil; or a distortion in our fingerprints are signs of impending death. Finally, and most importantly, if the locus of our self-awareness feels diffuse, or altered, or shifts from one place in the body to another, death is approaching.

This discussion on the signs of approaching death occurs in the context of reclaiming *vibhuti*, our extraordinary power and privilege. Merely forecasting our death is of no use in this regard. As skilled practitioners, we use this information either to prolong our life so we can complete our sadhana, or to methodically cast off our body without dying helplessly and so retain the privilege of creating our own destiny. Understanding the implications of omens is a blessing for those who deploy all their resources to expedite their spiritual progress, but a curse for those who are frightened by the prospect of death.

Those of us not well established in yoga sadhana can adopt a set of practices that do not require expertise in yoga as our life nears its end. We can spend our remaining life in the healthiest manner possible and deploy all our spiritual, intellectual, and worldly resources to serve the larger world. This is the time to drop all disputes and instill in the mind the virtues of friendliness, compassion, joy, and most importantly, a non-judgmental attitude toward those whose values and conduct are in stark contrast to our own. If, by the time these omens begin to appear, we have realized that the origin of the life force is far beyond the domain of the material world, we will shift our attention and loyalty from our material and emotional possessions to the reality that gives birth to the life force itself.

During this limited time, our body, mind, and senses may be fragile and thus unfit to undertake any methodical practice to further strengthen our bond with the higher reality. But based on our current knowledge and convictions, we can organize a group practice designed to infuse our immediate surroundings with consciousness capable of strengthening our convictions. For example, we can sponsor group practices that center around mantras such as the *maha mrityunjaya* and *navarna* mantras or suktas such as Shiva Sankalpa Sukta. Acts of charity aimed at preserving and disseminating knowledge of higher reality, promoting peace, nurturing mother nature, and expressing our gratitude to nature's finer forces are all helpful practices as we go through the time of transition.

SUTRA 3:23

मैत्र्यादिषु बलानि ।।२३।।

maitryādiṣu balāni ॥ 23 ॥

maitryādiṣu, on friendliness and so on; *balāni*, capacities

[From samyama] on friendliness and so on, capacities.

This is the third time Patanjali mentions a practice directly associated with the idea of friendliness and similar virtues: compassion, joyfulness, and a non-judgmental attitude. The first mention occurs in sutra 1:33. There the goal of the practice is to cleanse the mind of impurities engendered by feelings of animosity toward others, particularly those who appear to be more fortunate, and consequently happier, than we are. The practice of friendliness is contemplative. We are guided to reflect on our irrational justification for animosity. Furthermore, we are reminded of the importance of cultivating a crystal-clear, balanced mind, which we can then deploy to practice meditation as described in sutras 1:36 through 1:39 and in chapter 3. In other words, the practice of friendliness in sutra 1:33 is for the purification of the mind (*chitta prasadanam*).

In sutras 2:33 and 2:34, the practice of friendliness is somewhat more advanced. It is for transforming the element of animosity into friendship. Here we are guided to discover the root cause of the feeling of animosity and eradicate it by actively cultivating an antidote. To discover the subtle cause of animosity, we are led to reflect on the dynamics of our mind and its role not only in committing violence but also in promulgating it by inspiring others to violence or by consenting to it. The purpose of the practice in these two sutras is to become cognizant of greed, anger, and confusion, all of which fuel violence, as well as to become cognizant of the afflicting qualities of these tendencies. By replacing them with the opposite virtues, we transcend the unending chain of afflictions.

The process and purpose of practicing samyama on the virtue of friendliness as described here in sutra 3:23 is completely different from what has come before. Practicing samyama on an object requires that the object is familiar to the mind and not abstract. Friendship between friends is based on friendly feelings and interactions. It is two-sided and abstract. Comprehending the exact strand of our own friendly feelings is difficult, let alone comprehending the friendly feelings of our friends. Practicing concentration on friendliness and taking it all the way to samadhi is practically impossible. And yet, this is what Patanjali wishes us to do in order to awaken the extraordinary capacities inherent in the virtue of friendliness.

According to the tradition, the key to practicing samyama on an abstract principle such as friendliness has been presented in sutra 3:14, which states that the substratum conforms to the changes occurring in its attributes. The mind is the substratum, or locus, of its samskaras and the thoughts and feelings arising from them. Changes occurring in our thoughts and feelings reshape our mind. We are the locus of our mind. Transformation of our mind reshapes us.

Take the example of Buddha. Buddha began his spiritual quest with a mind vacillating between sensual cravings and renunciation. He was disturbed by the sight of disease, old age, and death.

With practice, his cravings cooled. His mind conformed to this change, and thus became clear and stable. As his practice progressed, his mind was further purified, and eventually all his samskaras were purged. His mind was fully illuminated. Buddha as a person became the locus of this enlightened mind. Buddha had the capacity to trace each step of change that occurred in his tendencies, in his mind, and in himself. He had the capacity to focus on those changes because they were an integral part of his memory. He could retrieve them through his sheer intention. Buddha could pull the experience of both animosity and friendliness from his memory and see the difference between the two. He could isolate one from the other and meditate only on friendliness. We, on the other hand, lack such capacities and the changes brought by them.

Because Buddha is the locus of his mind as well as of all the virtues his mind embodies, meditation on Buddha is meditating on what his mind is made of. Enlightenment, perfect knowledge, is the essence of Buddhahood. Before reaching this state of enlightenment, Buddha passed through the stages of yogic achievement characterized by friendliness, compassion, joy, and a non-judgmental attitude. His mind became the locus of these virtues.

As the locus of such an enlightened mind, Buddha is an embodiment of these virtues and so can be used as an object of our practice of samyama. Similarly, any of the other masters who embody these virtues can be used as an object of samyama. Following the rules of mental absorption as described in sutra 1:41, as our mind dissolves into the object of its focus, it becomes infused with the intrinsic properties of that object. To what degree properties such as friendliness and compassion are going to manifest by practicing samyama on the beings who embody these virtues will always be in proportion to the maturity of the practice.

It is important to remember that this practice, like many of those to come, posits the attainment of a highly concentrated mind as described in sutra 3:12. That kind of mind protects us from falling into the trap of blind faith in the spiritual accomplishments of others. Furthermore, that kind of mind enables us to deconstruct a variety of emotions associated with the person who is the object of our samyama, and thus we can focus only on the friendly, compassionate, or joyful aspect of the qualities in that person. It is also important to remember that by the time we have mastered the content of sutras 3:1 through 3:12, we are fairly well established in our pure essence. We are no longer smeared by negative, afflicting qualities. Sheer intention alone is enough to bring forward the power hidden in friendliness, compassion, and other related virtues.

SUTRA 3:24

बलेषु हस्तिबलादीनि ॥२४॥

baleṣu hastibalādīni ॥ 24 ॥

baleṣu, on powers; *hastibalādīni*, powers of an elephant, and so on

[From samyama] on powers, the powers of an elephant, and so on.

Cultivating extraordinary strength and stamina is the objective of the practice referred to in this sutra. The fundamental principle behind the practice is that absorption in the object of samyama infuses the mind with the property intrinsic to that object. Like friendliness, compassion, and so on, described in the previous sutra, strength, stamina, and power are abstract properties of their substratum. The presence of these capacities is known by the influence the powers hidden in the substratum exert on others. Samyama—concentration, meditation, and samadhi—on a power in isolation from the substratum embodying it is utterly impossible.

This takes us to the central doctrine of tantra sadhana: the practices of *shakti*, power, and *shaktiman*, the locus of the power, are one and the same. By meditating on shakti, we automatically meditate on shaktiman, and vice versa. Achieving the strength of an elephant by practicing samyama on power is merely an example—this sutra is not recommending that we actually meditate on the strength of an elephant.

To put this sutra into practice, we must first select an object that embodies power befitting the standards of yoga. The locus of this power must be pure, pristine, and uplifting. Furthermore, there must be a mechanism for pulling that locus into our mind field, and a time-tested way of meditating on it. In tantric literature, divinities such as Parashurama, Buddha, Narasimha, Hanuman, Bhairava, Vainateya (Garuda), Virabhadra, and several emanations of Rudra are said to be the epitome of power. However, power—the ability to bring change—is an unspecific shakti. What is meant here by acquiring power is acquisition of a specific ability—retentive power, physical strength, intellectual sharpness, healing power, or laser-focused capacities such as attracting wild animals, curing snakebite, or developing artistic talents.

The divinities just mentioned are non-human entities. They are as imperceptible and as intangible as the powers they embody. To bring them into our awareness and enable the mind to perceive them as an object of samyama, meditation on their mantric body is recommended.

The specificities of these divinities are brought into focus by the specific mantras for invoking their presence. For example, *Parashurama gayatri* is the mantra for meditating on Parashurama. According to the tradition, Parashurama is an all-pervading light of *dharma*, unalterable essential attributes; *jnana*, knowledge; *vairagya*, unsmearability; and *aishvarya*, absolute power to command. Due to his pervasive nature, he fills every nook and cranny of the universe, including our body, mind, and senses. *Parashurama gayatri* specifically invokes three of his unique powers: the capacity to forgive, the capacity to conquer, and the capacity to contain others in his heart. These three powers are contained in the mantra in three words: *jamadagnyaya*, *mahaviraya*, and *ramah*. Similarly, one of the many mantras for Buddha, the *Buddha gayatri*, is specifically for invoking and meditating on Buddha's power of omniscience.

Further precision in meditating on the powers of these "power wielders" is brought to focus through ancillary practices such as *dhyana* mantras, mantras that make an imperceptible, formless deity perceptible; *nyasa*, bringing awareness to a specific spot in the body; and special fire offerings. Success in these power-driven practices is highly dependent on selecting the divinity embodying the specific power and mantrically awakening and meditating on it.

SUTRA 3:25

प्रवृत्त्यालोकन्यासात्
सूक्ष्मव्यवहितविप्रकृष्टज्ञानम् ॥२५॥

pravṛttyālokanyāsāt sūkṣmavyavahitaviprakṛṣṭajñānam
॥ 25 ॥

pravṛttyālokanyāsāt, by directing the light of extrasensory cognition; *sūkṣmavyavahitaviprakṛṣṭajñānam*, knowledge of subtle, obstructed, and distant objects

By directing the light born of extrasensory cognition, knowledge of subtle, obstructed, and distant objects.

The practice referred to in sutras 1:34 through 1:36, and thoroughly elaborated on in the last five sutras of chapter 2 and the first five sutras of chapter 3, provides access to the practice mentioned in this sutra and the nineteen sutras that follow.

The practice this sutra refers to leads a yogi to acquire the extraordinary power to gain knowledge of objects imperceptible to the senses either because they are too subtle or because they are obstructed by other objects or are too distant. In effect, the yogi is able to perceive an object without using the senses by directing his inner light, which is born of extrasensory cognition. Patanjali calls this extrasensory cognition *jyotishmati* (YS 1:36).

Jyotishmati means "filled with light, endowed with light, accompanied by light." It is a meditative state that arises when the mind is united with prana and guided to ascend and descend between the opening of the nostrils and the center of the forehead in unison with the ascending and descending currents of prana shakti. While following the current of prana, the mind is guided to be extra cognizant of specific spots located along the pathway of the ascending and descending pranic currents. Finally, the united forces of mind and prana are confined to the space corresponding to the region of the forehead. As described in sutras 3:1 through 3:5, the space of consciousness corresponding to the physical region of the forehead becomes the center of pranic pulsation. The mind is constantly engaged in witnessing this pranic pulsation, which allows the space of consciousness in the region of the forehead to become saturated with the unique glow of prana shakti. This pranic luminosity is jyotishmati.

Cognition of this luminosity is beyond the domain of the senses; thus, it is called extrasensory cognition. Extrasensory cognition emerges when the mind has already transcended all afflicting samskaras and the tendencies they breed. During this extrasensory cognitive state, the mind is free of fear, attachment, anger, sorrow, and remorse, and drenched in *vishoka*, absolute sorrowless joy. Practices leading to this state of experience are called vishoka or jyotishmati (YS 1:36). The more established we are in the state of vishoka or jyotishmati, the more clear, perceptive, concentrated, and penetrating is the mind.

Jyotishmati is a state of experiencing our own inner luminosity. It is *buddhi sattva*, the essence of the self-revealing power of our faculty of discernment. As elaborated on in sutras 1:36, 1:47–49, 2:27, and 3:5, the inner luminosity arising in the center of the forehead is *prajna shakti*, the power of intuition. Through sustained practice, this luminosity intensifies and becomes firm. Even though this shakti has always been there, with practice it becomes manifest and is at our disposal to be used in the manner we wish.

Following the principle described in sutra 3:14, this inner luminosity is the mind's attribute, and the mind is its locus. When it is dormant, that aspect of the mind is also dormant. As soon as this power awakens and becomes manifest, the mind wakes up. Transformation of the mind is always in proportion to the transformation in its attributes—in this case, inner luminosity.

We are the locus of this highly empowered mind. With the combined force of technique and intention, we can direct this light to a place of our choice within or outside the body. The intentional and precise deployment of the light of jyotishmati enables us to comprehend an object without the aid of the senses. The term for this precise deployment of inner light is *nyasa*.

Nyasa means "bringing awareness to an identifiable spot and anchoring it there." During the practice of the *Sri Vidya* mantra, for example, we are guided to do a variety of nyasas. In a nyasa known as *rishyadi nyasa*, we direct awareness filled with the feeling of the seer of the mantra to our head, the meter of the mantra to our throat center, and the locus of the mantra to the heart. To practice a nyasa known as *shadanga*, we split the mantra into six parts and then direct the awareness of those parts to our heart, head, top of the head, shoulders, eyes, and the space surrounding our body. Similarly, there is *anga nyasa*, bringing awareness to different parts of the body; *kara nyasa*, bringing awareness to our hands; and *matrika nyasa*, directing awareness of fifty letters of the Sanskrit alphabet to different parts of the body.

Merging with a mantra, the seeing power of the seer, the meter, the letters of the Sanskrit alphabet, and so on, is the crux of nyasa practice. The purpose of these nyasas in mantra sadhana is to gain a concrete experience of the powers inherent in the mantra. The purpose of the nyasa described here is to gain a concrete experience of an object that is beyond the reach of the senses.

The precise term for the the nyasa referred to in this sutra is *pravritti aloka nyasa*. It involves directing and anchoring the light born of extrasensory cognition. This extrasensory cognition refers to the experience of pranic luminosity radiating from the highly concentrated, pranically charged space of consciousness in the region of the forehead. Before we attempt to mentally transport and anchor this luminosity somewhere beyond the reach of the senses, we must gain proficiency in the practice by directing this shakti to different spots in our own body—a process known as *sthana nyasa* or *sthana anusandhana* (*Svacchanda Tantra* 1:59–60). This practice, in concert with *prapancha vyapti* and *pranava anusandhana*, enables us to become cognizant of the space inside our body as well as of the twelve-finger-width expanse surrounding our body. The ability to sense, navigate, and eventually cross the threshold where this space ends allows us to project the light of jyotishmati without the obstruction posed by our highly concentrated and psychologically concrete *asmita*, our sense of self-identity.

The capacity of the senses to perceive their objects comes from the deeper power of buddhi sattva. Because their range is limited, the senses have a limited capacity to contain and exercise this power. Thus, they cannot perceive an object if it is too close, too far, too small, too big, and so on. Jyotishmati, which is the radiance of buddhi sattva itself, has no such limitation. Our strong sense of self-identity, which binds our consciousness to the body, is the barrier preventing jyotishmati from illuminating the world and all worldly objects. Once we cross this barrier, jyotishmati can travel and illuminate any object of any size or shape. The notions of time and space familiar to our ordinary mind and senses do not apply to the light of jyotishmati. It can comprehend an object the size of an atom or a mighty star. It can comprehend an object of any size on the other side of a mountain or on the other side of the earth. Simply put, the extraordinary power described in this sutra depends solely on how firmly we are established in the experience of vishoka and jyotishmati.

SUTRA 3:26

भुवनज्ञानं सूर्ये संयमात् ॥२६॥

bhuvanajñānaṁ sūrye saṁyamāt ॥ 26 ॥

bhuvanajñānaṁ, knowledge of the spheres of existence; *sūrye*, on the sun; *saṁyamāt*, from samyama

From samyama on the sun, knowledge of the spheres of existence.

For those unfamiliar with tantric philosophy and practice in general, and with the Sri Vidya, Shaiva, and Natha traditions in particular, this sutra and the commentary on it are shrouded in mystery. Here Patanjali claims that by concentrating on the sun it is possible to gain knowledge of the fourteen *bhuvanas*, spheres of existence. Complicating matters, Vyasa introduces the idea of seven hells and an earth consisting of seven islands. He goes on to describe Sumeru, the king of mountains, which is made of gold and capped by peaks of precious gems.

Vyasa then elaborates. On the south side of Mount Sumeru is the island of Jambu, where day and night are regulated by the movement of the sun. The peaks of three mountains on the northern part of this island stretch for thousands of miles and emit blue and white rays. Beyond these mountains lie three continents: Ramanaka, Hiranmaya, and Uttarakuru. Beyond these continents lies another mountain range. On the other side of that range are three more continents, bordered by yet another range of mountains. This entire landmass is surrounded by a saltwater ocean. On the north, east, and west sides of Mount Sumeru is a landmass of shining mountains and continents, surrounded by oceans of sugarcane juice, wine, ghee, yogurt, starchy liquid, milk, and water.

These lands and oceans are populated by clusters of celestial beings, demonic beings, invisible beings, beings that look like humans, and mythical beings, such as *yakshas*, *rakshasas*, *bhutas*, *pishachas*, and so on. Mount Sumeru itself is the playground of celestial beings. It houses four sacred groves; a celestial city, Sudarshana; a celestial assembly hall, Sudharma; and a celestial palace, Vaijayanta.

Vyasa goes on to describe an even vaster world located in different tiers of Mount Sumeru and above. He also details the quality, capacity, and state of experience of the residents living in those worlds. He concludes his commentary with a description of the fourteen tiers of existence. Below the base of Mount Sumeru are the seven tiers of hell. Earth, the eighth tier, extends from the seashore all the way to the base of Sumeru. From the base of the mountain to the pole star is *antariksha*, the space filled with planets, stars, and constellations. This constitutes the ninth tier. It and the remaining five tiers—*mahendra*, *prajapatya*, *janaloka*, *tapoloka*, and *satyaloka*—are celestial realms.

Those who have earned only afflicting karmas and are thus entitled to reap only pain are consigned to one of the seven hells. The earth is populated by those who have earned a mixture of good and bad karmas. Mount Sumeru and the realm of existence beyond its peak is the playground of celestial beings. Depending on their degree of spiritual development, these beings reside in relatively lower or higher realms of these celestial planes. The higher the plane, the greater the concentration of joy. The life span of those inhabiting higher celestial planes is longer than the life span of those in the lower planes. There is also a difference in the levels of their knowledge and capacities to command different aspects of creation. For example, souls living in higher planes are endowed with the ability to know everything that lies below them. Souls in the thirteenth realm, tapoloka, have the capacity to command the five gross elements, the mind, and the senses, as well as primordial unmanifest prakriti, whereas souls in the twelfth realm, janaloka, have the capacity to command only the five elements, the mind, and the senses.

Souls with the privilege of residing in the highest realm, satyaloka, anchor their consciousness in a locus they themselves create. They transcend the entirety of prakriti, both unmanifest and manifest, and everything evolving from it. They are in prakriti, yet prakriti is not in them. The joy intrinsic to the different levels of meditation is their diet. They watch over prakriti and the phenomenal world evolving from it.

According to Vyasa, "Experiencing these fourteen tiers of existence is within the scope of yoga sadhana, and a yogi should aspire to experience them. A yogi can accomplish this by practicing samyama at the doorway of the sun. From there, he can lead his samyama to other places and should continue practicing until all this is experienced."

It is important to understand that Vyasa's description of the fourteen tiers of existence has nothing to do with the geography or cosmology of our universe. Drawing from a time-honored style of describing yogic experience, he is using metaphorical imagery to elucidate the varying degrees of experience engendered by the practice mentioned in this sutra. These metaphorical images are the basis of what is known in mystical literature as *sandhya bhasha*, twilight language, or *sanketika bhasha*, indicative language.

The custom of using this style predates Vyasa and Patanjali and has been frequently employed by mystics writing in Sanskrit as well as in India's regional languages. Here, in speaking of Mount Sumeru, Vyasa is referring to the spinal cord—the physical counterpart of the pranic current moving up and down—and the fourteen different stages of consciousness engendered by meditation on the sun.

Similarly, Patanjali is not prescribing the external sun as an object of concentration and meditation. Rather, he is referring to our internal sun, which rises and sets each time we inhale and exhale, and to a unique meditation on it leading to fourteen levels of experience. The system of samyama leading to this experience is grounded in the following principles of tantra: As in the universe so in the body; the sun in the cosmos and the sun in the body are identical—the same is true of the moon. The principle of movement is prana. It is intelligent and self-propelled. The pole star, the sun, the moon, the stars, the planets, and the entire realm of existence located on Mount Sumeru are anchored in and propelled by this self-regulated force.

In the last paragraph in his commentary, Vyasa provides a clue as to where and how to begin the practice of samyama on the sun. He says the practice begins "at the doorway of the sun." He further states that the practice is not confined to the doorway of the sun; rather, a yogi should practice samyama at other spots in the body as well, and continue practicing until all fourteen levels of existence are in his full view.

There are differing opinions in regard to the doorway of the sun. Yogis belonging to the Kaula school of tantra identify the *muladhara chakra* as the doorway of the sun. The Mishra school of tantra identifies it as the *anahata chakra*, whereas the Samaya school identifies it as the *ajna chakra*. In the tradition of Sri Vidya, all these locations converge in the sun, which, according to scriptures such as *Svacchanda Tantra* and *Saundaryalahari*, is part of a continuum of the *sahasrara chakra*. From the standpoint of practice, however, the opening of the nostrils is the doorway of the sun.

The following summary of the practice of samyama on the sun, which begins at the opening of the nostrils and continues to other locations—such as the center of the forehead, the region of the soft palate, the heart center, the crown center, and so on—is derived primarily from *Svacchanda Tantra*, chapters 1–4 and 7; *Yoga Vashishtha*, "Upashama Prakarana," chapters 78 and 91, and "Nirvana Prakarana," chapters 18, 24–26, and 69; and Lakshmidhara's commentary on *Saundaryalahari*, verses 8, 9, 10, 11, 14, 32, and 41.

Drawing from these texts and the living tradition of Sri Vidya, it is clear that the relationship between prana and mind is eternal. The mind follows the pranic movement and receives its nourishment from prana. Mental quietude is always in proportion to the quietude of pranic pulsation. Prana is the life force. It embodies sankalpa, the primeval intention of Ishvara. It is as intelligent and omniscient as Ishvara. It fills every nook and cranny of the body as well as the twelve-finger-width space surrounding the body. Prana can be described as the sun. Just as the energy emitting from the sun fills the entire solar system, the pranic sun permeates our entire being. However, there are greater concentrations of prana shakti in certain locations in the body known as *marmasthanas*. The mind more easily senses the presence of prana in these locations. There are 108 of these vital centers. In the practice of meditation, 28 of them are the most significant. Each of these is *surya dvara*, a doorway of the sun.

In this sutra, neither Patanjali nor Vyasa specifies which doorway to use as an object of samyama. However, from Vyasa's remark,

"From there, [the yogi] can lead his samyama to other places, and should continue practicing until all this is experienced," it is clear that we can begin our practice at any easily accessible doorway. As Patanjali himself has demonstrated in sutras 2:51 through 2:55 and 3:1 through 3:5, the opening of the nostrils is the most accessible doorway of the pranic sun.

As elaborated on in the first five sutras of this chapter, the formal practice of samyama on prana shakti begins at the opening of the nostrils. As we inhale, we bring our attention to the region corresponding to the opening of the nostrils, mentally registering the touch of the incoming breath in this region and allowing the mind to follow the flow of the breath through the nostrils all the way to the center of the forehead. We then allow the mind to descend with the exhalation, making a deliberate effort to follow the flow of the breath as far from the opening of the nostrils as possible.

In the beginning, we may be able to follow the breath only an inch or two from the nostrils, but eventually we reach a point in space twelve finger-widths away from the face, which the scriptures call *dvadashanta*. For the sake of simplicity, we call it "the zero point." Exploring the zero point is crucial to the practice of samyama on the doorway of the sun. The texts mentioned above consider the zero point to be the first doorway of the sun for entering the vast landscape of sadhana described in this sutra.

While ascending and descending between the zero point and the center of the forehead, we are guided to pay extra attention to the regions of the opening of the nostrils, the inner corners of the eyes, and the center between the eyebrows. The goal at this stage of the practice is to concentrate the united forces of prana and mind at the center of the forehead. This leads to the emergence of the states of vishoka and jyotishmati. The more established we are in the experience of vishoka and jyotishmati, the greater our success in practicing samyama on doorways of the sun elsewhere in our body.

The practice described in this sutra begins with gaining proficiency in the states of vishoka and jyotishmati. As far as the precise practice is concerned, we stretch the experience of the inner luminosity of jyotishmati concentrically from the center of the forehead. The practice demands special attention to the lower reaches of the field of jyotishmati in the region of the heart. This is done by employing our power of intention. No power of intention is employed to experience the higher reaches of the field of jyotishmati. According to the self-propelled and self-regulated law of prana shakti, as our attention expands downward from the region of the forehead, in the same proportion it automatically moves upward.

Allowing the mind to become fully established in the pranically lit space encompassing the region of the forehead and the heart center is crucial to this practice. Once that is accomplished, we remove our attention from the pranic movement between the zero point and the forehead and allow the mind to follow the ascent and descent of prana shakti between the center of the forehead and the heart.

Once the mind has become fully familiar with the pranic conveyor belt continuously moving up and down between the heart and the forehead, special attention is brought to the region of the soft palate. This region, known as the *talu chakra*, is another doorway of the sun. Here, according to *Svacchanda Tantra*, we are guided to apply *divyakarana mudra*. Keeping the upper and lower jaws together and placing the tip of the tongue at the junction of the hard palate and the gumline is the core of this mudra. Precision in the practice demands that we make no effort to keep the jaws together or to place the tip of the tongue on the hard palate.

The lower and upper lips remain relaxed while slightly touching (*Svacchanda Tantra* 4:365–367).

Divyakarana mudra is maintained throughout the practice of samyama on the prana shakti descending and ascending between the forehead and the heart. Just as *mula bandha* forces prana shakti to move upward through the muladhara, divyakarana forces the mind accompanying the pranic flow to move through the talu chakra. Once the combined currents of mind and prana enter the talu chakra, they have no choice but to pierce the bindu at the center of the forehead—a process known as *bindu bhedana*. Bindu bhedana transports the united mind and prana to the innermost doorway of the sun, located in the lower regions of the sahasrara chakra. Reaching this particular doorway and becoming fully established there is the goal of the practice described in this sutra.

Mastery over samyama on the doorway of the sun saturates the mind with the immense power intrinsic to this particular doorway. According to the scriptures mentioned above, there are four streams of prana shakti originating from and subsiding in the sun at this center. Two of them, *nivritti kala* and *pratishtha kala*, manifest as exhalation. Nivritti kala, originating from the pranic sun, releases our mind and consciousness from the fivefold affliction. It destroys our samskaras and the mental tendencies they churn up. Pratishtha kala enables our mind and consciousness to become established in their own essence. This brings firmness to our limbs and organs and accelerates the process of inner healing. Furthermore, it fills the mind with an extraordinary level of willpower and spiritual ambition.

The remaining two streams of prana shakti—*vidya kala* and *shanta kala*—manifest as inhalation. As their names indicate, vidya kala, originating from the pranic sun, infuses the mind with intuitive knowledge. This allows the mind to comprehend extrasensory dimensions of reality. Shanta kala infuses the mind with patience and fortitude—qualities that build the foundation for inner peace and tranquility (*Svacchanda Tantra* 4:242–246).

Together, these four streams of prana shakti, originating from the sun located in the sahasrara chakra, boost our spiritual ambition at an extremely subtle level. We are naturally and spontaneously motivated to reach a point in the space of consciousness far above the doorway of the pranic sun, known as *shantyatita*. As the name suggests, this particular pranic pulsation is "beyond peacefulness." This is where the four pranic streams propelling inhalation and exhalation originate and subside. This experience is the ground for comprehending the absolute reality—the substratum of prana. Numberless pranic pulsations, including the four principal ones filling our body and the universe within and without, are attributes of this substratum. Upon knowing this substratum, all of its attributes are known.

Charged with the courage, curiosity, and limitless enthusiasm intrinsic to the experience of this substratum, we continue exploring the limitless expanse of consciousness. Unlike yogis interested in finding their personal freedom and fulfillment, adepts of the sadhana described in this sutra embark on this exploration for the purpose of seeing and embracing the full spectrum of reality, from the lowest to the highest.

Patanjali and Vyasa describe the experience pertaining to the full spectrum of reality while following the model of fourteen *bhuvanas*, tiers of existence. Enthused by the prospect of knowing the fullness of the truth, and charged with the confidence of being untouched by what she touches, the yogi directs her mind to different doorways of the sun, including those located in the lowest realms of consciousness. For example, pairing the mind with prana, she focuses on the pranic center far below the muladhara. Her proficiency in reaching the twelve-finger-width space away from the physical frame of the body enables her to enter the world abounding in and ruled by subhuman tendencies. She is able to connect herself with those who are drowning in the bottomless ocean of fear, doubt, insecurity, anger, grief, and regret. She is able to feel the pain of hunger and starvation; she is able to feel the desperate urge to die and the pain of being unable to die. A yogi of this caliber is able to volunteer her pure and pristine vishoka-filled mind to fully embrace the pain of other creatures who are being eaten alive—physically and emotionally.

The entire range of pain and sorrow and the inability of souls to escape it is what Vyasa means by seven spheres of hell. While seated at the highest peak of spiritual safety and joy, the yogi swims, drowns, and floats along with the suffering souls.

To explore the nature of consciousness and experiences common to human beings, the yogi practices samyama on the space of consciousness known as *rudra granthi*. It covers the *muladhara*, *svadhishthana*, and *manipura* chakras, as well as several secondary vital centers in the abdominal region. This leads the yogi to understand the dynamics of consciousness, the behavior, and the impetus behind the conduct of humans who are neither fully in hell nor fully in heaven. He is able to connect his consciousness with the consciousness of those who are neither fully ignorant nor fully enlightened. He is able to relate to those who are caught between wanting and not wanting, like and dislike, pleasure and pain, love and hatred, compassion and cruelty, forgiveness and revenge. He is able to see the clashing currents of honoring obligations and avoiding them, and the damage these clashes inflict on the conscience. He sees the limitless gifts humans are endowed with as well as the forces that prevent them from using these gifts.

This knowledge and the ability not to be adversely affected by it guides the yogi's thoughts, speech, and actions, enabling him to function as *kalyana-mitra*, benevolent friend, to those around him. A yogi of this caliber lives among those who are struggling, helps them, and yet remains unaffected at a deeper level. This is what Vyasa means by the eighth tier of existence.

The remaining six tiers of existence in yogic cosmology represent increasingly higher grades of yogic experience. In "Samadhi Pada," Patanjali details different levels of samadhi. First, he divides the total range into two main categories: *sabija* and *nirbija* samadhi. He further divides sabija samadhi into four categories: *vikalpa anugata*, *vichara anugata*, *ananda anugata*, and *asmita anugata*. He then describes *dharma megha samadhi*, the transitional state between sabija and nirbija. Thereafter comes nirbija samadhi. These are the six tiers of existence that Vyasa terms "celestial realms" in his commentary on this sutra. (Theologians and religionists call them "heaven.") Vyasa explains how the higher levels of samadhi automatically subsume the experiences of the lower levels, and finally, how the experiences of all thirteen levels of existence are subsumed in nirbija samadhi, which is the fourteenth tier—satyaloka.

The difference between what is described in "Samadhi Pada" and what is described here in this sutra is that in "Samadhi Pada" we get the sense that once we reach nirbija samadhi, our quest is over. However, in this sutra, it becomes clear that the quest to explore the limitless expanse of consciousness begins only after we are no longer concerned with our personal fulfillment and freedom. This is a joy-driven quest of self-exploration. The descent from higher levels of awareness to revisit the world we once worked so hard to leave behind is propelled by divine will. The yogi engaged in the sadhana referred to in this sutra goes from one doorway of the sun to another, basking in the full brilliance of each one. By meditating on different doorways of the pranic sun, the yogi gains a direct experience of the dynamics pertaining to the consciousness filling the space around each doorway. It also enables her to understand why some benefit from the life-giving luminosity of the sun and others do not. In the sutras that follow, Patanjali introduces samyama on other significant pranic locations and explains the resulting experiences.

SUTRA 3:27

चन्द्रे ताराव्यूहज्ञानम् ॥२७॥

candre tārāvyūhajñānam ॥ 27 ॥

candre, on the moon; *tārāvyūhajñānam*, knowledge of the arrangement of the stars

[From samyama] on the moon, knowledge pertaining to the arrangement of the stars.

The practice mentioned in this sutra builds on what has been described in the preceding sutra. There samyama on the inner sun results in knowledge of the fourteen tiers of existence. That sun is located in the lower regions of the sahasrara chakra. Now Patanjali is prescribing the practice of samyama on the inner moon, which results in acquiring knowledge of the arrangement of the inner stars.

Where is the inner moon? According to Lakshmidhara on *Saundaryalahari* verses 9, 10, and 14, the inner moon is located in the center of the sahasrara chakra. In the Sri Vidya tradition, which describes the practice and experience of kundalini yoga while following the model of Sri Chakra, the moon is equated with *bindu*, the central point of reference in the most interior space of Sri Chakra. The technical term for *bindu* in the Sri Vidya tradition is *chandra kala*. According to Lakshmidhara, this moon is *nishkala*, without parts. It is indivisible, beginningless, and endless. It is also equated with *sudha-sindhu*, the ocean of ambrosia. This is the central playground of Sri Vidya, the kundalini shakti.

According to the *Rig Veda* (10:85:1–5), this indivisible moon (known also as *soma*) presides over the celestial realm. While drinking the celestial elixir flowing from the moon incessantly, the sun and its offspring—the planets—remain healthy and energized. This elixir also provides nourishment to other stars and constellations. All entities in the cosmos and in our body drink this elixir, yet it remains undiminished.

Tantric literature, especially that of the Sri Vidya, Shaiva, Natha, and Siddha traditions, is replete with information related to the inner moon. What follows is a succinct summary drawn from Sri Vidya texts.

The inner moon is located above the inner sun. By passing through the doorway of the sun located in the lower part of the sahasrara chakra, we reach the inner moon, located in its higher reaches. As a space of consciousness, the sahasrara chakra is devoid of physicality, so the terms "higher" and "lower," "inner" and "outer" are not to be understood as spatial references.

In the beginning stages of sadhana, the region of the fontanelle can be used as a physical correlate of the space of consciousness indicated by the term *sahasrara chakra*. Experientially, however, we can access this space only after we have transcended the awareness of our body. In that non-physical space, the moon is above the pranic sun yet still far below the outermost edge of the dvadashanta. The four streams of prana shakti (nivritti kala, pratishtha kala, vidya kala, and shanta kala), which originate from the sun and subside in it, receive their nourishment from the moon located in this region. By practicing samyama on the moon here, a yogi is able to comprehend the arrangement of the stars in the body.

What are these stars and where are they? The stars are chakras and marmasthanas. Chakras are the most significant junctions of prana shakti. They consist of a myriad of crisscrossing pranic currents. They can be compared with massive self-luminous stars—they are highly concentrated energy fields in our body. Endowed with unique qualities and characteristics, they exert their influence on our body, mind, and senses. Marmasthanas are relatively less significant junctions of prana shakti. Their range of influence is pronounced but narrower than that of the chakras. There are also millions of simple junctions, known as *sandhis*, where a few less significant pranic currents cross.

The human body is governed, guided, and energetically sustained by these chakras, marmasthanas, and sandhis. In this sutra, the way they are arranged, the way they communicate with each other, and the way they receive and execute orders issued in the regions of the sun and moon in the sahasrara are referred to as *vyuha*, arrangement. Why does a yogi gain the knowledge of *taravyuha*, the arrangement of these stars in the body, while practicing samyama on the moon?

The practice of samyama on the moon matures into *samapatti*, mental absorption, in the moon. During this state of absorption, the mind becomes saturated with the inherent qualities and attributes of the moon. Following the pranic currents, which receive their nourishment and guidance from the moon, the yogi is able to mentally travel to every nook and cranny of the body. In the process, she passes through the entire network of stars. During this journey, she can stop and practice samyama on any star and, as a result, become familiar with its unique qualities and attributes. Then she may move on to other stars and practice samyama there. This way, a yogi can eventually gain knowledge of all, some, or a few significant centers of prana shakti in the body. The step beyond simply knowing the stars is the subject of the next sutra.

SUTRA 3:28

ध्रुवे तद्गतिज्ञानम् ॥२८॥

dhruve tadgatijñānam ॥ 28 ॥

dhruve, on the pole star; *tadgatijñānam*, knowledge pertaining to their movement

[From samyama] on the pole star, knowledge of their [the stars'] movement.

In sutra 3:26, Vyasa tells us that the stars, planets, and constellations are anchored in Dhruva, the pole star. Their movement is regulated by *vayu-vikshepa*, pranic thrust. That is how the stars, planets, and constellations located on, around, and above Mount Sumeru, rotate. As we have seen, the spinal cord is Mount Sumeru. The sahasrara chakra is located on the highest peak of this mountain, figuratively speaking. The doorway of the sun mentioned in sutra 3:26 is located in the lower regions of the sahasrara chakra. Above this doorway is the moon. Above the moon is Dhruva.

In epic literature, Dhruva refers to a young prince who committed himself to an extremely intense meditation. As the story goes, this meditation led him to conquer hunger and thirst. Finally, his breath (more accurately, pranic pulsation) reached a state of absolute stillness. In this state, he found himself totally immersed in all-pervading consciousness. As he began to descend from this immersive state, he became cognizant of the entire universe, from minute atoms to the intricate network of constellations and galaxies. In the twilight of his sabija samadhi, he saw how his own body, mind, and senses are pervaded and permeated by consciousness, how consciousness breathes life into matter, and how, thereafter, prana shakti executes all physical, mental, sensory, and spiritual activities.

In light of this story, the term *dhruva* came to represent the epitome of determination, stability, and perfection. Dhruva is a symbol of reality characterized by the principle of constancy. It is a state of unmoving consciousness; yet it is the center of all that moves. In the context of yoga sadhana as described in this sutra, dhruva is above the sun and moon. It is the immutable space of consciousness located where the sahasrara ends and the realm of dvadashanta begins. In other words, it is located in the space above the highest peak of Mount Sumeru. It does not have a physical correlate other than the space above the fontanelle.

Samyama on the moon, as described in sutra 3:27, enables us to comprehend the locations of different stars—chakras, marmasthanas, and sandhis. The immersive state arising from samyama on dhruva empowers the mind to comprehend the dynamic activity of the entire network of constellations and planets in the body as well as the dynamics of each and every part of this network.

Due to deep and prolonged immersion in dhruva, the mind crosses the threshold of its natural and innate fluttering behavior engendered by nature's fundamental forces of sattva, rajas, and tamas. The mind becomes as still and immutable as the consciousness unique to the state of dhruva. Saturated with the quality of this immutable constancy, the mind follows the stream of pranic pulsation originating from the center of dhruva. Traveling along the pathways of nadis, the mind reaches and pierces the chakras, marmasthanas, and sandhis before entering clusters of tissues and cells where prana shakti is less concentrated.

In this state of awareness, the yogi can pause at any of these significantly charged pranic centers and assess its condition. He can see whether a vital center is sluggish or hyperactive and whether or not it is acting in coordination with other vital centers. He can see whether a vital center is in a state of chaos or harmony, whether or not it is exerting its influence over all the cells and tissues in its orbit equally, and whether or not it is retaining full control over all the cells in its domain. A yogi is able to know whether the changes occurring in the vital centers and the systems associated with them are healthy or unhealthy. This is what is meant by "movement of the stars."

However, the extraordinary power gained from samyama on dhruva is not sufficient to accelerate, reverse, or harmonize the conditions that have already affected the functions of the vital centers in the body. For that, the yogi needs to gain additional capacity, which he can use either to accelerate or slow the flow of prana shakti—charged with the power of the sun or moon, or both—to these vital centers. How to gain that capacity is the subject of the next sutra.

SUTRA 3:29

नाभिचक्रे कायव्यूहज्ञानम् ॥२९॥

nābhicakre kāyavyūhajñānam ॥ 29 ॥

nābhicakre, on the navel plexus; *kāyavyūhajñānam*, knowledge of the systems of the body

[From samyama] on the navel plexus, knowledge of the systems of the body.

From the standpoint of yoga sadhana leading to the acquisition of extraordinary powers, the navel center is the most mysterious and least understood pranic center. In yoga shastra, the navel center is known as *rudra granthi*, the knot of rudra, the vibrant life force. It refers to the entire abdominal region and the unique energy and consciousness that regulate the functions of all the visceral organs in this region. It is the center of the four primitive urges: hunger, sleep, sex, and self-preservation. Through the vagus nerve, it is directly connected to the part of the brain that controls and regulates the functions of our autonomic nervous system.

According to yogis, the abdominal region is the worksite of the part of the brain that deals with our unconscious behaviors and deep-rooted habits and urges. The consciousness of this region is vested with the power to make and execute decisions independently, which is why the functions of our heart, liver, kidneys, bladder, lungs, ovaries, testes, and digestive system remain outside our conscious awareness. Similarly, our circulatory and endocrine systems are primarily governed by the power unique to the abdominal region. *Nabhi chakra*, the navel center, refers to the core of the network of shaktis that fill this space. According to Patanjali, samyama on this center results in the knowledge of the body's complex systems and their functions.

The practice of samyama mentioned in this sutra is a continuation of what has been described in the three preceding sutras. By following the method of sadhana described in sutra 3:28, a yogi is able to comprehend the current conditions of the stars—the pranic centers—in his body. By focusing on a particular pranic center, he can gather the details of that center. If he wishes to gain a comprehensive knowledge of his bodily systems, he is advised to focus on the navel center.

Yogis who draw from both Sri Vidya and Aghora Marga delineate the steps for practicing samyama on the navel. The first step is to gain proficiency in the general practice of hatha yoga. The practice of *goraksha asana*, *matsyendra asana*, *agni sara*, *ganesha mudra*, and *vajrayogini mudra* builds the foundation for the pranayamas essential for practicing samyama on the navel center.

The most important of these pranayamas is *urdhvadhah-tiryan-pravahi*. It consists of a cluster of techniques to pull the prana shakti up, down, and diagonally in different parts of the body. This allows the yogi to cultivate an acute sensitivity to the flow of prana in the parts of the body that have fallen outside the domain of his conscious awareness. With the help of this pranayama, the yogi pulls the pranic force from different parts of the body to the navel center. The practice of goraksha asana, matsyendra asana, and so on enhances the efficacy of urdhvadhah-tiryan-pravahi pranayama.

For the second step, the yogi is advised to do *prana manthana*, churning of prana, at the navel center. She does this by practicing *bhastrika*, *anuloma*, *viloma*, *pratiloma*, and *surya bhedi*. The third step is to quiet the pranic activity at the navel center. This is done by applying the principles of *prayatna shaithilya*, effortlessness, and *ananta samapatti*, absorption in the inner space, as described in sutra 2:47. Finally, she does *pracchardana vidharana*, as described in sutra 1:34. This pranayama saturates the ajna chakra with prana shakti, allowing her to reach the state of vishoka and jyotishmati quickly.

These practices are necessary to prepare the body to carry the prana shakti from the higher spheres of the sahasrara to the navel center without contamination or interruption. The prana shakti flowing from the sahasrara becomes cognizant of the healthy and unhealthy conditions of everything it passes through. It senses the conditions not only of the pranic centers but also, as Vyasa says, of the skin, blood, muscles, nervous system, bones, marrow, and sexual secretions. Now the yogi is not only able to stop at those troubled places but also to decide how to fix the problems. This capacity comes from practicing samyama on the navel center, because the navel center is the abode of *rudrani*, the healing power of Rudra. The practices described in sutras 3:26 through 3:29 constitute the core of *surya vijnana*, the central practice of the yogis of Aghora Marga.

SUTRA 3:30

कण्ठकूपे क्षुत्पिपासानिवृत्तिः ॥३०॥

kaṇṭhakūpe kṣutpipāsānivṛttiḥ ॥ 30 ॥

kaṇṭhakūpe, on the well of the throat; *kṣutpipāsānivṛttiḥ*, relief from hunger and thirst

[From samyama] on the well of the throat, relief from hunger and thirst.

SUTRA 3:31

कूर्मनाड्यां स्थैर्यम् ॥३१॥

kūrmanāḍyāṁ sthairyam ॥ 31 ॥

kūrmanāḍyāṁ, on the kurma nadi; *sthairyam*, stability

[From samyama] on the kurma nadi, stability.

SUTRA 3:32

मूर्धज्योतिषि सिद्धदर्शनम् ॥३२॥

mūrdhajyotiṣi siddhadarśanam ॥ 32 ॥

mūrdhajyotiṣi, on the light of the crown; *siddhadarśanam*, a vision of siddha

[From samyama] on the light of the crown, a vision of the siddhas.

These three sutras are an elaboration of sutra 3:29, which explains the dynamics of the navel center and how a yogi is able to unravel the subtle anatomy of his body by meditating on it. Due to enhanced sensitivity to the pranic flow and the mind's ability to follow the flow, the yogi is able to comprehend the subtle dimensions of his body, mentally isolate a particular spot from the region surrounding it, and practice samyama on that spot. Out of hundreds of such spots, here Patanjali chooses three: *kantha kupa*, the well of the throat; the *kurma nadi*; and *murdha jyotish*, the light at the crown, and describes the result of practicing samyama on each of them.

None of these spots is physical. The physical location is merely a tool for pinpointing the pranically charged space of consciousness corresponding to that physical region. Thus, in his commentary on sutra 3:30, Vyasa takes pains to describe the exact location of the well of the throat. According to him, there is a space of awareness underneath the tongue that corresponds to the general vicinity of the cord anchoring the base of the tongue. Further down is the throat. The kantha kupa lies in the lower regions of the throat.

Practicing samyama on the space corresponding to the well of the throat empowers the yogi to transcend the urges of hunger and thirst, because the space corresponding to this region is imbued with the power of nourishment. In kundalini yoga, this is the region of the *vishuddhi chakra*, the center of purity. As seen in sutra 3:27, the moon is located in the region above the doorway of the sun. The four streams of prana shakti receive their nourishment from this inner moon. According to verse 37 of *Saundaryalahari*, the space corresponding to the region of the well of the throat is the first recipient of the nectar flowing from the moon—it is the container of the nectar flowing from the transcendental moon and is thus the secondary domain of the moon. The greater and more intense his mental absorption in this center, the longer the yogi is able to sustain his body without food or water.

Sutra 3:31 states that practicing samyama on the kurma nadi leads to stability. Commenting on this sutra, Vyasa tells us that the kurma nadi lies below the well of the throat and above the heart. However, according to kundalini and tantric texts, the kurma nadi runs between this region and the perineum. Concentration on the lower region of this nadi results in physical stability; concentration on the higher region results in mental and spiritual stability. Because the practice of samyama is by definition of a meditative nature, Vyasa pinpoints the upper end of the kurma nadi in his commentary on this sutra.

In sutra 3:32, Patanjali focuses on the self-luminous space corresponding to the region of the crown. This area is part of the sahasrara chakra, which, as we have seen, transcends the physical dimension of the body. The *murdha jyotish*, the light of the sahasrara chakra, is the spot in space where the domain of the dvadashanta begins. As described earlier, *dvadashanta* means "twelve-finger-width space." According to tantric scriptures, "twelve finger-widths" refers to a continuum of twelve levels of experience known as *samana*, *unmana*, *ardha chandra*, *nirodhini*, and so on. All twelve levels of experience are imbued with the luminosity of pure consciousness.

The practice of samyama on this luminosity is associated with a spectrum that lies between the transcendent and immanent. This is the realm of siddha masters. In terms of yogic anatomy, this realm sits on the top of Dhruva, the pole star mentioned in sutra 3:28. The distinction between the realm of Dhruva and the self-luminous space of the sahasrara chakra is extremely subtle, and the spatial distance between the two is not literal.

Like the practices described in sutras 3:30 and 3:31, the practice of samyama on this light builds upon the practice of samyama on the doorways of the sun, the moon, and the pole star. Thereafter, as we see in the "Nirvana Prakarana" of the *Yoga Vashishtha* (81:50–56), the yogi pushes prana to flow only through the *brahma nadi*, blocking the flow of prana in all other nadis. She does this with a unique application of *rechaka*, pranayama empowered by exhalation. This enables the yogi to reach the self-luminous field of consciousness, where she must remain fully focused for a minimum of forty-eight minutes. This unique practice of samyama awakens the yogi's ability to see the siddha masters. The key to success in this practice lies in the yogi's perfection in sensing the presence of the twelve-finger-width space in front of her face, as well as above the skull. This particular practice brings firmness to the practice of svadhyaya as described in sutra 2:44 and is the precursor to nirbija samadhi.

SUTRA 3:33

प्रातिभाद्वा सर्वम् ।।३३।।

prātibhādvā sarvam ॥ 33 ॥

prātibhāt, from that which is rooted in intuition; *vā*, or; *sarvam*, everything

Or from intuitive knowledge, everything is known.

Here Patanjali reiterates the most inclusive outcome of samyama. As described in the first five sutras, the practice of samyama is representative of the full range of the practice of dharana, dhyana, and samadhi. In its final stage, samyama results in *prajnaloka*, the emergence of intuitive light (YS 3:5). By the time this light dawns, the mind has attained a high degree of clarity, purity, and stability. It is no longer subject to its roaming tendencies because the afflicting samskaras propelling them have been purged. The experience of self-luminous light in the space corresponding to the center of the forehead is the sign that the intuitive light is emerging. With sustained practice, this light takes on a distinct form. The extremely subtle pranic pulsation becomes the locus of this discrete ball of light.

As described in sutra 1:36, this self-luminous meditative state is called jyotishmati. Because jyotishmati nullifies afflicting feelings of fear, doubt, grief, and remorse, it is known as vishoka, sorrowless joy. In advanced stages of the practice, the mind becomes absorbed in the self-luminous light characterized by the experience of vishoka and jyotishmati. This is the source of *pratibha-jnana*, intuitive knowledge. Mental absorption in this light allows the mind to absorb intuitive knowledge. This intuitive capacity is the ground for clearly comprehending the objects of samyama described in sutras 3:16 through 3:32.

Patanjali now states that a fully and firmly matured intuitive knowledge subsumes the outcome of all forms of samyama so far described. A yogi aspiring to less than nirbija samadhi may invest his attention in identifying distinct objects of samyama and use the mental power engendered by the inner luminosity to concentrate on those objects and reap the benefits. However, a highly motivated and wise yogi remains aware of the short-lived and unfulfilling nature of these siddhis and thus pays no heed when they present themselves of their own accord during his quest for nirbija samadhi. As a codifier of a broad range of yoga traditions, Patanjali mentions the practices leading to these siddhis, but as we will see in sutra 3:37, he tells us that these siddhis are merely distractions on the path to the highest state of samadhi.

SUTRA 3:34

हृदये चित्तसंवित् ॥३४॥

hṛdaye cittasaṁvit ॥ 34 ॥

[From samyama] on the heart, the knowing power of chitta.

With this sutra, Patanjali completes the practice presented in sutra 1:36 as well as the supporting practices introduced in sutras 1:33–35, 2:51–55, 3:1–5, and 3:26–33. Like sutras 1:36 and 3:26, this sutra is compact—its brevity belies the magnitude of its content. In light of Patanjali's definition of yoga, sutra 3:34 is the heart of yoga sadhana. Patanjali tells us that mastery over the roaming tendencies of the mind is yoga (YS 1:2). There are various techniques for conquering the mind's roaming tendencies, making it one-pointed, and focusing it on an object with the capacity to illuminate the mind's hidden grandeur. As we have seen in sutra 1:36, Patanjali's preferred technique for accomplishing this is to meditate on a state of consciousness free from sorrow and anguish and infused with inner light. According to Vyasa, this highly sought state of consciousness emerges when we meditate on the lotus of the heart, which he describes as meditation on vishoka and jyotishmati.

In sutra 1:36, however, neither Patanjali nor Vyasa tells us why meditation on the lotus of the heart is identical to meditation on vishoka and jyotishmati. Furthermore, neither master explains why they consider this precise system of meditation to be the most efficient tool for achieving the highest goal of yoga—samadhi. When studied in the context of what immediately precedes it, sutra 3:34 explains why meditation on the lotus of the heart is meditation on vishoka and jyotishmati, and why that serves as a doorway to the highest goal of yoga.

Samadhi is the highest goal. It is a perfectly still state of mind. This state of perfect stillness arises only when the mind is free of its roaming tendencies. Attempting to quiet, curb, or completely eliminate the mind's roaming tendencies without knowing their source is like shooting at a target without knowing its characteristics and location. With this sutra, Patanjali takes us directly to the bull's-eye—chitta—and teaches us how to hit it.

Chitta is the sum total of all aspects of the mind—the thinking mind, the discerning mind, the mind that identifies itself with the objects of its experiences, and the mind that serves as the storehouse of the memories of all experiences. Chitta is also the locus of pure and pristine self-awareness and its relationship with all-pervading, beginningless, undecaying, immutable, transcendental consciousness. It is the substratum of the intrinsic attribute of intelligence inherited from transcendental consciousness, as well as of the attributes acquired by identifying itself with the objects of the phenomenal world. When we ponder on what has been presented so far in this text, it is clear that the purpose of yoga sadhana is to cleanse the mind of its acquired attributes, allowing its intrinsic attributes to illuminate reality unimpeded. As this sutra tells us, meditation on the heart leads to the emergence of *chitta samvit*.

Experiencing the knowing power of chitta is chitta samvit. The subtlety of this experience is communicated by the term *samvit*. *Samvit* is a composite of *sam* and *vit*. As a prefix, *sam* means "complete, completely, along with, mutually interactive." As a verb, *vit* means "knowing"; as a noun, it means "one who knows, the knower." As sutra 2:20 states, the sheer power of seeing is the seer. There Vyasa explains that the knowing power in us is the knower, and this power is the locus of chitta. This locus is chitta samvit.

Because of this knowing power, chitta is able to know itself and the experiences of the phenomenal world brought to it by the senses. This knowing power enables the mind to think, discern, and identify. The same power enables the mind to transform its experiences into memory; preserve them in its deepest recess (*shanta*); bring them to the surface as a recollection (*udita*); and intuit what is to be experienced in the future (*avyapadeshya*)—a process and phenomenon outlined in sutra 3:14. Meditation on the heart results in experiencing chitta samvit as well as its intrinsic and acquired attributes. In other words, meditation on the heart leads us to knowing the knower and the objects of knowledge, which include all cognitions of past, present, and future.

In the circle of adepts, the practice of samyama on the heart described in this sutra is referred to as *akhanda yoga* as opposed to *khanda yoga*. In khanda yoga, a segment of a larger practice is treated as an independent technique. One or more such techniques can be arranged in a sequence to achieve a specific goal, but that sequence can be changed or altered to achieve a completely different result. In akhanda yoga, the different components of the practice are arranged in an undivided, unbreakable, and unalterable sequence. The practice of samyama on the heart is akhanda yoga, a series of techniques fixed in an undivided, unbreakable, unalterable sequence melded into a single practice.

Earlier in the text, Patanjali introduces several practices, all of which belong to the category of khanda yoga, the practice of yoga in parts. All are narrow in scope and lead to a focused result. For example, the practice of friendliness, compassion, and so on described in sutra 1:33 leads to mental purification. The practice of pracchardana vidharana (1:34) leads to mental stability. Concentration on the tip of the nose, the tip of the tongue, the middle of the tongue, the root of the tongue, and the region corresponding to the soft palate also engenders mental stability (1:35). Concentration on someone free from all desires (1:37) and concentration on cognitions gained from dreams and sleep (1:38) are for mental stability as well. From the practice of *ahimsa*, non-violence, comes the removal of animosity (2:35); from *brahmacharya*, continence, comes the capacity to transmit knowledge (2:38); from *aparigraha*, non-possessiveness, comes understanding of the reason behind birth (2:39); from *shaucha*, purity, comes purity of mind, mastery over the senses, and qualification to gain direct experience of oneself (2:41); from *tapas*, austerity, comes bodily perfection (2:43); and *svadhyaya*, self-study, leads to the company of siddhas (2:44). These practices are all examples of khanda yoga.

The practices described in sutras 3:16 through 3:32 engender specific experiences, but none lead to samadhi unless they are placed in the larger structure of practice described in sutras 1:36 and 3:34. When they are pulled into the larger body of meditation on the heart, they are no longer independent practices but inseparable limbs and organs of the body of meditation on the heart.

The practice described in this sutra demands a clear and correct understanding of the heart—its location and its unique qualities. It also demands that we understand the dynamics of chitta, its location, and its relationship with prana. Further, we need to know the sequence of the practices leading to the main body of meditation on the heart and understand the rationale behind arranging these practices in that particular sequence.

In regard to describing the location of the heart, its unique attributes, and how to meditate on it, Vyasa's commentary on this sutra is almost as succinct and compact as the sutra itself.

He views the body as the city of *brahman*, consciousness. In that city, there is a cavity of the heart. That is the lotus and that is the shrine. This lotus shrine embodies *vijnana*, supremely refined knowledge. Samyama on that lotus leads to chitta samvit.

Relying on what I have received from the living tradition of Sri Vidya, of which Patanjali and Vyasa themselves are an integral part, I have dared to elaborate on this sutra and on Vyasa's commentary. This elaboration is further supported by the following texts: *Shiva Sutra*, *Saddharma-Pundarika Sutra*, *Katha Upanishad*, *Yoga Vashishtha*, *Bhagavad Gita*, *Svacchanda Tantra*, *Saundaryalahari*, and *Gorakh Bani*.

In yogic and tantric literature, the body is described as a temple. In a physical temple, the inner sanctum occupies the central place, spiritually speaking. Normally, the inner sanctum of a temple contains an altar. On this altar an object—such as a flame, scripture, idol, yantra, or mandala—is installed. The entire temple is sacred, and the object installed on the altar is the highest embodiment of sanctity. It is the soul of the temple, the locus of the power inherent in the temple.

In the human body, the heart is the inner sanctum and *chiti shakti*, the power of consciousness, is the highest embodiment of sanctity. Consciousness is the soul, the locus of the body and everything associated with it. The power of consciousness residing in the inner sanctum of the heart is the substratum of our multifaceted existence. We think, feel, reason, discern, and aspire to be because our thinking, feeling, reasoning, discerning, and aspiring self is anchored in this substratum. The instant we become disconnected from this substratum, our existence collapses—we are dead. When our thinking, feeling, reasoning, discerning, and aspiring self is consciously reabsorbed in this substratum, we are free and fulfilled—we are in samadhi.

A highly simplistic and general understanding holds that the heart, as the abode of the supremely potent substratum of our existence, is located in the chest cavity. According to the sources cited above, however, it is only after rising above this simplistic view that we can grasp the enormity of the content of this sutra and many of the others to come.

Vyasa calls the body *brahmapura*, the city of brahman. *Brahman* means "the principle of pervasiveness." This pervasive reality is *sat*, existent. It is intrinsically *chit*, intelligent, and *ananda*, blissful. Thus, brahman is often described as *satchidananda*, and the human body is described as the city of satchidananda—pervasive existence, intelligence, and joy. In every sense, the heart lies at the center of this city.

A city is a conglomerate of intricate structures. Individually and collectively, these structures serve a common purpose—the safety and comfort of those living in the city. In the safe, comfortable atmosphere of the city, the citizens aspire to achieve life's purpose: fulfillment and freedom. Life is a complex phenomenon. In part we know what it is; in part we do not. This city of brahman, the human body, is fitted with everything we need to know about the dynamics of life and its source. It is fitted with the tools that enable us to discover the reason we are born as a human and why certain circumstances walk into our life. Most importantly, it is fitted with the tools we need to navigate the intermingled streams of sorrow and joy and achieve our highest goal. The heart is at the center of this complex and perfectly made city.

Vyasa describes the heart as *dahara*, cavity or space; *pundarika*, lotus; and *veshma*, shrine. The idea of meditating on the cave of the heart or the lotus of the heart has its source in many ancient texts. All these sources tell us that the heart is the center of consciousness. It has nothing to do with the physical heart located in the chest cavity. To describe its non-physical characteristic, yogis call it *chidakasha*, the space of consciousness. It is intrinsically imbued with omniscience. It is samvit, the knowing power of the knower. It is the substratum of our existence and of all that exists. The practice of samyama—dharana, dhyana, and samadhi—leads the mind to *samvit samapatti*, mental absorption in samvit.

In the higher stages of mental absorption, the mind's knowing power is identical to the knowing power of samvit—pure all-pervading consciousness. The mind is no longer outside the self-revealing power of consciousness but has become one with it. The mind does not experience the purest, transcendental, all-pervading, intelligent samvit as an object of cognition. In this unified state of oneness, the mind is samvit and samvit is the mind. The mind is no longer *antahkarana*, the inner instrument for experiencing pure consciousness. It is transformed into the self-revealing power of consciousness.

In this state, the mind knows itself exactly the way pure consciousness knows it. The intensity of the mind's self-revealing power as well as the joy emitting from this revelation is equal to that of pure consciousness. In this state of self-realization, the mind is aware not only of the personal life of its segregated world but also of the collective life of all that exists. This mind is no longer the mind of an individual person; it is samvit, the self-revealing power of supreme consciousness. This is the subject of sutra 3:54.

The practice of samyama mentioned here in sutra 3:34 focuses on a limited spectrum of samvit, which infuses chitta with the power to think, perceive, and comprehend; the power to discriminate, discern, and decide; the power to identify and superimpose value on what it identifies; and the power to transform its experiences into memory, store the memory, preserve it, and retrieve it. This limited spectrum of consciousness is called chitta samvit.

The experience arising from it makes the mind aware of the personal life of its segregated world. It comes to know the deeper causes of its thought patterns and gains the capacity to face and conquer its most potent and subtle self-defeating tendencies. In other words, the meditation introduced in this sutra empowers the mind with the complete understanding of itself and the vast personal world associated with it.

According to the *Yoga Vashishtha* ("Upashama Parkarana" 91:20–22), samvit is subtler than the subtlest. It fills the entire universe as well as every nook and cranny in our body. It is beyond mental comprehension, yet it is known through the pulsation of prana shakti. Pranic pulsation condenses pure, all-pervading consciousness and makes it available to the seer by awakening its *darshana shakti*, seeing power. The greatest concentration of pranic pulsation in the human body is in the heart. Thus, from the standpoint of yoga sadhana, the heart is the matrix of consciousness. The innate concentration of prana shakti in the heart makes it the perfect place to practice samyama. Mental absorption in the power unique to the heart infuses the mind with samvit, the seeing power of consciousness. This empowers the mind to see the seer within, to know the knower within.

There are hundreds of places in the body with significant concentrations of pranic pulsation. The most prominent 108 are known as *marmasthanas*, vital centers. The most significant of these are known as chakras, all of which are characterized by highly concentrated pranic pulsation. In the popular literature of yoga and tantra, the chakra corresponding to the physical heart is the heart center. However, this is only a partial truth.

According to the texts cited earlier, the lotus of the heart is of two kinds: *urdhva-hrit-padma*, the higher lotus of the heart, and *adhah-hrit-padma*, the lower lotus of the heart. The sahasrara chakra is the higher lotus of the heart. This lotus is described as having a thousand petals. A thousand signifies infinity. The chakra corresponding to the physical heart located in the chest cavity is the lower lotus of the heart. It is described as having eight petals. These eight petals signify *ashtadha prakriti*, the eightfold prakriti: the five *tanmatras*, the subtle elements; *manas*, the thinking mind; *buddhi*, the discerning mind; and *ahamkara*, the aspect of the mind that identifies with its experiences. The higher lotus of the heart is the locus of *shuddha samvit*, the knowing power of pure consciousness. The lower lotus of the heart is the locus of chitta samvit, the knowing power of chitta.

The higher lotus is beyond the realm of time, space, number, and linearity. It transcends the idea of more or less. Its being and non-being, existence and non-existence, cannot be comprehended by any standard. Here the knower, knowing power, and knowable are indistinguishable. The experiencing power of consciousness is the object of the experience, and that same consciousness is the experiencer. It is beginningless and the source of the beginning. It is pure being and the locus of the principle of constancy. It is unborn and undecaying and yet is the ground for constant change. It is above and beyond *pindanda*, the microcosm of our body and mind, as well as *brahmanda*, the entire universe; yet, at the subtlest level, the entire universe, including our body and mind, is anchored in it. Through its sheer intention, it is connected with the phenomenal world and yet remains untouched by it. Prana shakti is its intention. Through prana shakti, it breathes life into the inert world. It is cognizant of itself and the phenomenal world pervaded and enlivened by it. It knows the world; the world does not know it. This is the nature of shuddha samvit, pure consciousness, the locus of the pure and transcendental heart. Meditation on this higher heart is beyond the range of this sutra.

The lower lotus, corresponding to the physical heart, is the locus of chitta samvit. The pool of consciousness at this center is innately capable of knowing everything about the mind. It has the capacity to know everything that exists in the mind. It knows the mind's past, present, and future contents. The consciousness here is able to track the series of changes that have already occurred in every segment of memory stored in the mind. It is able to foresee the awakening of samskaras and their role in shaping our destiny in both the present and the future. It has the capacity to monitor the progress of the changes occurring in the mind and its inherent attributes and to envision a plan to slow, accelerate, or alter the course of those changes. However, the consciousness intrinsic to this lower lotus is incapable of knowing what lies beyond the mind and the contents buried in it.

The all-knowing power of consciousness at the lower heart is marred by time, space, number, linearity, and notions of less and more. The mind is a direct evolute of prakriti, primordial nature. Prakriti is pure and perfect in every respect. As a direct evolute of prakriti, the mind should be as pure and perfect as prakriti. Its intelligence should be as pervasive, penetrating, and discerning as prakriti's intelligence. The mind's omniscience should be as unbounded and unrestricted as prakriti's locus—consciousness. But it is not, because consciousness here is confounded by the forces of time, space, number, linearity, and the notion of less and more.

Consciousness mingled with the limiting factors of time and space is chitta samvit. These inherent attributes distinguish chitta samvit from shuddha samvit—the unbounded, unrestricted, pure, and perfect consciousness of the higher lotus of the heart. Due to these inherent limiting factors, chitta samvit of the lower heart is able to infuse the mind with the capacity to know only itself and the vast universe contained in it.

From the description above, it may appear that the lower lotus of the heart is inferior to the higher lotus, but from the standpoint of sadhana, it is by no means inferior. Gaining access to the innate power of consciousness, especially the aspect that enables the mind to know itself and its vast contents, is a significant achievement. Without access to this power, we remain unfamiliar with our inner strengths and weaknesses and fail to grasp the magnitude of our dormant tendencies. We cannot identify and distinguish between afflicting and constructive tendencies. We also fail to foresee when, how, and under what circumstances these tendencies will become active, stirring up our inner world. Pursuing our inner quest without sufficient understanding of our mind and its strengths and weaknesses leaves us groping in darkness.

Blossoming of the lower lotus gives the mind the insight and courage to see itself. In the light of chitta samvit intrinsic to this lotus, the mind is able to see the tight, complex knots of samskaras, unresolved issues, cravings, attractions, and repulsions. When sustained by the illuminating and nurturing light of chitta samvit, the mind has the courage and patience to loosen and untie these knots. The mind can pursue its inner quest without encountering obstacles only after it is free from the binding forces of its contents. Freedom from the mind's binding forces comes from meditation on the lower lotus of the heart.

Success in practicing samyama on the lotus of the heart is largely dependent on the precision and perfection of meditation at the center of the forehead, the physiological correlate of the ajna chakra. The ajna chakra is the locus of *buddhi samvit*, the knowing power of buddhi. The main function of buddhi is discernment. Because of this discerning power, buddhi is able to distinguish right from wrong, good from bad, and happiness from mere pleasure. The discerning power of buddhi is as sharp and illuminating as the self-luminous light of pure consciousness. This is why buddhi is called intellect, the instrument of inner intelligence. Meditation on the ajna chakra leads to buddhi samvit, the awakening of the power behind self-luminous inner intelligence.

Buddhi is imbued with eight attributes. The first four are *dharma*, the ability to nourish and anchor itself; *jnana*, the ability to know itself and everything that exists; *vairagya*, the ability to identify its intrinsic attributes and distinguish them from acquired attributes; and *aishvarya*, the ability to imbibe and exercise the power of Ishvara, including Ishvara's power of intention. The remaining four attributes are *adharma*, the inability to nourish and anchor itself; *ajnana*, the inability to know itself; *avairagya*, the inability to identify its intrinsic attributes; and *anaishvarya*, the inability to imbibe and exercise the power of Ishvara.

The first four attributes come from the all-pervading, pristine prakriti of Ishvara. They are a direct manifestation of *anugraha shakti*, the unconditional power of Ishvara's love and grace. They are gifts to our buddhi. The remaining four attributes are the work of our deep-rooted samskaras. These inabilities are the direct manifestation of our fivefold affliction: avidya, asmita, raga, dvesha, and abhinivesha. They are intermingled with the inherent abilities of buddhi in various proportions and intensities. This intermingling of abilities and inabilities undermines buddhi's self-revealing, discerning power. The purpose of meditation on the ajna chakra is to free our buddhi from its acquired limitations.

Entering the lower lotus of the heart requires a clear, calm, pure, and highly concentrated mind, which comes from meditation on the ajna chakra, the center of *buddhi sattva*, the pure and pristine knowing power of buddhi. We can bypass the ajna chakra and enter our heart by using the brute force of hatha yoga, pranayama, kundalini yoga, and tantra yoga, but there is a strong possibility that there will be adverse consequences. Commenting on sutra 3:18, Vyasa cites the example of Jaigishavya, a yogi who entered the vast field of his chitta. There, thousands of lifetimes of samskaras came into his view in a non-linear manner. To help him disentangle himself from the numberless currents and cross-currents of his past memories, another yogi, Bhagavan Avatya, entered Jaigishavya's mind and illuminated it with buddhi sattva. Without Avatya's assistance, Jaigishavya may well have lost his way in the jungle of his endless memories.

The practice of samyama on the lotus of the heart requires that we have already cultivated vishoka, a sorrowless mind, as well as a mind saturated with jyotishmati, inner luminosity. A sorrowless mind infused with the inner luminosity of pure consciousness is naturally drawn to joyful experiences. It is full of enthusiasm and courage. When confronted with unpleasant and undesirable thoughts, feelings, and memories, such a mind spontaneously puts a positive spin on them and seeks a liberating lesson. Cultivation of such a mind is the domain of meditation at the ajna chakra. For this reason, the practice of samyama on the lotus of the heart begins at the ajna chakra.

Reiterating what has been described in sutras 1:36 and 3:1 through 3:5, meditation on the ajna chakra begins as soon as we pay attention to the movement of the breath between the opening of the nostrils and the center of the forehead. As this awareness deepens, we are able to comprehend the subtle pranic dimension of the physical breath. This allows the mind to withdraw itself from the phenomenal world, including the physical frame of our body, and focus on non-physical pranic pulsation. This results in the union of the mind and prana.

The united forces of the mind and prana now travel back and forth between the opening of the nostrils and the center of the forehead. Once this process is settled, while exhaling we stretch the feeling of our outbound breath as far from the opening of the nostrils as possible. In the beginning, it may be only a few inches. As practice continues, we discover a point in space six to nine inches from the nostrils, where our outgoing breath finally diffuses into space. Yogis call this the zero point.

Now our breath is flowing between the zero point and the ajna chakra. Between the zero point and the ajna chakra, there are three significant points: the opening of the nostrils, the inner corners of the eyes, and the center between the eyebrows. The effortless effort invested in paying attention to these points allows the mind to discover and become absorbed in increasingly subtle dimensions of pranic pulsation. Finally, the entire space from the zero point all the way to the ajna chakra becomes one undivided continuum of pranic pulsation.

The practice of samyama on this continuum eventually leads to the manifestation of self-luminous light in the region of the ajna chakra. As the practice progresses, this luminosity becomes defined. For lack of a better image, this self-luminous pranic field is described as a ball of light. The more we meditate on this ball of light, the brighter it becomes. Mental absorption in this light leads the mind to transcend the familiar frame of time and space. Transcendence of time and space allows the mind to enter a space of consciousness not characterized by shape, size, number, or the notions of near and far.

The consciousness that forms the locus of this ball of light and gives it definition is not confined by direction. There is nothing like above, below, left, right, inside, or outside. It is whatever it is and wherever it is, and yet, even in a deep state of meditation we remain subliminally aware of ambient space. This is because, as long as we are alive, consciousness is inseparably intermingled with our body, mind, senses, and prana shakti. There is an innate relationship among them. According to the *Shiva Sutra*, the life of this relationship is exactly the length of the life of creation. This relationship is what makes unborn, undying, eternal, all-pervading pure being become *jiva*, the individual soul.

This relationship comes to an end only with the annihilation of the cycle of creation or when we enter nirbija samadhi. Until then, the consciousness intrinsic to jiva maintains the awareness of the sense of time, space, number, and direction. That is why, even while deeply absorbed in the self-luminous ball of light, there is still a sense of above and below, here and there. According to yoga shastra, this self-luminous ball of light is the locus of our consciousness; thus, spiritually speaking, it is the heart.

From the standpoint of sadhana, yogis identify the upper edge of this self-luminous light as the higher lotus of the heart and the lower edge as the lower lotus. The highest concentration of awareness is in the regions corresponding to our crown and our physical heart. Samyama on the higher heart leads to shuddha samvit, the knowing power of pure consciousness, while samyama on the lower heart leads to chitta samvit, the knowing power of chitta. Access to both the higher and the lower heart is through the ajna chakra.

Success in finding the way to our heart—in this case, the lower heart—and entering it is dependent on how proficient we are at keeping our mind focused on the pranically charged luminous field of the ajna chakra. The longer we stay focused on the ajna chakra, the brighter and more defined that luminous field becomes.

As described in sutras 3:1 through 3:3, by the time we reach dhyana, the second stage of samyama, the mind is primarily aware of the pranic pulsation moving up and down in the center of that field, and subliminally aware of the luminosity surrounding it. Now the cognitions pertaining to previous pranic pulsations and those rising in the present are identical. This uninterrupted chain of identical cognitions results in a highly concentrated state of mind (YS 3:12). The mind is charged with a high degree of clarity and precision. Its discerning power is unfailing. Its intelligence is free from preoccupations and preconceived notions of good and bad, vice and virtue, likes and dislikes. It is strong, perceptive, and keenly interested in discovering its essential nature and hidden contents—a qualification for safely entering the heart.

The process of practicing samyama at the heart center begins with bringing the mind from the ajna chakra to the heart center while exhaling. Experientially, the ball of light in the space of consciousness corresponding to the region of the ajna chakra is fully formed. The mind is fully engaged in witnessing the ascending and descending pranic pulsation at the center of this ball and subliminally aware of the entire luminous field surrounding it. Breath has become extremely subtle—to the point that we are only subliminally aware of the physical dimension of our breathing.

While maintaining this meditative state, we invoke the power of volition to mentally stretch the descending wave of pranic pulsation during exhalation. How far we allow our mind to follow the descending wave of pranic pulsation is not as important as allowing the mind to register the fact that it is making an effort to follow the descending wave. Furthermore, we make this effort effortlessly. Because we have the intention of lengthening the pranic pulsation downward, it will occur by itself.

At the end of the exhalation, we begin to inhale. The inhalation originates exactly where the exhalation terminates. Pranically speaking, the ascent of pranic pulsation begins from where the descent terminates. Our intention is to descend a little further with each exhalation, but we do not use our power of intention to ascend beyond the ajna chakra with the inhalation. Eventually, we are exhaling and inhaling between the ajna chakra and the heart center. We are fully aware of the ascent and descent of pranic pulsation in the space of consciousness that stretches between the ajna chakra and the heart center.

As we attempt to bring our awareness from the ajna chakra to the heart, it is important to refrain from using imagery or visualization. The wave of pranic pulsation has no parallel in the phenomenal world. It has no shape, size, color, or form. It is a feeling comprehensible only to a highly concentrated and inwardly turned mind. This feeling evolves when we engage ourselves in ajna-chakra-centered meditation. As described in sutras 1:36 and 3:1 through 3:3, meditation at the ajna chakra initially involves following the movement of the breath between the zero point and the ajna chakra while paying special attention to the sensations unique to the opening of the nostrils, the inner corners of the eyes, and the center between the eyebrows.

As practice deepens, we transcend the physical dimension of the breath and are aware only of the united force of the mind and prana ascending and descending between the zero point and the ajna chakra. The feeling that is vivid in the mind is *prana samvedana*, pranic sensitivity. The feeling associated with the movement of pranic sensitivity is *prana sanchara*, pranic movement. The process of sustained meditation leads to *prana sanchaya*, pranic concentration at the ajna chakra. In this particular meditation on the heart, we are transporting pranic concentration from the ajna chakra to the heart center.

In order to gain an experiential understanding of pranic concentration and how it is transported from the ajna chakra to the heart center while allowing our mind to follow the descent and ascent of pranic pulsation, yogis prescribe a technique for moving prana shakti from the ajna chakra to the crown. This technique is known as *utkramana kriya* (*Katha Upanishad* 26:6:16). It serves as a bridge between meditation on the ajna chakra and meditation on the lower lotus of the heart in two ways. First, it engenders a direct experience of the pranic conveyor belt moving up and down in the region where it is naturally most pronounced. We gain this experience, deposit it in our memory, and later use our familiarity with this experience to feel the pranic movement in a region of the body where it is not so pronounced. Second, this technique pushes the center of pranic pulsation up and slightly back toward the interior of our head.

During meditation on the ajna chakra, the pranically lit space of consciousness appears to be in front of our face. The center of the ball of light is parallel to the center of the forehead. The meditative energy filling the region of our eyes gravitates toward the center of the light, filling the space in front of the eyebrows and forehead. Utkramana kriya transports this pranically lit space in front of the face to the center of the brain and aligns it with *murdha*, the fontanelle; with the *talu*, the soft palate; and with the heart. When this kriya is applied and has taken effect, the ball of light has shifted from in front of the eyebrows and forehead to the fontanelle and the space around it.

Apply this kriya at the end of your meditation on the ajna chakra. When the self-luminous ball of light is already formed in the region of the ajna chakra and the mind is following the pranic pulsation at its center, invoke the power of intention to stretch the ascending pranic pulsation upward a little. Do this while inhaling. With the exhalation, descend from where the inhalation ended. Come down all the way to the core of the self-luminous field. With the next inhalation, allow your mind to follow the ascending pranic pulsation, and this time, try to go a little higher but do not attempt to go higher than the fontanelle. Repeat this a few more times.

You will notice there is a unique feeling of energy pushing its way upward and, in the process, lifting everything in its path. This feeling is most pronounced in the eyes and in the bioenergetic field corresponding to the eyes and the region above the eyes. During each inhalation, it feels as though the upward pull of prana is pushing the eyeballs upward toward the fontanelle. Physiologically, the eyeballs may not be rolling upward, but mentally it feels as though they are. Let your mind register this feeling. With each breath, this feeling intensifies. The upward pull of awareness becomes more vivid. You may even feel some pressure building in your eyeballs. If the pressure is uncomfortable in any way, discontinue the practice. Never set a deadline for reaching the fontanelle and, under all circumstances, refrain from setting a deadline for going beyond the fontanelle.

With consistent and sustained practice, utkramana kriya intensifies. When it does, the pranic sensitivity increases. You will feel as though the self-luminous ball of light has moved deeper into the brain, and its core has settled in the region corresponding to the fontanelle. The movement of pranic pulsation is so vivid that the mind cannot escape it. At this point, the purpose of applying utkramana kriya is complete. The formal practice of samyama on the lotus of the heart begins from here.

With the exhalation, bring the mind from the center of the ball of light to the heart center. Without pausing, begin inhaling. Let your mind follow the upward movement of your inhalation until it reaches the center of the ball of light in the region of the brain, and without pausing, descend all the way to the heart center.

If you have not done enough meditation on the ajna chakra and your sensitivity to pranic movement has not matured, your experience of the pranic conveyor belt moving between the ajna chakra and the heart center may be vague. Normally, that is the case with practitioners who have little or no experience with pranic sensitivity at, above, and around the ajna chakra. Utkramana kriya intensifies pranic sensitivity and enables you to have a vivid experience of the upward movement of prana.

During the upward movement of prana, the pressure you feel in your eyes and in the region above your eyes is very firmly registered in your mind. While exhaling, pull the experience of pranic movement downward. Do not apply effort in doing so but use your power of intention.

To enhance your sensitivity to the downward movement of the pranic force, use the power of memory associated with the upwardly moving, intense pranic pulsation you experienced during utkramana kriya. The intention-driven awakening of memory will help your mind recognize how it feels when the pranic pulsation flows downward. You will notice a natural urge to release the pressure that built up in your eyes during utkramana kriya. Thus, the downward flow of pranic pulsation from the ajna chakra to the heart will be accompanied by a feeling of comfort. This way, with each exhalation, allow your mind to travel from the ball of light filling the interior space of your brain to the heart, and with each inhalation, travel from the heart to the ball of light.

Due to the heightened pranic sensitivity engendered by utkramana kriya, the mind will become oblivious of the anatomical movement of the breath. In the same proportion, the mind's comprehension of the pranic dimension of the breath will increase. Eventually, it will become absorbed in the ascending and descending wave of the pranic force.

As this absorption deepens, the mind transcends body consciousness. It is now aware only of the space that exists between the region of the heart and the fontanelle. The feeling of self-existence has settled in the space of consciousness saturated with self-luminous brilliance. This pranic brilliance is the locus of our self-awareness. It is the field of consciousness. Its upper edge, which is bordered by the fontanelle and the space above it, is *urdhva-hrit-padma*, the upper lotus of the heart. The lower edge, which is bordered by the physical heart and the space below it, is *adhah-hrit-padma*, the lower lotus of the heart. The pranic conveyor belt is moving between these two hearts. As the practice deepens, the movement of inhalation and exhalation begins to follow the movement of the pranic conveyor belt. In advanced stages, the feeling of one following the other disappears. The mind and pranic movement have merged. As one inseparable unit, the mind and prana shakti move up and down in the self-luminous space of consciousness. This process and the experience engendered by it is meditation on the lotus of the heart.

During meditation on the ajna chakra, yogis advise us to pay special attention to the inner corners of the eyes and the center between the eyebrows while mentally traveling between the zero point and the ajna chakra. Here, during meditation on the lotus of the heart, we are advised to pay special attention to the talu chakra, the region associated with the soft palate. In his commentary on sutra 1:35, Vyasa mentions the unique nature of the talu chakra. According to him, the talu chakra is the center of *rupa samvit*, the knowing power of form. Thus, samyama on the talu chakra results in the awakening of the power that enables the mind to comprehend the form of formless space.

Samyama on the ajna chakra awakens buddhi samvit, the consciousness that infuses our intellect with the power of comprehension. This power enables buddhi to sense the presence of an object, including its own presence. Buddhi's ability to comprehend defining characteristics of an object comes from secondary pools of intelligence that are vested with unique powers of comprehension.

In this case, the shakti unique to the ajna chakra enables the intellect to sense the presence of pranic pulsation and the pranic field surrounding it. However, comprehension of the exact form of pranic pulsation and the surrounding pranic field is due to the awakening of rupa samvit, the knowing power of form, which is unique to the consciousness at the talu chakra. The talu chakra and a few minor chakras in the region of our forehead and above are integral to the ajna chakra. Therefore, meditation on the ajna chakra automatically includes the talu chakra.

Paying special attention to the talu chakra during meditation on the heart reinforces the manifestation of the ball of light and infuses it with specificity. It allows our inner intelligence to comprehend the distinctive qualities of that light. It pulls the self-luminous ball of light to the center of the brain, as opposed to allowing the mind to feel its presence in front of our face. Furthermore, it engages the mind to focus so deeply on the well-defined form of light at the center of our brain that by default it is withdrawn from its long-cherished association with the sense organ of seeing and the cortex.

During meditation on the ajna chakra, the perception of the self-luminous ball of light in the space of consciousness in front of the face triggers a subtle, yet recognizable, neurological activity in our eyes and cortex. This activity is due to the mind's lifelong dependence on the eyes and the cortex. Meditation on the talu chakra frees the mind from this dependence, allowing it to enter the space of consciousness that houses the lower and higher hearts.

To convey the importance of the talu chakra and its special place in meditation on the lotus of the heart, yogis equate the talu chakra with *abhijita muhurta*. According to Indian astrology, abhijita muhurta is the most auspicious time, for it confers victory in every regard. This auspicious time emerges at the conjunction of several celestial forces. The key factor is that the sun is at its peak. Because the earth is tilted on its axis, the timing of this auspicious moment differs from place to place and season to season.

According to yoga shastra, a human being is a miniature universe. In the human body, the place of sunrise and sunset is always fixed: the sun rises at the heart and sets at the dvadashanta, twelve finger-widths above the fontanelle. Prana is the sun. It rises as we inhale and continues moving upward until it reaches the dvadashanta. It sets there and descends as we exhale. The talu chakra is at the exact center of our ascending and descending breath. Each time the united forces of the mind and prana pass through the region of the talu chakra, yogically speaking it is abhijita muhurta, the most auspicious time for achieving success. In the macrocosm, this auspicious time lasts for forty-eight minutes. In our microcosm, it lasts but for a moment, but this moment is equal to forty-eight minutes in the external world. Every day, this auspicious moment walks into our life approximately 21,600 times.

Practicing samyama on the talu chakra means paying attention to this auspicious time and place as we inhale and exhale. This brief moment of attention to this auspicious time and place is enough to drench the mind in the power unique to the talu chakra; the power unique to the talu chakra is rupa samvit, the power that enables the mind to comprehend the form of formless space. In other words, the power of intelligence unique to the talu chakra enables the mind to comprehend an abstract experience concretely.

To amplify pranic sensitivity at the talu chakra, the adepts advise us to apply *divyakarana mudra* throughout the practice of meditation on the lotus of the heart. To apply divyakarana mudra, first relax your jaw. You will notice your upper and lower teeth touch lightly. Place the tip of your tongue on the hard palate. Make sure there is no effort involved. Your lower and upper lips are relaxed and lightly touching. Once this mudra is set, make no effort to maintain it. This mudra forces the ascending and descending streams of prana to flow through the center of the space of consciousness between the lower and upper hearts. It prevents the mind from following its established habit of accompanying the breath between the zero point and the ajna chakra.

Figuratively speaking, divyakarana mudra stands like a wall between the pranically charged space in the center of our body and the space in front of our face. In other words, it blocks the mind from being distracted by the pranically lit space in front of the face, thus allowing our entire awareness to travel up and down in the space of consciousness corresponding to the interior of the space occupied by our head. The talu chakra, the region of the soft palate, is the doorway for entering that space while inhaling. It is also the doorway for entering the space occupied by our neck, throat, and chest cavity while exhaling. Divyakarana mudra forces the mind to remain fully united only with the central current of prana ascending and descending between the lower and upper hearts.

In sutras 3:26 and 3:27, we have observed the role of divyakarana mudra in lifting our awareness from the ajna chakra to the doorways of the sun and moon. There the practices of samyama on the doorways of the sun and moon are described as independent practices, each leading to a different experience. Here, in the practice of meditation on the lotus of the heart, divyakarana mudra allows the combined forces of our mind and prana to sweep through both doorways. But unlike the practices described in sutras 3:26 and 3:27, here pay no attention to either doorway, but instead give special attention to the talu chakra.

While inhaling, allow your mind to follow the ascent of prana. When passing through the talu chakra, pay attention to the unique character of the space corresponding to this region. Do not make any change in your breathing pattern. Continue inhaling upward without stopping or slowing at the talu chakra. Once you have passed through this region, make no effort to reach a certain summit. You may feel the pranic ascent just a little above the talu chakra, or all the way to the crown, or any point in between. From wherever your inhalation comes to an end, begin your exhalation and descend. When you reach the region of your talu chakra, pay attention to the unique pranic sensitivity filling that space and make some effort to carry that pranic sensitivity to your heart. By the time you reach your heart, your exhalation has come to an end.

Without pausing, begin inhaling. During your ascent, pay attention to the unique feeling that fills the region of the talu chakra and continue moving upward effortlessly. Upon completing the inhalation, descend. During the descent, again pay attention to the unique feeling that surrounds the talu chakra and continue descending to the lotus of the heart. Repeat this process for three to five minutes.

As we have seen, the lotus of the heart refers to the general region of the space housing the heart, liver, and lungs. This space is saturated with chitta samvit, the unique power of intelligence that enables the mind to know itself and the complete range of its attributes. Because of this unique power of intelligence, the organs occupying this space have an acute ability to sense the slightest fluctuation in our thoughts, feelings, and sentiments.

Chitta samvit is always aware of changes that have occurred in the past, are occurring in the present, and will occur in the future. Because of the presence of this power, the physical heart occupying this space responds to the mind's past, present, and anticipated experiences. This response triggers a series of changes in the function of the heart. Changes in heart patterns trigger a cascade of changes in the function of the liver and lungs.

The power of intelligence corresponding to the general region of the chest cavity is the lotus of the heart and is described by a unique term: *hrit-padma-yantra-tritayam*. *Hrit* means "heart"; *padma*, "lotus"; *yantra*, "machine"; and *tritayam*, "cluster of three." Thus, "the lotus of the heart is a three-part machine made of the heart, liver, and lungs."

At a deeper level, the lotus of the heart is the power of intelligence that enables the mind to comprehend itself and its active and dormant tendencies. At the physical level, it enables the heart, liver, and lungs to communicate with each other and work in unison. This power of intelligence further links all visceral organs and facilitates their communication with the brain, which falls in the domain of the ajna chakra. The literal meaning of *ajna chakra* is "command center." The power unique to the heart has the ability to comprehend and execute both explicit and implicit messages coming from the ajna chakra.

Because the blossoming of this unique power unveils the mystery of our life in the past, present, and future, the heart center is described as a lotus. The lotus is a symbol of beauty and tenderness. Rooted in mud, it rises above the water. Its floating leaves, with their smooth and shiny surfaces, remain untouched by the water. The opening and closing of its blossoms are synchronized with sunrise and sunset and follow the path of the sun. Thus, "lotus" describes the unique capacity of intelligence to transform the mind so it learns to receive nutrients from muddy circumstances, reclaim its buoyancy, and rise while remaining unsmeared. This intelligence resets the mind's clock, which comprehends the laws of nature—when to be active and when to rest, when to engage and when to withdraw, when to receive and when to let go, when to retain and when to renounce, when to advance and when to retreat. Empowered by these gifts, the mind is able to loosen and eventually release itself from both known and unknown, manifest and unmanifest aspects of bondage.

As described earlier, meditation on the lower lotus of the heart begins with mentally watching the movement of prana shakti between the fontanelle and the general vicinity of the physical heart. Divyakarana mudra pulls the pranically lit ball of light from the front of the face to the center of the brain. Special attention to the talu chakra ensures that the mind is following the ascent and descent of prana shakti along the natural axis of alignment between the heart and the fontanelle without distraction. As we employ the mind in attending the pranic pulsation moving up and down in this space of consciousness, *prana samapatti*—mental absorption in prana shakti—arises.

In the deeper stages of this mental absorption, the mind is no longer aware of the physical dimension of inhalation and exhalation. It is cognizant only of the ascent and descent of prana shakti. Furthermore, in this state, the mind is barely aware of the body. All it knows and feels is the space of consciousness in which prana shakti is moving up and down. Eventually, the mind settles and becomes predominantly aware of the space corresponding to the region of the physical heart and only subliminally aware of the space extending all the way to the fontanelle and beyond. The emergence of this experience is due solely to the power of intention.

Understanding what guides our power of intention to condense our consciousness so vividly in the general vicinity of our physical heart requires revisiting the mystery of the four streams of prana shakti mentioned briefly in sutra 3:26. Above the ajna chakra lies the domain of the sahasrara, the thousand-petaled lotus of the crown chakra. The space corresponding to the upper ridge of the ajna chakra and the lower ridge of the sahasrara is extremely significant. This space is neither fully part of our phenomenal world nor completely transcendent. The doorways of the inner moon and inner sun are located here. The four streams of prana shakti originating from the sahasrara pass through this space.

The first two streams of prana shakti are known as *nivritti* and *pratishtha*. They are associated with exhalation. These two streams receive their names from their unique qualities and attributes. *Nivritti* means "release, liberation, emancipation, freedom." This stream of pranic flow infuses our mind with the ability to release itself from afflicting samskaras and the agitating tendencies they churn up. *Pratishtha* means "state of stability, groundedness." This pranic flow enables the mind to become grounded, reclaim its power of concentration, and become firm in its resolve.

The other two pranic streams are *vidya* and *shanta*. They are associated with inhalation. *Vidya* means "knowledge, understanding, comprehension, ability to intuit, discernment." This pranic stream infuses the mind with the power to intuit its vast treasury of samskaras as well as the current conditions of the body, mind, and senses. *Shanta* means "state of peacefulness, tranquility, quietude." This pranic stream infuses the mind with the power to relax, rest, and rise above the effects of internal or external disturbances.

Together, these four pranic streams originating from the higher lotus of the heart in the sahasrara chakra awaken chitta samvit, the knowing power of all aspects of the mind. These pranic streams are fully aware of our intention. When, as part of our meditation on the lower lotus of the heart, we inhale and exhale between the lower and higher hearts, these pranic forces exercise their power and privilege in unison with our intention.

Thus, as meditation matures, in their own mysterious way, the innate properties of these pranic forces facilitate the condensation of consciousness in the region of our physical heart. Furthermore, as we follow the ascent and descent of the pranic force passing through the talu chakra, the mind assimilates the balancing and irrepressible power of intelligence unique to the talu chakra.

As practice progresses, dharana evolves into dhyana. When dhyana matures into samadhi, the mind is totally absorbed in the pranic radiance in the region of the heart. Eventually, the mind is immersed in the pranic pulsation at the center of this radiance and is only subliminally aware of the ring of luminosity surrounding it. Maintaining this awareness is the final step in meditation on the lotus of the heart.

Sustained meditation on the lotus of the heart leads the mind to experience chitta samvit. The longer it maintains this meditative state, the firmer this experience becomes. The firmer this experience, the more effortlessly and clearly the mind invokes its intrinsic power to know itself and its attributes. It has the ability to see its pristine nature, which mirrors the purity of Ishvara, the transcendental being. The mind is thrilled with the realization that it is a direct extension of Ishvara's prakriti and, as such, is untouched by karmic impurities. It is thrilled by the realization that from its inception it has been a conduit for prakriti's intelligence.

The knowing power of chitta samvit also infuses the mind with the power to intuit its acquired attributes—samskaras, the subtle karmic impressions. It is able to see the causal relationship between samskaras and conditions manifesting in the present. Because it has discovered its beginningless relationship with Ishvara and primordial prakriti, the mind is not perturbed by seeing the causal relationship between its samskaras and present conditions. Furthermore, it is able to see the future and remain unaffected.

The awakening of the mind's knowing power at the lotus of the heart is accompanied by the power of retaining and assimilating it. Most importantly, chitta samvit is mingled with the constant awareness that all powers, including the mind's power to know itself and its attributes, come from primordial prakriti, Ishvara's own essence. This awareness fills the mind with humility and gratitude and empowers the mind to free itself from its mistaken identity as the knower. The mind knows and is happy that it knows but claims no ownership over the knowledge or the power of knowing. Trustful surrender is the spontaneous and effortless fruit of this realization. This realization is the core of chitta samvit—the ultimate experience resulting from samyama on the lotus of the lower heart.

SUTRA 3:35

सत्त्वपुरुषयोरत्यन्तासंकीर्णयोः प्रत्ययाविशेषो भोगः परार्थत्वात्स्वार्थसंयमात्पुरुषज्ञानम् ॥३५॥

sattvapuruṣayoratyantāsaṁkīrṇayoḥ pratyayāviśeṣo bhogaḥ parārthatvātsvārthasaṁyamātpuruṣajñānam ॥ 35 ॥

sattvapuruṣayoḥ, of mind and consciousness; *atyantāsaṁkīrṇayoḥ*, of two totally fused entities; *pratyayāviśeṣaḥ*, lack of difference between cognitions; *bhogaḥ*, experience; *parārthatvāt*, owing to fulfilling the purpose of someone or something other than itself; *svārthasaṁyamāt*, from samyama on self-awareness; *puruṣa-jñānam*, knowledge pertaining to pure consciousness

The mind and consciousness are so intensely fused that there is no difference between their cognitions. [This conflated cognition is] experience. An aspect of experience is smeared with the sense of being an object. [Withdrawing the mind from that and] practicing samyama on the other, which is accompanied by the sense of I-am-ness, engenders the knowledge of pure consciousness.

In the preceding sutra, Patanjali tells us what happens when we practice samyama on the lotus of the heart. Now he explains how to apply the power engendered by that practice and what happens when we do.

Samyama on the lotus of the heart results in chitta samvit, experiencing the knowing power of chitta. The range of chitta samvit includes a clear understanding of all aspects of the mind: the thinking mind, the discerning mind, the mind that identifies itself with the objects of its experiences, and the mind that serves as a storehouse of memories. It also includes the ability to comprehend pure consciousness. In other words, the experience of chitta samvit empowers us to comprehend all aspects of our mind as well as the power of comprehension itself. Chitta samvit enables us to know the mind as an object of our knowledge. It also enables us to know the knower. In yoga, the term for the knower is *purusha*, pure consciousness.

As detailed in sutra 2:20, the knowing power of pure consciousness is the knower. The power to know is intrinsic to purusha. Purusha (more clearly, its intrinsic knowing power) and the mind are intensely intermingled. Thus, in our day-to-day experience we fail to comprehend the difference between the two. Through their interaction with objects, the senses gather experiences and—so we are told—pass them on to the mind. This process is so subtle that we fail to notice it. The mind is an instrument of comprehension that passes sensory experiences to consciousness; this is even subtler and, in fact, inconceivable.

How the mind discerns and decides; how the mind identifies itself with the objects of its experiences; and how it collects, preserves, retrieves, and brings the memories to the forefront of our consciousness is an impenetrable mystery. All we know is that, as a living being, we are conscious of our existence. We have been perennially identifying this self-conscious living being as "we," "ourselves," "our soul." While having an experience, we never feel the urge to see who is experiencing it—pure consciousness, the mind, or both. We are not aware of whether consciousness is enabling the mind or the mind is enabling consciousness. We are not even aware that we are composed of two separate entities—consciousness and the conduit of consciousness.

The experience of chitta samvit gives us the ability to comprehend this intensely intermingled relationship between consciousness and the mind as well as the subtle distinction between the two. In this sutra, Patanjali tells us how to use this ability to practice samyama on pure consciousness, further sharpening our knowledge and experience of purusha.

The practice referred to here begins with dharana. As elaborated on in sutras 3:1 through 3:5, we practice dharana by anchoring the mind in a well-defined space. We can choose to anchor our mind in the space corresponding to any physical region inside or outside our body. For reasons discussed in sutra 3:1, the tradition prefers anchoring the mind in the space of consciousness corresponding to the center of the forehead. Practicing samyama according to the method elaborated on in sutras 3:1 through 3:5, we begin by focusing our mind on the breath flowing between the zero point and the center of the forehead. We pass through stages where we are guided to pay special attention to the spaces corresponding to the general region of the opening of the nostrils, the inner corners of the eyes, and the center between the eyebrows. By doing so, we intensify the bond between the mind and the breath, collect the intelligence unique to those spots in our body, and intensify our pranic sensitivity in the space of consciousness corresponding to the region of our forehead.

The sustained practice of dharana at the center of the forehead evolves into dhyana as the mind begins to comprehend the pranic counterpart of the breath. In the truest sense, this is when the mind and the life force become fully united. The longer the mind and prana remain in a mutual embrace, the more vivid is the experience of the pranically lit space in the forehead. As practice progresses, the mind becomes anchored in this ball of light. As it does, the core of this ball of light is more predominantly in the mind's view while the pranically lit space around it recedes into the background. Eventually, the mind and the pranic pulsation at the core begin to merge. This deeply immersive state is dhyana.

At this point, the practice described in sutra 3:34 is introduced. By applying divyakarana mudra, we gently pull the cognition of the pranically lit space from the center of the forehead deeper into our brain center. The space corresponding to the center of the brain now becomes the focal point of our practice of dhyana. As practice deepens, the pranically lit space begins to expand and fills the region between our fontanelle and the region of the physical heart. At this point, we are guided to pay special attention to the space corresponding to the region of the soft palate. This allows the united forces of our mind and breath to travel along the natural axis of alignment between the heart and the soft palate. Eventually, the core of this pranically lit space shifts closer to the heart.

A sustained practice of meditation on the lotus of the heart evolves into an immersive state. The process of meditation, the object of meditation, and the awareness of ourselves as the meditator begin to blend. Awareness pertaining to the process of meditation is the first to fade. We are left with two cognitions: one pertaining to the object of meditation, and the other pertaining to ourselves as the meditator. Pranic pulsation is the object of meditation and the awareness of our self-existence is the meditator. The mind is occupied by both of these cognitions.

During this immersive state, sometimes the cognition pertaining to pranic pulsation occupies the mind more strongly, and at other times, the cognition pertaining to our self-existence is dominant. This alternating dominance of subject and object is part of the meditative process. A prolonged and consistent practice brings refinement. As sutra 1:47 tells us, refinement in meditation results in *adhyatma-prasada*, spiritual transparency. A high degree of clarity and joy is an indicator of spiritual transparency. The mind is lit by *prajna*, the self-luminous field of consciousness (YS 1:48 and 3:5). In this immersive state, both cognitions—one pertaining to the object and the other to the subject—are about to merge.

At this stage, the mind is predominantly aware of the conflated cognitions of the pranic pulsation and the knowing power of self-awareness. But at the same time, it is subliminally aware of the distinction between pranic pulsation and self-awareness. This subliminal distinction is due to the mind's long-cherished habit of comprehending cognitions either as object or as subject. The force of meditation on the lotus of the heart destroys this entrenched habit. This is what results in chitta samvit, as described in the previous sutra.

At this stage, we can look back and see—through the eye of the seeing power of chitta—which aspect of this conflated cognition is smeared with objective awareness and which aspect is the seer, the sheer power of seeing. Experientially speaking, we are at the furthest frontier of sabija samadhi and at the very threshold of nirbija samadhi. We are able to see both object and subject—pranic pulsation and consciousness sensing it—from an equal distance. The awareness pertaining to pranic pulsation is at once there and not there. Similarly, as a conscious being we are simultaneously aware of our self-existence and unaware of it. This hard-to-describe, intensely conflated state of two cognitions—one pertaining to the mind and the other pertaining to pure consciousness—is *jiva*, the individual soul. *Chitta* is another term for this individual soul (*Shiva Sutra* 3:1).

During this highly immersive state, we can isolate the aspect of chitta that serves as a conduit for consciousness from consciousness itself. The secret of the practice described in this sutra lies in withdrawing the mind from objective awareness associated with pranic pulsation and anchoring it exclusively in sheer self-presence. This leads to *purusha samapatti*, absorption in the sheer power of seeing, which allows the mind to become infused with the seeing power of the seer. This transformative state is characterized by *purusha jnanam*, knowledge of purusha.

If we reverse the process during this same highly immersive state, withdrawing our mind from the sheer experience of self-presence and anchoring it exclusively in objective awareness, the resulting transformation will open doors to extraordinary powers. That is the subject of the next sutra.

SUTRA 3:36

ततः प्रातिभश्रावणवेदनादर्शास्वादवार्ता जायन्ते ॥३६॥

tataḥ prātibhaśrāvaṇavedanādarśāsvādavārtā jāyante ॥ 36 ॥

tataḥ, from that; *prātibhaśrāvaṇavedanādarśāsvādavārtāḥ*, intuitive hearing, touching, seeing, tasting, and smelling; *jāyante*, arises

From that arises [the power of] intuitive hearing, touching, seeing, tasting, and smelling.

As in sutra 3:35, here Patanjali describes the experience resulting from applying the power gained by chitta samvit, which comes from practicing samyama on the lotus of the heart (YS 3:34). In the normal course of life, the deep-rooted habit of identifying a cognition as an object and ourselves as a subject gives birth to duality, forcing the mind to operate within the confines of subject-object awareness. But in the immersive state of chitta samvit, this deep-rooted habit is transformed into *shakti matra*, sheer power.

Through chitta samvit, the seeing power of the mind, we are able to see pure awareness and the object of awareness clearly. By practicing samyama as described in sutra 3:35, we gain the knowledge of purusha, pure awareness. But by practicing samyama on the object of awareness, we gain the knowledge of that object. That is the subject of this sutra.

The range of our experience of the objective world can be divided into five categories. We experience objects of the world by hearing, touching, seeing, tasting, and smelling—the mind is dependent on the senses for its cognitions. According to yoga, the senses are an extension of the mind; the sense organs are the physical locus of the mental power coursing through them. From the standpoint of contacting and experiencing the objects of the phenomenal world, the mind is the subject and the experience is the object.

But in the immersive state of chitta samvit, the mind along with the senses and sensory experiences is the object, and chitta samvit, the mind's knowing power, is the subject. This is how chitta samvit, the knowing power of the mind, elevates the mind to the point where it begins to comprehend the vast universe of cognitions related to numberless sensory experiences, including those stored in the mind as memories. This highly empowered mind rises above its dependence on the senses and is thus capable of comprehending the objects of the world directly.

Intuitive light is the ground for the mind's ability to transcend sensory limitations. The Sanskrit word for intuitive light is *pratibha*, "reflecting or responding to *bha*, pure light." In the state of chitta samvit, the mind is so pure and pristine that it mirrors the luminosity of purusha without distortion. For all intents and purposes, in this state the mind is as self-luminous and pervasive as purusha itself. Thus, it reaches everywhere without moving. As described in sutras 3:25 and 3:33, time and space pose no barrier to this highly evolved mind. It can comprehend objects too subtle to be detected by the senses.

This state of comprehension is not an ordinary cognition but rather a pure intuitive understanding of an object or a conglomerate of objects appearing on the horizon of a mind that is fully lit by the glow of pure consciousness. This understanding encompasses the objects not only of the phenomenal world but also of the world incomprehensible to our ordinary mind and senses. By employing the unique power of chitta samvit, we are able to unveil *shabda samvit*, the knowing power of sound; *sparsha samvit*, the knowing power of touch; *rupa samvit*, the knowing power of form; *rasa samvit*, the knowing power of taste; and *gandha samvit*, the knowing power of smell. By employing these unique manifestations of chitta samvit, we are able to comprehend celestial sound, touch, form, taste, and smell. We gain these powers either by harnessing the intuitive light of pure consciousness, or by cultivating them through the practice of samyama on specific centers of consciousness in our body, such as the tip of the nostrils, the tip of the tongue, the soft palate, the middle of the tongue, or the base of the tongue (Vyasa's commentary on sutra 1:35).

What purpose these extraordinary accomplishments serve and whether or not they are essential to achieving the highest goal of yoga is the subject of the next sutra.

SUTRA 3:37

ते समाधावुपसर्गा व्युत्थाने सिद्धयः ॥३७॥

te samādhāvupasargā vyutthāne siddhayaḥ ॥ 37 ॥

te, they; *samādhau*, in samadhi; *upasargāḥ*, obstacles; *vyutthāne*, in an outwardly running mind; *siddhayaḥ*, accomplishments

For one with an outwardly running mind, these are extraordinary accomplishments, but for one aspiring to samadhi, they are obstacles.

In this sutra, Patanjali clarifies the relative value of practicing samyama on different objects and the experiences gained from those practices. In sutra 3:34, he introduces the practice of samyama on the lotus of the heart, which leads to the unfoldment of the knowing power of the mind. In sutra 3:35, he explains how to employ the knowing power of the mind to comprehend the distinction between the mind and its knowing power, which enables it to know itself. He further explains how to withdraw the mind from itself and allow an immersive state to arise in which nothing other than pure consciousness is in the view of consciousness. This immersive state eventually matures into nirbija, the highest state of samadhi.

With the exception of the practices described in these two sutras, all practices described in sutras 3:16 through 3:36 lead to the development of unique mental abilities, which may or may not be directly associated with the attainment of samadhi. The basic thrust of these practices is to unveil the mystery of the mind, discover its strengths and weaknesses, gain a clear understanding of potential pitfalls, and devise a strategy to complete the samadhi-bound quest with the fewest distractions. However, taking human frailty into account, Patanjali warns us not to mistake the means for the goal, advising us instead to remain focused on samadhi, the highest goal of yoga.

SUTRA 3:38

बन्धकारणशैथिल्यात्प्रचारसंवेदनाच् च चित्तस्य परशरीरावेशः ॥३८॥

bandhakāraṇaśaithilyātpracārasaṁvedanāc ca cittasya paraśarīrāveśaḥ ॥ 38 ॥

bandhakāraṇaśaithilyāt, from the loosening of the cause of bondage; *pracārasaṁvedanāt*, from sensitivity to pranic flow; *ca*, and; *cittasaya*, of the mind; *paraśarīrāveśaḥ*, entry into and infusion of another body

From the loosening of the cause of bondage and from sensitivity to pranic flow, the mind is able to enter and infuse another body.

Here Patanjali introduces *parakaya pravesha*, a fascinating practice that can be understood only by those familiar with the practices and experiences described in sutras 3:34 and 3:35. *Parakaya pravesha* is a composite of *para*, *kaya*, and *pravesha*. *Para* means "another"; *kaya* means "body"; and *pravesha* means "process or act of entering." Thus, *parakaya pravesha* means "the process or act of entering another body." It is the term most commonly used for the act of consciously leaving one's body and entering another body. This practice is for separating the mind from the body and pulling it out before the force of death severs the pranic link holding the body and mind together. In this sutra, Patanjali uses the more nuanced term, *para-shariravesha*, instead of *parakaya pravesha* to highlight the subtlety of this process.

Para-shariravesha is a composite of *para*, *sharira*, and *avesha*. Para means "another"; *sharira* means "body" and carries the etymological implication of shredding, disintegrating, or deteriorating; *avesha* means "penetrating from every direction, at every level, in every manner." Thus, *para-shariravesha* means "descending into another body and fully infusing it with self-awareness."

High-caliber yogis undertake this practice for two reasons. The first is to gain a direct experience of the limitless mystery of both their mind and mother nature. It enables them to understand why consciousness needs a physical entity to carry out its quest for fulfillment and freedom and how it feels when consciousness has no physical locus.

The second reason they undertake this practice is to outrun death. Death sucks us into nothingness. It buries our consciousness in a bottomless void, but before doing so, it withdraws the life force from the physical elements that comprise our body. It demands that the senses return their unique abilities to the mind. Death shreds our memories into numberless pieces and nullifies the linearity of time and space. It puts chitta samvit, the knowing power of the mind, to sleep. Death hands consciousness over to destiny. Thereafter, how long we stay in that state; when, where, and how we are reborn; how much of our memory returns; and how we restart our life-bound journey is in the hands of destiny. To avoid this condition of helplessness, yogis practice parakaya pravesha.

Parakaya pravesha entails keeping the mind intact, protecting it from the influence of death, leaving the body without falling into unconsciousness, guiding the mind to descend into another body, and infusing that body with chitta samvit along with the entire knowledge it contains. Yogis acquire these capacities with the practice of parakaya pravesha but use them only as a last resort. As described in the previous sutra, the value of extraordinary powers, including those arising from the practice of parakaya pravesha, lies in their application to attaining samadhi.

By using the knowledge gained from the practice described in sutra 3:22, we can get a clear sense of our impending death. Upon realizing that death will inevitably come before we have gained maturity in our meditation and are fully established in our essential nature, we invoke the power gained from the practice of parakaya pravesha and cast off our body before death can touch it. By doing this, we preserve our meditative samskaras. We descend into a new body and infuse it with our chitta samvit and the meditative samskaras it contains. This allows us to continue our practice of meditation without disruption. This is the yogic way of transporting the flame of consciousness from one body to another.

The formal practice of parakaya pravesha begins with dharana, dhyana, and samadhi. As described in sutras 3:1 through 3:5, the practice of dharana begins with confining the mind to a well-defined space—in this context, the center of the forehead. The details of dharana include uniting the mind with the flow of the breath and witnessing the movement of the mind and breath from the zero point to a space corresponding to the center of the forehead. Eventually, dharana matures into dhyana, leading the mind to be absorbed in the pranic pulsation that fills the space in and around the center of the forehead.

In the second stage of the practice, we skillfully transport this meditative state deeper into our brain center and, as described in sutra 3:34, from there we bring it to the lotus of the heart. Perfection in meditation on the lotus of the heart is the secret of parakaya pravesha. If we become fully absorbed in the consciousness unique to the lotus of the heart, we gain the experience of chitta samvit. This allows us to know the knowing power of the mind. It enables us to know the knower within as well as the object of our awareness.

By employing the power of chitta samvit as described in sutra 3:35, we can focus our awareness on the knower within. This leads to *purusha jnanam*, the knowledge of pure consciousness. If we focus on the object of awareness, as described in sutra 3:36, we gain knowledge of the objective world including our body, senses, mind, and the vast field of memory. With the exception of when we are deeply immersed in the unique stages of samadhi as described in sutras 3:35 and 3:36, there is always an intensely conflated awareness of both the knower and the knowable. This conflated awareness of the knower and knowable is *jiva*, the individual self. This individual self is the one who is engaged in parakaya pravesha.

From the standpoint of technique, parakaya pravesha is divided into two parts: the process of getting out of our body and the process of entering another body. According to this sutra, the process of getting out of our body requires loosening the force that binds jiva to the body. We accomplish this by attenuating and eventually nullifying the impact of the fivefold affliction on our mind and consciousness (YS 2:2–13). The process of entering another body requires cultivating sensitivity to the pranic movement in our own body and in the space our body occupies. We fulfill this requirement by practicing and eventually mastering prana dharana, as described in sutra 3:1.

As Vyasa elaborates, the mind, lacking clarity and concentration, fails to comprehend its immense power and its relationship with the body. In principle, the mind is the master of the body. The more dull and dense the mind, the less capacity it has to command the forces that govern and guide the functions of the body. The practice of meditation as described in sutras 1:36, 3:1

through 3:5, and most importantly, 3:34, enables us to transcend our mental dullness and reach an immersive state marked by the experience of chitta samvit.

In the light of chitta samvit, we are able to see the most subtle and potent streams of samskaras that determine the particular body we are born in, our life span, and the unavoidable circumstances that walk into our life. Only after we have a direct experience of our chitta samvit do we gain true understanding of the conflated experience of an object and the consciousness experiencing it. Chitta samvit empowers us to comprehend our body as an object of our cognition, as well as to comprehend the cognizant force behind cognition. Chitta samvit also empowers us to measure how intensely our body and that cognizant force are fused. By applying the practice described in sutra 3:35, we can isolate that cognizant force from the body, and by using the combined forces of vairagya and prana shakti, we can pull consciousness—the cognizant force—out of the body voluntarily. It is important to remember that the backdrop of this simple-sounding process is perfection in experiencing our disassociation from the external world, including our own body. This backdrop also includes maturity in comprehending our innate connection with prana shakti.

The practice of prana dharana is the key to success in parakaya pravesha. Perfection in prana dharana comes from merging the mind and prana—a process known as *manah-prana-aikyanusandhana*. Once this merger has taken place and has matured, we can begin the practice of parakaya pravesha.

The first step in this practice is to lead the combined forces of the mind and prana back and forth from one part of the body to another with full conscious awareness. The second step is to lead them back and forth from one marmasthana to the next. The third step is to lead them back and forth from the lower lotus of the heart to the doorway of the sun and moon as described in sutras 3:26 and 3:27. The fourth step is to remain in the region of the sun and moon until awareness of the physical body vanishes and is replaced by the palpable experience of space outside the body, an experience described in sutra 3:43. This is a self-born experience and contains no trace of imagination. Furthermore, the space of consciousness outside our body serving as a locus for this experience has no association with our familiar space. We are guided to place our consciousness—jiva, the individuated self—in this space. This completes the process of exiting our body voluntarily.

Initially, we get out of the body, touch that locus, and return to the body without lingering. As practice progresses, we embrace the locus longer and longer before returning to the body. Eventually, we become as comfortable with this locus as we are with our physical body.

Seated firmly in this locus, we witness our body, its past and present experiences, and its current condition. We witness dharma, lakshana, and avastha—the threefold change occurring in the body (YS 3:13). We also witness how our body is somewhat in a state of suspended animation. Our vital organs and the nervous system are completely relaxed and are functioning in a manner similar to hibernation. This quasi hibernation is sustained by the initial intention of prana shakti to maintain its connection with the body until the karmic thrust that initiated the process of our birth is exhausted.

With practice, we increase the duration of our stay in this self-born locus outside our body. This is a slow, gradual process. At some point, we are guided to reflect on the history of our body—how we were born; how we passed through the various stages of infancy, childhood, adolescence, and adulthood; how emotional factors helped us build and destroy our relationships with others;

and how we fell into, sank, floated, and got out of the torrents of pleasure and pain.

Anchored in this locus, we reflect on how our relationship with our body and everything and everyone associated with it is only as real as the objects of our dreams and is as transitory as a drop of dew on a blade of grass. In this state of consciousness, these reflections on life and its relationship with the body bring perfection to the most precious principle of yoga sadhana: vairagya. Armed with the power of vairagya, we cut asunder the most subtle and potent ropes of karma binding the jiva to the body. This frees us from all our actions, done and undone. We are free from the subtlest of all binding forces—fear and remorse. This degree of freedom enables us to stay outside our body as long as we wish. The degree of clarity engendered by this reflection enables us to assess the body's capacity to remain in a state of quasi hibernation without shutting down completely. This completes the first half of the practice of parakaya pravesha.

Entering another body is the second half of the practice. This involves allowing the locus of our self-existence to descend into another body. It is important to remember that at this point in our practice, the space of pure consciousness is the locus. Our self-existence—the intensely conflated essence of our senses, different faculties of our mind, and prana shakti—is anchored in the locus outside our body. The descent of this locus into another body automatically includes the descent of our entire self-existence. Just as in the first part of the practice we learned how to get out of the body, touch the self-born locus, and re-enter our original body, in the second part of the practice we touch the other body without lingering and then quickly allow the locus to distance itself from that body. Following the rules we applied in the first part, we slowly and gradually increase our capacity to allow the locus to embrace and saturate the body for longer periods.

In the initial stages, we are advised to choose a body that is occupied by a diffused consciousness and contains the least complex nervous system and simple vital organs—a plant or a butterfly, for example. We—our locus and all of its attributes—descend into the body of a plant or a butterfly, superimpose ourselves, gain firsthand experience of the pranic movement in that body, and then quickly extricate our locus from that body. Thereafter, either we live in that locus for a while or we immediately return to our original body. This journey of our locus of consciousness from one body to another is continuously repeated. Only after we have gained considerable experience and are confident that we will not make a mistake do we venture to enter the body of more evolved creatures, such as the higher order of animals or human beings.

Entering a complex body presents both ethical and procedural problems. We overcome the ethical problem by choosing to enter a dead body—one no longer claimed by the original occupant. However, the procedural problems remain. Accidents aside, humans die of disease, organ failure, or contact with a toxic substance. Soon after death, the body begins to decompose. Even the freshest corpse contains the residue of the cause of death. Thus, the preparation for practicing parakaya pravesha from this point and beyond requires perfection not only in prana dharana, but also in *rasayana vidya*, the science of alchemy precisely designed to detoxify and heal the damage caused before, during, and after death.

As mentioned in the commentaries on sutras 3:26 and 3:34, four streams of prana shakti flow from the sahasrara chakra: nivritti kala, pratishtha kala, vidya kala, and shanta kala. Passing through the doorways of the moon, sun, and talu chakra, they reach the lower lotus of the heart. Together, these four streams not only nourish our physical heart, liver, and lungs, which are located in the general region of the lower lotus of the heart, they also free these vital organs and the rest of the body from the obstructions engendered by hunger, thirst, exhaustion, disease, and toxins. This freedom is the unique property of nivritti kala, the first pranic stream. The second stream, pratishtha kala, brings stability to our body, mind, and senses. We become comfortably seated in our body. Because of this particular pranic stream, our chitta samvit and body are completely conflated. The third pranic stream, vidya kala, infuses our body, mind, and senses with self-awareness. We become aware that we exist, and this awareness pervades every nook and cranny of our body. We become an intelligent being. The fourth stream, shanta kala, makes us feel at home. Our body, mind, and senses become the center of our personal universe.

In the first part of parakaya pravesha, when we leave our body and enter the self-born locus, these four streams of prana shakti naturally follow us. Similarly, when we transport our self-born locus into another body in the second part of the practice, these four streams of prana shakti come along.

According to what I have gathered from the living tradition and a host of scriptures, mainly *Svacchanda Tantra*, *Tantraraja Tantra*, *Srividyarnava*, and *Yoga Vashishtha*, we descend into a corpse through its tenth gate, the fontanelle. In a living body, this region, as well as the space above it, is known as the sahasrara chakra. Even after the body has become a corpse, the area corresponding to the sahasrara chakra remains the most conducive gate for parakaya pravesha.

Our chitta samvit is deeply familiar with the space belonging to the sahasrara chakra. Propelled by our sheer intention, as soon as our locus descends into this space, chitta samvit becomes engaged in opening the tenth gate in the corpse. The subtle force of our prana shakti triggers the flow of the four pranic streams.

As it does, the first pranic stream, nivritti kala, facilitates the release of any lingering sense of self-identity with the body's previous occupant. Instantly, the second stream, pratishtha kala, claims ownership of the body. Our self-born locus and the chitta samvit anchored in it become established in this new body, and that body becomes a living being. The third stream, vidya kala, infuses the space corresponding to the tenth gate with vidya, intelligence. Thus, the living being is transformed into an intelligent being. The fourth stream, shanta kala, makes our self-born locus and chitta samvit feel at home. The process of reviving and healing the rest of the body begins from here.

It takes weeks, months, and sometimes even years to detoxify the revived body and retrain the nervous system to properly serve the long-term goal of parakaya pravesha. The first and most important step in this process is to reactivate the three key interconnected organs in the region of the lower lotus of the heart: the heart, liver, and lungs. Once these three organs are revived and the toxins removed, healing and rejuvenation of the rest of the body can begin. The four streams of prana shakti begin to flow between the sahasrara—the higher lotus of the heart—and the lower lotus of the heart. The incessant and unobstructed flow of these four streams revives, detoxifies, and clears the body's major and minor pranic pathways. This completes the process of parakaya pravesha at the physical level.

At the psychological level, we still face a big hurdle. Before the previous occupant of that body was evicted by death, the vital organs, nervous system, brain, and sense organs had been trained to meet the physical, sensory, emotional, and spiritual needs of that occupant. With the revival of the body, the experiences gathered by the previous occupant are also revived. Meanwhile, our highly purified and spiritually driven chitta samvit is imposing its own rules and ambitions. This creates a clash between the samskaras the body accumulated before parakaya pravesha and the new set of samskaras of our chitta samvit. If we reach this far because we employed the technique of parakaya pravesha with perfection and precision, but we are not fully established in the exalted state of vashikara vairagya (YS 1:15), we may lose the battle, laying the ground for bipolar disorder, dissociative disorders, schizophrenia, or other psychological disorders.

To avoid this possibility, it is crucial to learn and practice parakaya pravesha under the close supervision of a master who has direct experience of this vidya and is fully familiar with all the ins and outs of this process. It is also mandatory that both the adept teaching this vidya and the highly qualified, confident aspirant test each other.

Additionally, we must be fully grounded in our *ishta* mantra, which we receive from a living tradition and which embodies the power to nullify our deep-rooted afflictions, engenders vashikara vairagya, and opens the door to dharma megha samadhi. While we are firmly seated in our *ishta* mantra, we complete the practice of a mantra or mantras that spontaneously come to our aid during emergencies that walk into our life unannounced. *Nrisimha*, *maha mrityunjaya*, and *navarna* are a few examples of mantras known for their power of protection.

The tradition tells us that the best way to practice parakaya pravesha is to re-enter our own body rather than entering the body of someone else. This necessitates learning to get out of our body and briefly placing our chitta samvit in the space of consciousness that emerges from an intense and prolonged meditation on the pranic pulsation in the region of our forehead and beyond. After months or years of daily practice, we stay in the space of consciousness for longer and longer periods. This helps us train our body to maintain its normal functions without the assistance of our mind. We also become cognizant of the threshold beyond which our mind's absence from the body will lead to death. Eventually, we cross that threshold.

While seated in the self-born locus, we watch how the body's systems are shutting down, and return to the body after the process of dying is complete. Re-entering the same body not only allows us to avoid ethical problems, it also confers the benefit of dealing with a body whose organs, nervous system, and senses we trained ourselves.

Parakaya pravesha opens the floodgate of infinite knowledge. It gives us firsthand experience of how prana shakti shakes off the inertia inherent in matter and transforms it into a living entity. It unveils the mystery of birth and death. It enables us to know how consciousness uses matter and energy to create tools to experience its infinite expanse. It gives us a direct experience not only of the immortal nature of our core being but also of how untouched we are by what we touch. Put simply, parakaya pravesha abolishes our fear of death and fills us with unbounded respect for the life force. It breaks down the wall between duality and non-duality, mortality and immortality, and fills us with the joy of being free here and now.

SUTRA 3:39

उदानजयाज्जलपङ्ककण्टकादिष्वसङ्ग उत्क्रान्तिश्च ॥३९॥

udānajayājjalapaṅkakaṇṭakādiṣvasaṅga utkrāntiśca ‖ 39 ‖

udānajayāt, from victory over udana; *jalapaṅkakaṇṭakādiṣu*, in regard to water, mud, thorns, and so on; *asaṅgaḥ*, state of unaffectedness; *utkrāntiḥ*, transitioning by rising above the body; *ca*, and

From the conquest of udana, [a yogi is able to remain] unaffected by water, mud, thorns, and so on, and leave the body while transcending death.

Here Patanjali describes the result of samyama on *udana*, the function of prana shakti characterized by upward movement, elevation, elation, uplifting feelings, and an upward pull. According to Vyasa, the domain of udana shakti extends from the lowest part of the body all the way to our head. Taking this a step further, scriptures such as the *Yoga Vashishtha* and *Svacchanda Tantra* tell us the domain of udana is the same as that of prana shakti, which pervades every nook and cranny of the body including the *dvadashanta*, the twelve-finger-width space surrounding the body. The upward pull or push and the uplifting feelings and experiences in this space are functions of udana. By practicing samyama on this dimension of prana shakti, we are able to pull our awareness from the lower part of the body, direct it to the crown, push it through the fontanelle during the final transition, and enter the higher reaches of the space of consciousness known as the sahasrara chakra.

According to this sutra, mastery over udana shakti enables us to remain unaffected by the obstructions caused by water, mud, and thorns. This refers to the imbalances caused by the five elements that constitute our body. At the time of death, the body is subject to numberless factors, the majority of which are beyond our comprehension. Disease, old age, toxins, and the unpredictable emotional havoc associated with dying throw our bodily fluids out of balance. Yogis call this "drowning in water." Too little or too many minerals and hormones starve or clog our vital organs. In yogic terminology, this is "becoming stuck in mud." Similarly, the nervous system's response to the pain of dying is referred to as "being pricked by thorns." Mastery over udana shakti enables us to push our way up through these conditions during our final departure. Gaining this mastery is particularly useful in parakaya pravesha, both when we are getting out of our own body and when we are entering another body.

As described in sutras 1:36 and 3:34, the space twelve finger-widths away from the nostrils ("the zero point"), the opening of the nostrils, the inner corners of the eyes, the center between the eyebrows, and the center of the forehead are extremely significant centers of consciousness. Each embodies unique powers and experiences. One of the most significant centers of udana shakti is *bhru-madhya*, the center between the eyebrows. The upward movement of awareness is most pronounced at this center. According to the *Bhagavad Gita* (8:10), by applying the power of yoga at the time of final departure, a yogi channels his prana shakti into the center between the eyebrows, and from there reaches the realm of absolute being.

When a yogi allows the udana shakti dimension of prana to lead the mind to the center of the forehead as part of meditation, he does so without exerting any effort. However, when the yogi resorts to udana shakti in the moments just preceding death and pushes the chitta samvit to the dvadashanta through the fontanelle, effort is involved. It is important to remember that the ability to deploy the power of udana during the last moments of life is highly dependent on mastery over udana, which comes from consistent and sustained practice. It is only when the practice has matured that a yogi can use this kriya to get out of the body without obstruction.

SUTRA 3:40

समानजयाज्ज्वलनम् ॥४०॥

samānajayājjvalanam ॥ 40 ॥

samānajayāt, from the conquest of samana; *jvalanam*, ignition

From the conquest of samana, [a yogi is able to] ignite.

Like the preceding sutra, this is a continuation of parakaya pravesha. Here Patanjali is emphasizing the importance of mastery over *samana*, the function of prana responsible for circulation, assimilation, and proper distribution of the healing and nourishing properties throughout the body. The region of the navel is the main center of samana shakti.

If, during the practice of parakaya pravesha, we realize we have committed a mistake so serious that our chitta samvit cannot extricate itself from the grip of matter, we resort to samana. Such mistakes are normally due to lack of mastery over udana as described in sutra 3:39—we have fallen prey to water, mud, or thorns. Concentration on samana at the navel center results in spontaneous combustion, freeing our chitta samvit from the grip of the body. The body is incinerated instantly, enabling chitta samvit to join the self-born locus of pure consciousness, from where it is free to continue its journey.

In standard tantric literature, the navel center is known as the *manipura chakra*, the center filled with self-shining gems. It is the center of the fire element. After the brain, this region is the center of the largest network of energy channels. The shakti concentrated here controls and guides the functions of all of our vital organs, including the digestive system. From the standpoint of bodily functions, the navel center is the core of our body.

As the process of dying gains momentum, our cortical functions quiet and the instinctual power and authority of the navel center take over. Mastery over the navel center, therefore, is an essential part of parakaya pravesha. Upon realizing that the deteriorating conditions of the body are no longer reversible, the yogi uses the force of samana to get out of the body by voluntarily igniting the fire at the navel center. The force of samana ignites and fuels this fire.

In the tantric tradition of Sri Vidya, gaining mastery over the manipura chakra is essential in raising kundalini shakti and leading it to the sahasrara chakra. According to Lakshmidhara's commentary on verse 41 of *Saundaryalahari*, the practice leading to the mastery over the manipura chakra is accomplished by receiving *mahavedha diksha*, initiation into the great penetration. With this initiation, the yogi gains a unique experience of kundalini shakti at the manipura chakra. After mahavedha diksha, the practitioner meditates on the fire at the navel center as part of her daily routine. Adepts of Sri Vidya keep this mastery in their tool kit and use it to strengthen their connection with the manipura chakra. During the time of parakaya pravesha, after exhausting all other options, the yogi invokes the power unique to the manipura chakra and incinerates the body, transporting chitta samvit into the space of consciousness.

SUTRA 3:41

श्रोत्राकाशयोः सम्बन्धसंयमाद्दिव्यं श्रोत्रम्
॥४१॥

śrotrākāśayoḥ sambandhasaṁyamāddivyaṁ śrotram
॥ 41 ॥

śrotrākāśayoḥ, of the sense of hearing and space; *sambandhasaṁyamāt*, from samyama on the relationship; *divyaṁ*, extraordinary; *śrotram*, sense of hearing

From samyama on the relationship between the sense of hearing and space, the extraordinary power of hearing.

Failure of vital organs and falling unconscious are signs of the dying process. Whether we are ordinary humans or accomplished yogis, once this process has begun, our ability to retain a self-chosen train of thought weakens and eventually evaporates. During parakaya pravesha, if we accidentally happen to fall into the vortex of the forces of death and fail to pierce the fontanelle and enter the dvadashanta, we fall into unconsciousness.

Parakaya pravesha requires that we drop all our karmic clutter, get out of the body without retaining any connection with the unwanted past, and enter another body with only the select memories needed for fulfilling the purpose of entering that body. When shrouded in unconsciousness, chitta samvit has no capacity to decide which set of memories to keep in the forefront of its awareness and which to drop while attempting to pierce the fontanelle and enter the dvadashanta. This is possible only if we do not become unconscious during the last few moments of exiting the body. To make sure that even in the worst-case scenario we are able to retain only select memories, Patanjali introduces the unique practice referred to in this sutra.

Memory means remembering an unbroken sequence of experiences. Each segment of experience is held on the thread of time and space. The thread's ability to hold the experience depends on an unbreakable link between time and space. The thread of time and space pierces the segments of experience, which, like the beads in a mala, are held fast by knots. The state of unconsciousness engendered by the forces of death weakens and eventually destroys the link between time and space, thus breaking the thread and shattering the knots that hold the experiences in sequence. The mind becomes blank; we hear no sound and cannot comprehend words and their meaning. This lack of comprehension results in loss of memory.

To avoid this possibility, the yogi transcends his reliance on time and space as a means of organizing his experiences and the memories associated with them. He accomplishes this by practicing samyama on the relationship between the sense of hearing and space.

The sense of hearing is directly linked to the part of the brain that comprehends sound. This part of the brain is also the center of learning through words. This center gives meaning to the segments of sound and their combinations. A word and its meaning always go hand in hand. Without a meaning, the word is only a sound. Space gives room to sounds, words, and their meanings. However, the space adjacent to our ears is independent of the laws governing the space inside our brain. The sound filling the space outside the organ of hearing is not comprehended by the auditory center in the brain. Even so, this space—an integral part of the dvadashanta—has the capacity to store sound and give meaning to the different segments of sound; it also has the capacity to preserve words and their meanings as memory.

To do this practice, the yogi isolates a minuscule and extremely precise portion of the dvadashanta adjacent to the organ of hearing and practices samyama on the relationship between the organ of hearing and that space. Perfection in this practice leads to acquiring the extraordinary power to comprehend sound and its subtle variants. This unique power also includes comprehending words and their meanings, which may or may not be compatible with the words and their meanings familiar to the auditory center in the brain. According to the tradition, this extraordinary power is *nada tattva*, the principle of transcendental sound—the primal pulsation of prana shakti.

During the last moments of parakaya pravesha, if a yogi notices he is losing control over his nervous system and the functions of his brain, he invokes this power and, through sheer intention, allows all words, their meanings, and their associated memories to dissolve into that power. He then submits himself to normal death and dies. However, before entering his chitta samvit, he retrieves the memories from nada tattva and masterfully deposits them in chitta samvit. Wherever and whenever the opportunity presents itself, he lets that chitta samvit descend into another body. Thus, he completes parakaya pravesha. Just as with the two previous sutras, the ability gained from doing the practice just described is used only during unpreventable circumstances arising during parakaya pravesha.

SUTRA 3:42

कायाकाशयोः सम्बन्धसंयमात्
लघुतूलसमापत्तेश्चाकाशगमनम् ॥४२॥

kāyākāśayoḥ sambandhasaṁyamāt
laghutūlasamāpatteścākāśagamanam ॥ 42 ॥

kāyākāśayoḥ, of body and space; *sambandhasaṁyamāt*, from samyama on the relationship; *laghutūlasamāpatteḥ*, from mental absorption in light cotton fiber; *ca*, and; *ākāśagamanam*, moving through space

From samyama on the relationship between the body and space or from mental absorption in light cotton fiber, [the power of] moving through space.

During the practice of parakaya pravesha, a situation may arise where we find ourselves in doubt about the precise course of moving through extremely subtle and delicate pranic pathways either in our own body or in the corpse into which we are descending. In these extraordinary moments, we need extraordinary help. Such help comes only from siddhas, devas, and rishis—accomplished beings who pervade the space which stretches between the earthly and celestial planes (YS 2:44). Their presence—more importantly, our ability to sense their presence—infuses us with the ability to receive their guidance and implement it in their living presence during these extraordinary moments.

Here, in sutra 3:42, Patanjali refers to the extraordinary ability to move through space. The practice leading to this extraordinary ability is similar to the practice referred to in sutra 3:41, where Patanjali refers to the practice of samyama on the relationship between the sense of hearing and the space in immediate contact with the sense of hearing. That results in the extraordinary ability to comprehend words belonging to or originating from the celestial realm. Here, in sutra 3:42, he advises us to practice samyama on the relationship between our body and the space in immediate contact with it. This practice results in the ability to move through space.

In the scriptures, the ability to move through space is known as *khechari siddhi*. There are several techniques leading to this extraordinary accomplishment. The one referred to in this sutra entails practicing dharana at the spot in the body where we can most easily feel the presence of space.

Space is an abstract substance characterized by its ability to make room for things to exist. The existence of space is felt in relation to the object occupying it. Our body is one such object. Our body exists in space and there is space inside our body. There is always space between two objects, which is what enables us to differentiate one object from another. In order to practice samyama on the relationship between our body and space, we first have to gain an experiential comprehension of the space surrounding and inside our body.

Our intense identification with the body obscures our feeling of the space constantly touching our body—a tendency we have cultivated from birth. We are caged in space, but we know only what has been caged, not the cage itself. Comprehending the space touching our body requires first displacing that space by bringing an object into close contact with the body. That object must be conducive to our purpose and must not be irritating.

One such object is the breath. One of the spots most sensitive to detecting the breath is the opening of the nostrils.

The incoming and outgoing breath changes the quality of the space in immediate contact with the general region of the opening of our nostrils. Even though the breath does not completely displace the space, it increases and decreases pranic pressure in that region. This pressure is registered by the sense of touch, which is highly active in this region. Touch is the property of air, not of space. Thus, the feeling of touch interposes itself between space and the skin sensing the touch. Concentration on this feeling allows the mind to comprehend that on one side of this feeling is the skin sensing the touch, and on the other side is pure space. This is known as *sparsha dharana*, concentration on touch.

The next step is to withdraw the mind from the object of sparsha dharana (i.e., touch). This is accomplished by taking the practice of dharana to the highest stage of dhyana, where the object of meditation dissolves into our feeling of being the meditator. In this case, the experience of touch merges with the meditating mind; thus, the mind is in direct contact with the space that was once filled with the feeling of touch. Before this experience, the mind was solely dependent on inference and postulation to comprehend the existence of space. Now the mind is able to comprehend space directly. At this point, we are guided to comprehend, and thereafter practice samyama on, the relationship between the body and space.

The process of reaching this level of comprehension occurs naturally as our meditation practice becomes refined—a subject discussed in detail in sutras 1:40 through 1:44. Mental sharpness and comprehension gained from meditative practice lead a yogi to a unique experience, which Patanjali calls *vashikara* (YS 1:40). According to Vyasa, the mind of such a yogi is able to enter a physical object of any size and is capable of penetrating each and every atom in that object. This ability helps us understand how an object—in this case our body and its constituents—relates to space. The practice of samyama on this relationship enables us to navigate through the thin spaces that exist within and between cells, atoms, and subatomic particles in our body. By using this ability, a yogi is able to travel through the infinitely vast universe packed into his finite-appearing body.

In this sutra, Patanjali also mentions another practice leading to the unfoldment of the capacity for moving through space. That practice consists of selecting an extremely light cotton fiber as an object of concentration. Following the course of meditation as described in sutras 1:40 through 1:44, as the mind becomes increasingly sharp and refined, it drops the physical dimension of the object of concentration—the cotton fiber—and becomes absorbed in its subtle counterpart. This subtle counterpart has no mass. Weight is a property of mass and exerts itself only in proportion to the gravitational force of another body of matter. Mental absorption in the non-physical, pure idea of the cotton fiber nullifies the relational value of weight, freeing the yogi to move through space without any obstruction. This could be in the vast universe, in the space around our body, inside our body, around a corpse, or inside a corpse.

According to Vyasa, concentration on cotton fiber is only an example. Penetrating the physicality of an object and reaching its most subtle counterpart—the pure idea pertaining to that object—constitutes the heart of this practice. The first significant stage of the practice is marked by *paramanu samapatti*, mental absorption in an atom (or atoms) of the object. Further refinement continues from there. Meanwhile, the yogi is guided to assess her progress by walking first on water, then on the filament of a spider's web, then on the rays of the sun, and finally, by walking in space without any physical support.

Based on what we have gathered from sutras 3:38 through 3:42 and Vyasa's commentary on them, parakaya pravesha is a practice meant to gain a deeper understanding of ourselves—our body, breath, mind, senses, and consciousness, and their relationship. It is the doorway to accessing the infinity packed in our finite body. It is one of the most reliable methods for understanding the dynamics of birth and death and how to transcend them. This practice gives us a firsthand experience of the complexity of our body, how perfectly and precisely our vital organs and systems function, and what an insignificant role we play in making the stream of life flow. This makes us humble. Those who reflect on this are effortlessly and spontaneously transported to a state of trustful surrender—the force that gently lifts and unites us with our creator, the lord of life and the universe.

SUTRA 3:43

बहिरकल्पिता वृत्तिर्महाविदेहा ततः
प्रकाशावरणक्षयः ॥४३॥

bahirakalpitā vṛttirmahāvidehā tataḥ
prakāśāvaraṇakṣayaḥ ॥ 43 ॥

bahiḥ, outside; *akalpitā*, unimagined; *vṛttiḥ*, cognition; *mahāvidehā*, the great experience that transcends the notion of being in the body; *tataḥ*, that; *prakāśāvaraṇakṣayaḥ*, the destruction of the veil that hides the light

Non-imaginary [fully palpable] cognition outside [the body] is *mahavideha*. From that [comes] the destruction of the veil that hides the light.

Here Patanjali introduces the bedrock of the advanced practices of yoga, parakaya pravesha included. He calls this bedrock *mahavideha*. *Maha* means "great, exalted"; *videha* means "beyond body." Thus, *mahavideha* means "the exalted state of awareness that transcends body consciousness." Once we are established in this field of awareness, the veil that hides our intrinsic luminosity is destroyed. This field of awareness unfolds and becomes available to us when we practice samyama on the space of consciousness outside our body.

Success in the practice leading to the unfoldment of this exalted state of awareness hinges on the fact that cognition of the space of consciousness is not a product of our imagination. It is self-born and fully palpable. Furthermore, while we meditate on this cognition, our chitta samvit is no longer anchored in our body—this cognition is itself the locus of our chitta samvit. We are fully immersed in the cognition pertaining to the space of consciousness outside our body.

From the vantage point of this immersive state, our body is like any other material object. It has lost its power to draw our attention—we have no particular interest in it. The mind has settled in a state of consciousness that is beyond the reach of biological urges, neurological responses, and physical comforts and discomforts. In other words, the locus of our chitta samvit has shifted from our body—more precisely from the lotus of the heart—to an extraordinary space of consciousness. Our chitta samvit is fully absorbed in the cognition of this space of consciousness. While anchored in this space, we simply witness our body. This witnessing is unintentional and subliminal.

The process leading to the realization of the space of consciousness outside our body has been described in sutra 1:36 and further elaborated on in sutra 3:34. The practice of meditation described in sutra 1:36 culminates in the emergence of a self-luminous ball of light in the general vicinity of our face and forehead. The consistent practice of meditation on this ball of light enables us to experience the non-physical counterpart of our breath. We become cognizant of the subtle dimension of pranic pulsation. As practice progresses, this subtle pranic pulsation forms the nucleus of the self-luminous ball of light. Mental absorption in this luminosity results in the experience of *buddhi samvit*, the knowing power of our faculty of discernment. Experientially, the space of consciousness corresponding to this self-luminous ball of light is free from even the subtlest shades of sorrow. Hence, Patanjali calls this experience *vishoka*, the cognition of sorrowless joy. Meditation on vishoka is the foundation of the practice described in this sutra.

The practice referred to here sits between the practice of vishoka described in sutra 1:36 and the practice described in sutra 3:34. As elaborated on in sutra 3:34, we stretch the experience of vishoka from the region of our forehead to the lower lotus of the heart. Eventually, we are led to experience the space of consciousness stretching from the lower lotus of the heart all the way to the sahasrara chakra. Continuous practice leads to concentration of consciousness to the point that this entire space begins to claim its independent identity. The extraordinary luminosity filling this space is distinct enough for our mind to register its existence in contradistinction to everything else, including our body. With further practice, we begin to feel the pranic pulsation in this space. The subtlest form of pranic pulsation becomes the locus of this space of consciousness. Complete immersion in this space leads to the experience of chitta samvit.

The experience of the space of consciousness is twofold: *kalpita*, imaginary; and *akalpita*, not imaginary, fully palpable. Akalpita, the non-imaginary cognition of space outside our body, is the subject of this sutra. However, the imaginary cognition of space outside our body is the doorway to the non-imaginary cognition. In fact, the non-imaginary cognition of space outside our body is the outcome of consistently practicing meditation on the imaginary cognition of space outside the body. This twofold cognition refers to two distinct stages of experiencing chitta samvit.

In sutra 3:35, Patanjali tells us that the mind and consciousness are so intensely fused that there is no difference in these cognitions. This conflated cognition is what we call experience. With the exception of the most exalted state of samadhi, one aspect of our experience is smeared with the sense of being an object, and another aspect of the same experience is smeared with the sense of ourselves being the experiencer. As long as the feeling of being in the body persists, these two experiences are bound to be conflated. We are simultaneously aware of these two fully conflated cognitions.

These conflated cognitions are innate. From the day of our birth, we have been experiencing the togetherness of our awareness and the object of our awareness. Numberless times we have said, thought, and felt, "This is me; this is my body; this is my mind." This "me" and "mine" is our most deeply ingrained samskara. Even in a highly immersive state, the feeling of "me" and "mine" persists. When the self-luminous space of consciousness manifests outside our body and we meditate on it, the feeling "I am meditating on this space" remains. This feeling is further accompanied by another cognition: "I am here in this body. While anchored in this body, I am focusing my mind on the space of consciousness outside my body."

In the advanced stages of this practice, once in a while and for brief moments, we rise above these conflated cognitions and become fully aware of our oneness with the space of consciousness outside the body, only to slide back into bodily awareness. Highly accomplished adepts consider this stage of experience to be kalpita, an imaginary cognition. However, further refinement brought by continuous practice transforms this imaginary cognition into a non-imaginary, fully palpable cognition. The term for this cognition is *mahavideha*.

A yogi fully established in this space of consciousness is not bound by the five afflictions, karmas, and the forces that bring karmas to fruition. Such yogis are able to go back and forth between their body and the space of consciousness outside their body with the same ease that we move from one room to another, from one house to another. For them, birth and death have no meaning. Guided by the will of Ishvara, they come and go. Guided by divine will, they venture into parakaya pravesha. They achieve nothing new from parakaya pravesha, as they have already achieved all that is to be achieved. For them, parakaya pravesha is simply one of the means of exploring and rejoicing in the limitless grandeur of Ishvara's prakriti. As Patanjali mentions in upcoming sutras, while living in the safety and comfort of the self-born, self-luminous space of consciousness, these high-caliber yogis discover and examine the most subtle aspects of nature, which are beyond the comprehension of a normal mind.

SUTRA 3:44

स्थूलस्वरूपसूक्ष्मान्वयार्थवत्त्वसंयमाद्भूतजयः ॥४४॥

sthūlasvarūpasūkṣmānvayārthavattvasaṁyamādbhūtajayaḥ ॥ 44 ॥

sthūlasvarūpasūkṣmānvayārthavattvasaṁyamād, from samyama on the tangible form, essential nature, and subtle form [of the elements]; *bhūtajayaḥ*, victory over the elements

From samyama on the tangible form, essential nature, and subtle form [of the elements, as well as on their comingled nature and their purposefulness], victory over the elements.

Here Patanjali refers to a practice that empowers a yogi to conquer the five elements: earth, water, fire, air, and space. It enables a yogi to remain unaffected by the elements and to command their behavior—to accelerate, decelerate, and even arrest their functions. Before we venture into elaborating on the dynamics of this practice, it is important to emphasize that the practice lies in the exclusive domain of the highest-caliber adepts. This and the practices described in the upcoming sutras in this chapter, and the practices introduced in the fourth chapter, are only for those who have mastered the practices described in sutras 3:34 and 3:43 and thus have gained an experiential understanding of chitta samvit.

As we saw in sutra 3:43, the advanced stage of meditation results in the manifestation of a self-luminous field of consciousness outside the body. With sustained practice, this self-luminous field eventually becomes the locus of our chitta samvit. Our chitta samvit is so firmly anchored in this field that our sensitivity to our body is no different than our sensitivity to any other object. Our chitta samvit, the knowing power of the mind, along with all of its past, present, and future attributes (YS 3:14), is totally absorbed in the pranic pulsation at the center of the self-luminous field outside the physical body. In other words, cognition of our self-awareness is centered in this non-imaginary, fully palpable, self-luminous space of consciousness. We are fully cognizant of ourselves as a living being; the self-luminous space is now our body. While residing in this body, we undertake the practice referred to in this sutra.

Anchored in this self-luminous space of consciousness, we practice samyama on one or more of the elements. According to Vyasa, the vast range of the properties and functions of the elements can be divided into five main categories. One set is associated with *sthula*, the tangible form of the element. Another is associated with *svarupa*, the essential nature of the element. Some properties and functions are associated with the element's *sukshma*, subtle form. Still others are associated with the element's *anvaya*, comingled nature—its natural ability to combine with other elements, penetrate other elements, absorb other elements, and assimilate the properties of other elements. Finally, some properties and functions are associated with the element's *arthavattva*, its intrinsic quality of serving the purpose of *bhoga* and *apavarga*, fulfillment and freedom. This intrinsic quality ensures that all of the element's properties and functions change purposefully.

Each of the five elements—earth, water, fire, air, and space—has five categories of properties and functions. Thus, there are twenty-five discrete categories of properties and functions for the practice of samyama. By following the principle of meditation described in sutra 3:12, we have gained a highly one-pointed mind. By employing this one-pointed mind—fully anchored in the self-luminous space of consciousness outside the body—we are able to comprehend the transformation of the defining qualities, symptoms, and conditions occurring in any of these five broad categories (YS 3:13). We can begin our practice of samyama with one broad category of one element and continue adding other categories as our practice progresses. Because our chitta samvit is not confounded by the limitations of the body and because it is not dependent on the senses for analysis, scrutiny, and dissection of the properties and functions of the elements, it can simultaneously bring the entire range of one or more properties or functions into laser focus.

For instance, we can focus on the physical form (*sthula*) of earth, water, fire, air, or space. We will use the earth element as an example. We can focus on the physical form of the earth element by concentrating on a lump of clay. With our sharp, highly concentrated mind, we can isolate a tiny particle of clay, split it further, directly perceive its atomic and subatomic form, and practice samyama on an atom, its relationship with other atoms, and the dynamics involved in bringing trillions of atoms together to form a lump of clay.

This form of samyama unveils the atomic and subatomic behavior of the earth element. It enables us to understand earth's essential nature (*svarupa*), which is solidity. It enables us to understand how a particular atomic sequence increases or decreases the density of matter, affecting its compactness and weight. It enables us to understand sukshma, the subtle counterpart of the gross form, and how changes occur in atoms, in their relationship with other atoms, and in the aggregate of atoms that form a lump of clay. This enables us to perceive the infinitely vast range of *gandha*, the tanmatra of smell, enabling us to detect the smell that distinguishes one atom from another and the collective smell of all the atoms that form a lump of clay.

Samyama on a lump of clay also entails focusing on *anvaya*, the comingled nature of the element. We are able to perceive how one atom combines with similar or dissimilar atoms or a chain of atoms within the earth element, how similar or dissimilar atoms in a lump of clay function, how they penetrate each other, how one absorbs the other, and how one type of union of elements is reversible or irreversible. Finally, this advanced practice of samyama focuses on *arthavattva*, the purposefulness of an element's properties and functions. This enables us to comprehend how the properties and functions of each and every atom in the clay—individually and collectively—are guided by the element's intrinsic urge to carry out the creator's intention: bhoga and apavarga, the fulfillment and freedom all sentient beings are seeking in the world.

According to Vyasa, conquering the five elements by practicing samyama on the five broad categories of the properties and functions of the elements means befriending the elements. The intimate acquaintance with the elements brought about by this practice engenders such a powerful bond between the yogi and the five elements that both parties find joy in serving each other unconditionally. The elements protect and nourish the yogi and the yogi protects and nourishes the elements.

SUTRA 3:45

ततोऽणिमादिप्रादुर्भावः
कायसम्पत्तद्धर्मानभिघातश्च ॥४५॥

tato'ṇimādiprādurbhāvaḥ
kāyasampattaddharmānabhighātaśca ॥ 45 ॥

tataḥ, from that; *aṇimādiprādurbhāvaḥ*, the rise of anima, and so on; *kāyasampat*, wealth of bodily perfection; *tat-dharmānabhighātaḥ*, being unhampered by the natural properties and functions of the elements; *ca*, and

From that [victory over the elements] arise [siddhis of] anima, and so on, the wealth of bodily perfection, and [the siddhi of] being unhampered by the properties and functions of the elements.

Sutras 3:43 and 3:44 describe the exalted experience of the fully palpable, self-luminous cognition of the space of consciousness outside the body and the empowerment that comes from being fully established in it. While anchored in this space, we are able to focus on the physical form of the elements as well as on their essential nature. We are also able to focus on the subtle tanmatras of the elements and their comingled nature. With our highly concentrated and pristine mind, we can comprehend and focus on the intrinsic urge of the elements to carry out the creator's intention of supplying the fulfillment and freedom all sentient beings are seeking.

As explained in the preceding sutra, this samyama allows us to gain a direct understanding of the atomic and subatomic behavior of the elements, what causes differences in the sequencing of atoms, and why atomic sequencing increases or decreases the density of matter. We are also able to comprehend the subtler dimension of the five elements, how one element absorbs another, and how these four broad categories of properties and functions of the elements are saturated with the fifth category of properties and functions—the purposefulness of the elements. This comprehension, and samyama on this comprehension, result in the manifestation of eight siddhis: *anima*, *laghima*, *mahima*, *prapti*, *prakamya*, *vashitva*, *ishitva*, and *yatra-kamavasayitva*.

Due to the victory over the five broad categories of the properties and functions of the elements, a yogi has the capacity to become as minute as he wishes—the extraordinary capacity known as *anima*. Similarly, the capacity to be light (*laghima*) and the capacity to be grand (*mahima*) are natural components of his accomplishment. He is capable of touching and grasping the smallest and biggest objects, unobstructed by distance (*prapti*). Without being obstructed by the natural properties and functions of the elements, a yogi of this caliber interacts with them as he wishes (*prakamya*). He also has the ability to control, alter, and guide the functions of the elements at will (*vashitva*). In regard to the elements, the yogi is capable of doing what he wishes to do, not doing what he does not wish to do, and reversing the changes that have already occurred in the elements (*ishitva*).

The most important accomplishment, however, is *yatra-kamavasayitva*, the yogi's ability to make the elements respond to her *sankalpa*, power of intention. Regarding this last siddhi, Vyasa tells us that despite this extraordinary capacity, a yogi of this caliber abides by the law of nature. In an extremely rare instance, she may manipulate the natural function of the elements, but under no circumstances will she disturb their fundamental structure and properties, which follow the design of Ishvara's sankalpa. A yogi who is not cognizant of Ishvara's sankalpa and has no respect for it cannot reach this far. And the fact that a yogi has reached this far is evidence that her sankalpa is always aligned with the sankalpa of Ishvara, whose command all the elements follow.

Victory over the elements also manifests in *kaya sampat*, acquisition of bodily wealth, a subject elaborated on in the following sutra.

SUTRA 3:46

रूपलावण्यबलवज्रसंहननत्वानि कायसम्पत्
॥४६॥

rūpalāvaṇyabalavajrasaṁhananatvāni kāyasampat
‖ 46 ‖

rūpalāvaṇyabalavajrasaṁhananatvāni, beauty, charm, vitality, and healing power; *kāyasampat*, bodily wealth

Beauty, charm, vitality, and healing power are bodily wealth.

The unfoldment of *kaya sampat*, bodily wealth, is a vast subject. Patanjali and Vyasa divide the range of kaya sampat into two parts. They elaborate on the first part in sutra 2:43, where it is introduced in the context of tapas. Tapas destroys our physical and mental impurities, leading to the unfoldment of *kaya siddhi*, bodily perfection, and *indriya siddhi*, perfection in the functions of our senses. As explained there, the practice leading to bodily perfection begins with *kaya kalpa*.

Kaya kalpa is a system of rejuvenation that derives its inspiration from ayurveda, siddha medicine, hatha yoga, and tantra. The yogis belonging to the Sri Vidya and Natha traditions have long been custodians of kaya kalpa. The purpose of kaya kalpa is to detoxify the body, restore its healing and rejuvenating power, and enable us to live a disease-free life. Cultivating a strong, energetic body with the capacity to remain unaffected by internal or external causes of disease is a great achievement. Such a body is a perfect container for a healthy mind. With the help of a healthy body and mind, we are able to enter a realm of yogic experience defined as *siddhi*, extraordinary accomplishment. This level of accomplishment originates from kaya kalpa and constitutes the first part of kaya sampat. It is a siddhi in its own right, but from the standpoint of yogis who have gained a direct experience of their chitta samvit and have made their locus the self-luminous space of consciousness outside their body, it is only the beginning.

The high-caliber yogis who have attained victory over the five elements (YS 3:44) and thus have attained eight siddhis (YS 3:45) are the natural recipients of the second part of kaya sampat. This is far beyond the first part, which merely involves the restoration of the body's natural beauty, charm, vitality, and healing power. To a yogi anchored in the fully palpable, self-luminous space of consciousness, these bodily attributes and conditions are meaningless. The second part of kaya sampat is not dependent on a technique or a practice but is an outgrowth of *bhuta jaya*, victory over the elements.

Earth, water, fire, air, and space are saturated with the properties needed to bring forward form, structure, attractiveness, vitality, stamina, and the ability to heal and rejuvenate. A yogi who has attained victory over the elements is conversant with the dynamics of the properties and functions of the elements. Using that knowledge and power, he can set his own standard of bodily wealth and use it in parakaya pravesha. Due to his mastery over the elements, he has the power to infuse the body of any sentient being with beauty, charm, vitality, and healing power. Therefore, during parakaya pravesha, the yogi is able to exercise this power to infuse a corpse with this shakti and bring forward the elements of beauty, charm, vitality, and healing power in the proportion and intensity he wishes. This power enables the yogi to bring changes in the body's overall form, structure, vitality, and immunity to diseases necessary to accomplish the purpose behind parakaya pravesha.

SUTRA 3:47

ग्रहणस्वरूपास्मितान्वयार्थवत्त्वसंयमाद्
न्द्रियजयः ॥४७॥

grahaṇasvarūpāsmitānvayārthavattvasaṁyamād indriyajayaḥ ॥ 47 ॥

grahaṇasvarūpāsmitānvayārthavattvasaṁyamāt, from samyama on [the senses'] perceiving power, essential nature, self-identification, comingled nature, and purposefulness; *indriyajayaḥ*, victory over the senses

From samyama on the perceiving power, essential nature, self-identification, comingled nature, and purposefulness [of the senses], victory over the senses.

Parallel to the practice described in sutra 3:44 leading to victory over the elements, the practice Patanjali refers to here empowers a yogi to attain victory over his senses. This practice and the victory it engenders over the senses are extraordinary.

Mastery over the senses usually implies an enhancement either in our capacity to smell, taste, see, touch, and hear, or in our capacity not to be distracted, disturbed, or overwhelmed by sensory experiences. The victory over the senses referred to in this sutra, however, includes complete knowledge of the senses: how they evolve, their relationship and interaction with the mind, how they bring specificity to the objects of cognition, how they give concrete form to our abstract comprehension of the objects, and how a unit or a series of cognitions is stored in the bed of memory with detailed identifying characteristics and attributes. Mastery over the senses also includes understanding how the mind uses the five senses to break down the cognitions of the phenomenal world into five broad categories and recoalesce these cognitions as necessary. In other words, mastery over the senses includes understanding the evolution and involution of the senses, the scope of their functions, and their subservience to the mind.

According to this sutra, the vast range of properties and functions of the senses can be divided into five categories: the perceiving power of the senses, their essential nature, their unique capacity to identify objects, their capacity to comingle and penetrate each other, and finally, their inherent capacity to assist consciousness in finding fulfillment and freedom. Because each of the five senses has five broad categories of properties and functions, together there are twenty-five discrete points for practicing samyama.

Seated in the pranically lit, radiant space of consciousness, an accomplished yogi employs her highly concentrated, penetrating mind to practice samyama on one discrete point of one sense. As practice progresses, she adds another point and then another. Eventually, she is able to pull the twenty-five discrete points into one continuum of samyama, thus reaching a state where she is able to see how the vast range of properties and functions of the senses flow from chitta samvit, how they are connected to chitta samvit, and how they are nourished by chitta samvit.

In advanced stages, the adept is able to gain firsthand knowledge of how the senses unfold from chitta samvit and how they dissolve back into it. This knowledge opens the floodgate to understanding how an individual chitta samvit relates to the infinitely vast field of prakriti, how it evolves from prakriti, and how it dissolves back into prakriti. As elaborated on in the next sutra, this entire range of revelation is what is described as *indriya jaya*, victory over the senses.

SUTRA 3:48

ततो मनोजवित्वं विकरणभावः प्रधानजयश्च
॥४८॥

tato manojavitvaṁ vikaraṇabhāvaḥ pradhānajayaśca
॥ 48 ॥

tataḥ, from that; *manojavitvaṁ*, ability to move at the speed of mind; *vikaraṇabhāvaḥ*, ability to comprehend without relying on sense organs; *pradhānajayaḥ*, ability to enter and explore primordial prakriti; *ca*, and

From that [victory over the senses], the ability to move at the speed of mind, the ability to comprehend without relying on sense organs, and the ability to enter and explore primordial prakriti.

This is a continuation of the preceding sutra. There Patanjali refers to a practice leading to perfect mastery over the senses, which leads to the unfoldment of numberless shades of extraordinary powers. For the sake of simplicity, Patanjali divides those powers into three broad categories: *manojavitva*, ability to move at the speed of mind; *vikaranabhava*, the ability to comprehend without relying on the sense organs; and *pradhana jaya*, the ability to enter and explore primordial prakriti. These siddhis are perfection par excellence.

As we have seen, an adept anchored in the self-luminous, self-born space of consciousness transcends the need to reside in a body made of elements and is qualified to practice samyama on the vast range of properties and functions of the senses. This practice charges the adept with *prajna*, the extraordinary intuitive understanding of the evolution of the senses, the need for their evolution, and ultimately, their transcendence of the sense organs. At this level of yogic accomplishment, there is no longer a difference between the senses and the mind.

Similarly, there are no differences between *manas*, the thinking mind; *ahamkara*, the mind that identifies itself with the objects of its cognition; *buddhi*, the discerning mind; and *chitta*, the vast field of memories. They have merged and re-emerged as chitta samvit. At this stage, the luminosity of chitta samvit is identical to the luminosity of *shuddha samvit*, the pure and pristine knowing power of Ishvara's prakriti. In other words, the mind of such an adept is as pure and pervasive as primordial prakriti. Such a mind is a natural container of the three broad categories of siddhis addressed in this sutra.

Having attained this level of mastery, a yogi is able to be anywhere at any point in time and space at the speed of his intention. He can also transport himself to realms of existence independent of our familiar laws of time, space, and causation. This capacity, along with its numberless offshoots, is *manojavitva*, the ability to move at the speed of mind.

Because he is fully established in chitta samvit and the world of numberless cognitions and recognitions it contains, the yogi is able to perceive the objects of his cognitions without the aid of the senses. The scriptures call this knowledge *sakshat-anubhuti*, direct experience without aid of the senses. A yogi is able to simultaneously comprehend the object of the entire experience, along with each distinct part. This capacity, along with its numberless offshoots, is *vikaranabhava*.

Because the purity and luminosity of his chitta samvit is identical to the purity and subtlety of primordial prakriti, the yogi is able to enter and explore the infinite field of unmanifest prakriti just as a beam of light moves into another field of light. Such a yogi is able to perceive even the most subtle physical, emotional, intellectual, and spiritual content lying dormant in the womb of unmanifest prakriti. Complying with higher will, he is able to selectively acquire such content and introduce it as a new reality. This capacity, along with its numberless offshoots, is *pradhana jaya*.

According to the Sri Vidya tradition, masters of this caliber are not individuals—they become masters only after their individuality vanishes. They are beyond our familiar concepts of time, space, number, and gender. They are a category of reality in their own right: they are neither one with nor separate from the absolute. They are whatever they are—they are here, there, everywhere, and yet nowhere.

Because they condense their presence in the realm of time and space at the flicker of intention, they are called *sadyojata*, born instantly. They are *bhava*, born; *abhava*, unborn; *atibhava*, transcendentally born; *natibhava*, transcendentally unborn; and *bhavodbhava*, the origin of all those ever born. Such a reality is *Vamadeva*, the emitter of creation; *Jyestha*, the eldest; *Shrestha*, the most venerable; *Rudra*, the protector; *Kala*, time; *Kalavikarna*, time-splitter or time-spreader; *Bala*, strength; *Balavikarna*, splitter and spreader of strength; *Bala-pramathana*, churner of strength; *Sarva-bhuta-damana*, suppressor or subduer of all living beings; *Manonmana*, beyond mind; *Ishana*, introducer of all fields of knowledge; and *Ishvara*, guru, guide, protector, and nurturer of all living beings. They are an open question: Are they one or many? Are they living or non-living? Are they identifiable or unidentifiable? Are they one with prakriti or separate from prakriti? Are they one with Ishvara or separate from Ishvara?

SUTRA 3:49

सत्त्वपुरुषान्यताख्यातिमात्रस्य
सर्वभावाधिष्ठातृत्वं सर्वज्ञातृत्वं च ॥४९॥

sattvapuruṣānyatākhyātimātrasya
sarvabhāvādhiṣṭhātṛtvaṁ sarvajñātṛtvaṁ ca ॥ 49 ॥

sattvapuruṣānyatākhyātimātrasya, to one who has gained direct realization of the distinction between buddhi and purusha; *sarvabhāvādhiṣṭhātṛtvaṁ*, capable of presiding over all samskaras; *sarvajñātṛtvaṁ*, the all-knowing power or quality; *ca*, and

One who has gained direct realization of the distinction between buddhi and purusha is capable of presiding over all samskaras and is endowed with omniscience.

Here Patanjali and Vyasa summarize sutras 3:34 through 3:48. They reiterate that meditation on vishoka and jyotishmati attenuates and eventually nullifies the rajasic and tamasic properties of our mind, resulting in the experience of *buddhi sattva*, the knowing power of buddhi (YS 1:36). Using the power of buddhi sattva, we meditate on the lotus of the heart, resulting in *chitta samvit*, the knowing power of the totality of our mind (YS 3:34).

The experience of chitta samvit empowers us to comprehend the distinction between the faculty of discernment and pure consciousness, as well as their intensely conflated states (YS 3:35).

This experience in turn enables us to comprehend how our samskaras propel the wheel of karma and place us in the torrent of birth and death. It also enables us to see clearly how afflicting samskaras bind our consciousness to our body, and how ultimately, by loosening our samskaras and cultivating sensitivity to pranic movement, we can pull our chitta samvit out of our body and place it in another body at will (YS 3:38).

By taking this practice to the next stage, we experience a self-luminous space of consciousness outside our body; in advanced stages, that space becomes fully palpable (YS 3:43). Thereafter, we continue our practices while anchored in that fully palpable, self-luminous space of consciousness. These highly advanced practices result in victory over the elements (YS 3:44) and victory over the senses (YS 3:47). These yogic victories are perfection par excellence. As described in the preceding sutra, perfection par excellence is characterized by the ability to move at the speed of mind, the ability to comprehend without relying on the senses, and the ability to enter and explore primordial prakriti.

According to sutra 3:46, all these practices and the experiences gained from them lead us to a state of enlightenment in which we truly understand the difference between our mind and pure consciousness. At this stage of realization, the understanding of our mind and consciousness is no longer intellectual—it is purely experiential and completely palpable. We are able to see how the conflated state of our chitta samvit and pure consciousness contains and retains our endless samskaras. Our highly enlightened chitta samvit is simultaneously aware of *shanta*, completely quiet, dormant samskaras; *udita*, fully awakened, active samskaras; and *avyapadeshya*, samskaras with the potential to claim their role in the future (YS 3:14). We also see how those samskaras were transformed into sheer shakti (YS 2:4) by the practice of vairagya known as *vashikara samjna* (YS 1:15).

We are no longer concerned with the presence of our samskaras, for we see them simply as *bhavas*, the essence of our past actions. We are confident they will exert their binding and releasing capacities only with our permission. In effect, we preside over them. We are their masters; they are in our service. They are in us; we are not in them. We know them; they do not know us. According to Vyasa, this is vishoka in the truest sense. Upon reaching this state, we embody omniscience. With this high degree of self-mastery, we move between states of awareness unobstructed.

SUTRA 3:50

तद्वैराग्यादपि दोषबीजक्षये कैवल्यम् ॥५०॥

tadvairāgyādapi doṣabījakṣaye kaivalyam ॥ 50 ॥

tadvairāgyāt, by renouncing attachment to that; *api*, even; *doṣabījakṣaye*, at the destruction of the seed of impurities; *kaivalyam*, absoluteness, the essence of the non-dual state

By renouncing attachment even to that attainment, destruction of the seed of impurities; that [leads to] kaivalya.

Having explained powerful practices that result in victory over the five elements (YS 3:44) and victory over the senses (YS 3:47), Patanjali again emphasizes yoga's ultimate objective: *kaivalya*. *Kaivalya* signifies the absence of everything other than the presence of consciousness. This state of consciousness dawns when cognitions other than the self-revealing power of intelligence vanish completely. For the sake of discussion, this state is characterized by the unalloyed experience of *chiti shakti*, the knowing power of consciousness. Reaching this state is the greatest of all yogic accomplishments and falling from this state is the greatest loss. In this sutra, Patanjali reminds us that the disappearance of avidya allows the state of kaivalya to rise, and the reappearance of avidya causes us to fall from the state of kaivalya.

As described in sutras 2:3 through 2:10, the fivefold affliction contaminates and distorts the intrinsic brilliance of our self-revealing power of intelligence. Avidya, loosely translated as "ignorance," is the mother of all afflictions. In effect, avidya is lack of awareness, or partial awareness, of our pure being. The most prominent quality of avidya is its ability to conceal its own existence. In its presence, the discerning power of our intelligence becomes dull. Our power of vigilance declines and carelessness takes over. The distinction between the goal and the means of achieving extraordinary accomplishments becomes blurry. This is how the subtle, highly potent seed of affliction is sown in chitta samvit. This compromises chitta samvit's ability to receive and absorb the omniscient light of *shuddha samvit*, the knowing power of pure consciousness. In this sutra, Patanjali gives us the tools to rule out the possibility of the re-emergence of avidya.

As we have seen in sutra 3:34, by the time we are able to comprehend and meditate on the lotus of the heart, we have cultivated a highly concentrated and discerning mind. This degree of concentration and discernment is the fruit of a well-structured practice and well-orchestrated vairagya. Meditation on the lotus of the heart results in the direct experience of chitta samvit. Further application of chitta samvit empowers us to clearly distinguish pure consciousness from the objects of cognition (YS 3:35). By further reinvesting this yogic accomplishment, we are able to secure a permanent home in the self-luminous space of consciousness (YS 3:43).

At this stage, we have transcended the frailty and limitations of our physical body. Anchored in the secure and fully nourished space of consciousness, we explore the mysteries of the phenomenal world. Patanjali cites two such mysteries: victory over the elements and victory over the senses (YS 3:44 and 3:47). These victories and the extraordinary powers manifesting from them (YS 3:45–46 and 3:48–49) can distract a yogi who is not supremely vigilant from the highest goal of yoga: kaivalya. This sutra tells us that vairagya is the key to avoiding even the slightest possibility that such distractions will emerge.

Just as the yogic accomplishments at this level and the potential distractions emerging from them are not of an ordinary nature, the principle of vairagya and its practice at this level are not ordinary either. If after gaining the direct experience of our chitta samvit, as described in sutra 3:34, we aspire to rise above the sphere of sabija samadhi and enter the state of nirbija, we must apply the principle of *vashikara vairagya* (YS 1:15 and 1:40) to wipe out the subtle traces of even meditative samskaras (YS 1:50–51 and 3:1–5).

When we deliberately postpone our journey to nirbija samadhi and decide to explore the infinite expanse of prakriti and mine some of its extraordinary riches, we must be extra vigilant. During the practices leading to victory over the elements and the senses, we must ensure that avidya is held at bay. This requires maintaining constant awareness that all the faculties of our mind as well as chitta samvit, the knowing power of the mind, belong to prakriti. Even our effort to explore the infinite kingdom of prakriti is propelled by prakriti's intrinsic power of sattva, rajas, and tamas. Therefore, in reality, we are not exploring the expanse of prakriti, but rather prakriti is exploring her own vast kingdom. It is a privilege to witness this exploration, not a right.

Constant non-identification of ourselves as a yogi engaged in this advanced practice is vairagya. The technical term for this level of vairagya is *vashikara samjna*. Humility and trustful surrender to the higher reality are the key to practicing this form of vairagya.

How the extremely subtle avidya-driven obstacle—our identification as a yogi—may arise and exactly how to apply vairagya to defeat it even before it arises is the subject of the next sutra.

SUTRA 3:51

स्थान्युपनिमन्त्रणे सङ्गस्मयाकरणं
पुनरनिष्टप्रसङ्गात् ॥५१॥

sthānyupanimantraṇe saṅgasmayākaraṇaṁ
punaraniṣṭaprasaṅgāt ॥ 51 ॥

sthānyupanimantraṇe, when honored or rewarded by the extraordinary powers associated with siddhis; *saṅgasmayākaraṇaṁ*, the process of avoiding attachment and pride; *punaḥ*, again; *aniṣṭaprasaṅgāt*, because of the possibility of unintended consequence[s]

When honored or rewarded by the extraordinary powers unique to siddhis, [a yogi] must avoid succumbing to attachment and pride lest unintended consequences ensue.

Here Patanjali is emphasizing the distractions and pitfalls in yoga sadhana. The practices leading to extraordinary siddhis presuppose that we have cultivated a highly purified and laser-focused mind, yet the possibility of getting derailed remains. Avidya is extremely subtle and potent—even highly accomplished masters can fall prey to it. Ishvara alone has complete mastery over avidya. Constant refinement of vairagya and trustful surrender to Ishvara are the only means of avoiding entanglement in the snares of this mysterious power.

At a practical level, avidya is outside the domain of our comprehension and thus undetectable. Its undetectability makes it unpreventable. The first evolute of avidya is the feeling "This is mine; this is what I am." This feeling is encapsulated in one word: *asmita*, I-am-ness. Asmita is somewhat within the range of our comprehension and is thus both detectable and preventable. In this sutra, Patanjali is cautioning that even in extremely advanced stages of yoga sadhana we must remain aware of the consequences of avidya-born asmita.

Walking through the doorways of the sun, moon, and polar star, for example, and unraveling the mysteries of the fourteen spheres of existence and the arrangements of stars and their movements (YS 3:26–28) are extraordinary achievements. But an even greater achievement lies in maintaining constant awareness that none of these accomplishments are our creation. Our body and mind are part of prakriti. Our sadhana is propelled by the inherent power of our body, mind, and prana shakti. Identifying ourselves as a practitioner and claiming ownership over the process of sadhana and its fruit are the epitome of asmita. Not only can asmita impede our progress, it can also push us backward. The scriptures are replete with accounts of yogis smitten with their own siddhis. Under the influence of avidya-born asmita, many adepts have misused and abused their extraordinary abilities. Some disrupted the laws of nature—even challenged the sankalpa of Ishvara—only to suffer grave consequences.

According to this sutra, the key to moving forward and reaching the state of consciousness from which there is no possibility of sliding backward is strict adherence to *para vairagya*, absolute non-attachment, and *Ishvara pranidhana*, trustful surrender to Ishvara.

SUTRA 3:52

क्षणतत्क्रमयोः संयमाद्विवेकजं ज्ञानम् ।।५२।।

kṣaṇatatkramayoḥ saṁyamādvivekajaṁ jñānaṁ ॥ 52 ॥

kṣaṇatatkramayoḥ, of instant[s] and their sequence; *saṁyamāt*, from samyama; *vivekajaṁ*, distinctive; *jñānaṁ*, knowledge

From samyama on instants and their sequence, distinctive knowledge.

In this and the next two sutras, Patanjali and Vyasa posit the existence of time and the result of practicing samyama on it. According to them, time is twofold: linear and non-linear. The linearity of time is a mental construct. Cognition of time as seconds, minutes, and hours, and as bigger units of time—such as days, weeks, months, and years—is a series of convenience-driven mental constructs. The mind conjures them up to distinguish one experience or event from another. Cognition pertaining to time is abstract, devoid of substance. It is completely imaginary.

The mind uses the five senses to interact with the phenomenal world. When the senses relay an experience of the objective world to the mind, it attaches the concept of time to add specificity to that experience. This specificity comes from assigning a segment of time to each experience. Each segment of time, along with the experience associated with it, is connected to the next segment of time and its associated experience. Thus, our experiences float on the current of a long chain of mental constructs. The smallest unit of a mental construct is known as *kshana*, instant.

According to yoga shastra, there is only one instant: the present. It is immutable—beginningless and endless. It is characterized by constancy. Fleeting experiences of the objective world pass across the horizon of this constancy, leaving the mind no choice but to remain occupied with the illusion of the appearance and disappearance of constancy. This forces the mind to conjure up the idea of instants, assign fleeting experiences to those instants, and string them together. The cognition of a cluster of such instants and the experiences superimposed on them gives the mind a sense of completion.

This sense of completion has three main components. The first consists of instants and associated experiences that are no longer in the forefront of the mind but exist as memory. A second component of this sense of completion consists of the instances and associated experiences that are in full view of the mind. The third portion consists of the anticipation of instances and associated experiences that are similar to those currently in full view of the mind. This is what gives rise to the notion of past, present, and future.

Our world is made of continuously appearing and disappearing chains of experiences held together by continuously flowing segments of time. Segments of time are the product of our mind. In the final analysis, our experience of the objective world is completely dependent both on the mind's skill in discerning the segments of time, which are the mind's self-created constructs, and on the experiences it superimposes on those constructs.

According to Patanjali and Vyasa, we cultivate the skill to discern those constructs by first comprehending the end stage of one instant and the beginning stage of the next. This comprehension results in *viveka jnana*, distinctive knowledge characterized by the experience of *pravaha nityata*, eternity in flux. This experience becomes the doorway to experiencing *kutastha nityata*, eternity in constancy, the subject of sutra 3:54.

In the next sutra, Patanjali explains why, if each moment and the objective experience associated with it is in constant flux, we have the sense that an experience lasts for minutes, hours, or even longer. And more importantly, he explains why this distinctive knowledge is so crucial in rising above the forces of time that rule our objective world and entering the state of consciousness characterized by non-linear eternity in constancy.

SUTRA 3:53

जातिलक्षणदेशैरन्यतानवच्छेदात् तुल्ययोस्ततः प्रतिपत्तिः ॥५३॥

jātilakṣaṇadeśairanyatānavacchedāt tulyayostataḥ pratipattiḥ ॥ 53 ॥

jātilakṣaṇadeśaiḥ, through common denominator, distinctive denominator, and location; *anyatānavacchedāt*, due to lack of interference by dissimilar; *tulyayoḥ*, in or within two identicals; *tataḥ*, from that; *pratipattiḥ*, conclusion

[An experience is cognized on three grounds:] common denominator, distinctive denominator, and location. Due to the lack of interference by dissimilar [common denominator, distinctive denominator, or location, there arises the cognition of] sameness of the experience. [From samyama on the instant that exists between two] seemingly identical cognitions, [distinctive knowledge] concludes.

Time is neither big nor small, long nor short. It has no beginning and no end. It is intrinsic to eternity—one, pervasive, and indivisible. Time transcends the notion of past, present, and future. Yet the mind apprehends it as long or short. It apprehends its beginning and its end. The mind remembers the time that has already passed, remains cognizant of the time that is giving room to current events, and conceives of the time that will give room to anticipated events. This allows the mind to perceive time in three broad categories: past, present, and future.

These three categories, both separately and in aggregate, may be extremely big or extremely small, extremely long or extremely short. The mind arbitrarily determines the beginning, middle, and end of the past, present, and future. This dimension of time is described as *pravaha nityata*, eternity in flux. It is totally imaginary, yet quite real to the ordinary mind. In spite of its abstract and substanceless nature, this dimension of time imbues our cognitions of the objective world with the notion of existence. Experiences begin to exist only when they fall in pravaha nityata, the constantly flowing realm of time. An experience's association with time is birth, the phenomenon of coming into existence. Birth lasts only for an instant and that instant is the present. Why the present is experienced as more than the thinnest slice of the smallest segment of time, and what causes the present to be pushed into the past or causes the thinnest slices of time to be perceived as the past, are the subjects of this sutra.

Mental cognitions are as abstract as the constantly flowing instants of time. The abstractness of cognitions is removed and replaced with a recognizable degree of substance when the mind identifies three inherent properties of the cognition: the common denominator, the distinctive denominator, and the location.

Let us take a cow as an example. The cognition of a cow is accompanied by a common denominator—the qualities and characteristics that all cows have in common. It is also accompanied by a distinctive denominator—such as that cow's particular color, height, subtle behavior, and capacities—which distinguishes it from other cows. Furthermore, the cognition of this particular cow is accompanied by the comprehension of the cow's location. In other words, the cognition of the space occupied by the cow is an integral part of the cognition of the cow.

According to this sutra, as long as an instant bearing a cognition is immediately followed by an instant bearing an identical cognition, and that is followed by another and another, we perceive that chain of cognitions as one cognition. As soon as there is an alteration either in the common denominator, the distinctive denominator, or the location, the flow of identical cognitions comes to an end and a new cognition or chain of cognitions begins. Thus, any sensory experience, regardless of how brief, consists of a cluster of cognitions. Furthermore, this cluster of cognitions is *kramavalambi*, dependent on sequence, and that must remain unobstructed by dissimilar cognitions.

An ordinary mind has no capacity to detect instants—the smallest indivisible units of time—let alone comprehend the instant that serves as a bridge between one instant and the next. But a yogi who has attained victory over the elements (YS 3:44) and victory over the senses (YS 3:47) and consequently is capable of entering and exploring the subtler dimensions of nature—such as atoms and unmanifest prakriti—can detect and isolate an instant of time and the cognition it bears from other instants.

Looking through the window of an instant separating the previous instant from the next, a yogi is able to comprehend *kutastha nityata*, eternity in constancy. This comprehension is what the previous sutra and the upcoming sutra describe as *viveka jnana*, distinctive knowledge—knowledge par excellence. This knowledge is the gateway to non-linear, indivisible, and immutable kutastha nityata, eternity in constancy, as opposed to pravaha nityata, eternity in flux, which facilitates and rules over the experiences pertaining to the phenomenal world. The next sutra details the nature of kutastha nityata.

SUTRA 3:54

तारकं सर्वविषयं सर्वथाविषयम अक्रमं चेति विवेकजज्ञानम् ॥५४॥

tārakaṁ sarvaviṣayaṁ sarvathāviṣayam akramaṁ ceti vivekaja-jñānaṁ ‖ 54 ‖

tārakaṁ, liberating; *sarvaviṣayaṁ*, having everything as its object; *sarvathāviṣayam*, that which is not the object of anything; *akramaṁ*, that which is beyond sequence; *ca*, and; *iti*, thus; *vivekaja-jñānaṁ*, born of distinctive knowledge

Distinctive knowledge is liberating, has everything as its object, is not the object of anything, and is beyond sequence.

As described in the two preceding sutras, time is a distinct reality. Complete comprehension of time is distinctive knowledge. Distinctive knowledge emerges from distinguishing two aspects of time: linear and non-linear.

Linear time consists of the uninterrupted flow of indivisible units of time. An indivisible unit of time is known as *kshana*, instant. Our cognitions float on the current of these indivisible instants. Instants and the experiences associated with these instants are too brief to be noticed by the mind. Our mind is designed to take cognizance of an experience only when a chain of identical experiences floats on the current of instants without interruption. In other words, cognition of an objective experience is made of a long chain of cognitions; each unit of cognition latches on to continuously flowing instants.

An ordinary mind does not have the capacity to distinguish one instant from another or one cognition associated with an instant from another cognition associated with another instant. An adept's accomplishment reaches its pinnacle when he succeeds in distinguishing one instant from another and is thus able to penetrate the smallest segments of experiences that give an appearance of one experience.

Two cognitions and the instants bearing them are two only because another instant separates the two instants. In the absence of this separating instant, the two become one, leading to the complete collapse of objective experience. Life is a long saga of objective experiences. The life of the universe is a long saga of the objective experiences of consciousness. This is what is meant by *pravaha nityata*, eternity in flux. This eternity is completely dependent on *kutastha nityata*, eternity in constancy, which is identical to the instant that remains constant: purusha, pure consciousness. A yogi with an intensely sharp and illuminating chitta samvit is able to identify continuously flowing instants as well as the unique instant holding two instants together. This process constitutes the soul of *viveka khyati*, unshakable discerning knowledge. The knowledge emerging from it is *viveka jnana*, distinctive knowledge.

Patanjali calls this distinctive knowledge *taraka*, the reality that enables us to cross the realm of pravaha nityata, eternity in flux, and reach kutastha nityata, eternity in constancy. Coming to this world, living here, and departing are part of eternity in flux. To be born, grow old, and die is the defining characteristic of this world. Transcending this characteristic and becoming established in never-changing eternal truth is immortality. A yogi fully established in this distinctive knowledge is immortal. He lives in that instant from which all instants evolve and into which all instants dissolve.

Further describing this distinctive knowledge, Patanjali tells us that it is *sarva vishaya*, inclusive of all objective experiences. Anything ever known in the past, present, and future is fully present in this knowledge. As a ground for constantly fleeting instants of time and the experiences associated with them, this beginningless, middleless, and never-ending distinctive knowledge is the eternal measure of all experiences, from the smallest component to the largest aggregate. Experiences pertaining to all twenty-four categories of reality—the five gross elements, five subtle elements, five senses of action, five senses of cognition, manas, ahamkara, buddhi, and prakriti—are within the domain of this distinctive knowledge.

This knowledge is also *sarvatha vishaya*, not an object of anything. It cannot be comprehended by perception, inference, or scriptural testimony. The mind cannot conceive it. The intellect cannot comprehend it. Scriptures cannot articulate it. It is self-revealed and known by its self-born, self-contained, and self-sustained effulgence. It illuminates the senses; the senses do not illuminate it. It illuminates our faculties of thought, identification, and discernment, but these faculties cannot grasp it. The entire objective world is known by it, yet the objective world does not know it.

Finally, this distinctive knowledge is *akrama*, beyond sequence. Experiences in the phenomenal world are dependent on and regulated by the sequence of ever-flowing units of indivisible instants. The unstoppable flow of these units of time and the unalterable process that allocates value to their sequence bring forward a consequence, which we call experience. All experiences are consequential. This consequentiality is the ground for destiny. Sequential sensory and emotional data are loaded onto sequentially flowing units of time. The cognitions of such units of time are then deposited in our mind as memory. Impelled by the force that ignites our memory (YS 2:3), these data come to the forefront of our mind, setting the wheel of karma in motion.

Distinctive knowledge transcends the linearity of time, yet preserves all cognitions and experiences belonging to the world of linearity. Akrama, non-linearity, is the defining attribute of distinctive knowledge. As soon as the cognitions and experiences and the linear instants bearing them enter the ambit of non-linear reality, their linearity collapses. They are embraced by the one and only beginningless, middleless, unending instant and absorbed into it.

The adepts who have reached this far are the highest-caliber siddhas. They are *yogishvaras*, lords of the yogis. They have crossed the realm of time and space meant for the inhabitants of the phenomenal world. They are *kalavit*, knowers of time; *kalabhit*, penetrators of time; *kalabhedya*, unpenetrated by time; and—due to their immersion in ever-present, beginningless, middleless, and unchanging transcendent time—they themselves are *kala*, time. They are known as *adhikari purusha*, distinguished beings vested with the power to create, maintain, destroy, cast the veil of inertia over what has been destroyed, and lift the veil, illuminating inert matter and non-living beings with life-exuding luminosity.

In the yoga tradition, these siddha masters are not Ishvara because they still retain their individuality, but they are like Ishvara because they are not subject to the limitations that accompany individuality. Divinities such as Brahma, Vishnu, Shiva, Dakshinamurti, Sadyojata, Vamadeva, Aghora, Tatpurusha, and Ishana are yogis of this caliber. They are simultaneously transcendent and immanent. They are one and many. They are at once fully in the world, guided and governed by linear time, and untouched by the world. In their *akrama sankalpa*, non-linear intention, reside an infinite number of linear intentions. This phenomenon is known as *akrama srishti*, non-linear creation. This non-linear intention is the *svabhava*, intrinsic nature, of the adept. In the realm of linear time, this single non-linear sankalpa continues manifesting linearly for eons.

Yogis with such non-linear sankalpa are Brahma, the creator of the phenomenal world. Their non-linear intention is imbued with unconditional love and compassion for souls suffering from afflicting samskaras; therefore, the creation ensuing from their primordial intention holds all the tools and means that suffering souls need to find freedom and fulfillment. The state of consciousness these yogis embody is known as *taraka*, the liberator.

The practice leading to the achievement of this state begins with meditation on vishoka and jyotishmati. The score of practices described in the third chapter of the *Yoga Sutra* simply fill the space that lies between the states of vishoka and taraka. Practically speaking, taraka is the final destination of the meditative journey that begins with vishoka.

Is the practice leading to this distinctive knowledge and the power engendered by it essential to the highest goal of yoga, which is nirbija samadhi? In the final sutra, Patanjali addresses this question.

SUTRA 3:55

सत्त्वपुरुषयोः शुद्धिसाम्ये कैवल्यमिति ॥५५॥

sattvapuruṣayoḥ śuddhisāmye kaivalyamiti ॥ 55 ॥

sattvapuruṣayoḥ, of mind and purusha; *śuddhisāmye*, upon having equality in purity; *kaivalyam*, absoluteness; *iti*, thus it concludes

When the purity of the mind becomes equal to the purity of purusha, absoluteness arises.

The mind is the greatest of all mysteries, the source of all known and unknown powers. Each of us has a natural urge to discover and reclaim the treasures hidden in our mind and the natural world. This requires a sharp, laser-focused mind. Yoga sadhana is the means of cultivating such a mind. As we commit ourselves to yoga sadhana, we are confronted with the mind's roaming tendencies. But with sustained practice, we gradually attenuate the subtle causes of the mental disturbances, roaming tendencies, and inertia that create obstacles to our practice of meditation.

According to Patanjali, the source of these mental disturbances, distractions, and stupefactions is the fivefold affliction. In conjunction with tapas, svadhyaya, and Ishvara pranidhana, the system of meditation described here in the third chapter calms the mind and turns it inward, allowing its intrinsic intelligence to see its own hidden potential. Each step of meditation is marked by its own unique intensity of concentration, revelation, and power of discernment. These varying degrees of intensity empower the mind to shake off its inertia and disown its dark, dull, and self-defeating tendencies. This results in the removal of mental impurities. With its newly found purity, clarity, concentration, and sharpness, the mind is able to identify the extraordinary gifts of nature buried within itself and within the phenomenal world. This process matures into the development of siddhis, extraordinary yogic powers.

Although siddhis are not the ultimate goal of yoga sadhana, the manifestation of siddhis validates our practice. In sutra 3:37, Patanjali warns: "For one with an outwardly running mind, they are extraordinary accomplishments, but for one aspiring to samadhi, they are obstacles." The goal of yoga sadhana is to gain such a high degree of mental purity and concentration that the mind is able to know its own knowing power. This degree of mental purity goes hand in hand with disowning the deep-rooted karmic impressions that give rise to our mental tendencies. This results in the experience of chitta samvit, the mind's knowing power (YS 3:34).

At this stage, the mind is fully illumined by the radiance of purusha, pure consciousness. This is a highly significant stage in the meditative process. Powered by the radiance of pure consciousness, the mind is able to rise above its identification with the body—an experience described in sutra 3:38. As this experience matures, a yogi is able to use the non-imaginary but fully palpable space of consciousness outside his body as a seat for higher meditative practice—an experience described in sutra 3:43. This practice allows a yogi to further refine his chitta samvit. This results in the next level of purity the mind needs to explore both the subtle dimensions of primordial prakriti and the two aspects of time: one characterized by linearity, the other non-linear.

Here, in the final sutra, Patanjali is stating that, after having attained the most refined state of chitta samvit, a yogi can—for the sake of his own pleasure—explore these subtle dimensions or ignore them altogether and enter the highest state of samadhi known as *nirbija*. The criterion for accessing nirbija samadhi is *shuddhi-samya*, an exalted state of yoga in which the purity of the mind is identical to the purity of purusha. This level of purity dawns when the mind no longer identifies itself even with its most revealing meditative samskaras. The distinction between this level of experience and the experience of *kutastha nityata*—the beginningless, middleless, unending instant from which the linearity of time issues and into which it dissolves—is detectable only by yogis whose mental purity is equal to that of Ishvara. For the rest of us, it is merely a game of words.

Summarizing this entire chapter, Patanjali states definitively that nirbija samadhi is the final goal of yoga, for it is in this state that *kaivalya*, absoluteness, is experienced. Vyasa says that in the state of kaivalya a yogi is *svarupa-matra-jyoti*, the sheer light of her own essence. Her essence is not contaminated by even the most subtle attributes of nature, let alone by the stains of samskaras. Thus, she is *amala*, stainless, and *kevali*, absolutely free. For such a yogi, there is nothing undone and nothing to be achieved. She is perfect in every respect.

APPENDIXES

APPENDIX A

Devanagari, Transliteration, and Translation

SUTRA 3:1

देशबन्धश्चित्तस्य धारणा ॥१॥

deśabandhaścittasya dhāraṇā ॥ 1 ॥

Confining the mind to an [assigned] field is *dharana*, concentration.

SUTRA 3:2

तत्र प्रत्ययैकतानता ध्यानम् ॥२॥

tatra pratyayaikatānatā dhyānam ॥ 2 ॥

There the continuous flow of a single cognition is *dhyana*, meditation.

SUTRA 3:3

तदेवार्थमात्रनिर्भासं स्वरूपशून्यमिव समाधिः ॥३॥

tadevārthamātranirbhāsaṁ svarūpaśūnyamiva samādhiḥ ॥ 3 ॥

When that [object of dharana and dhyana] seems to have lost its defining features and is expressive only of its meaning, it is *samadhi*.

SUTRA 3:4

त्रयमेकत्र संयमः ॥४॥

trayamekatra saṁyamaḥ ॥ 4 ॥

Together [these] three are called *samyama*.

SUTRA 3:5

तज्जयात्प्रज्ञालोकः ॥५॥

tajjayātprajñālokaḥ ॥ 5 ॥

From mastery over that [samyama], the light of intuitive wisdom [arises].

SUTRA 3:6

तस्य भूमिषु विनियोगः ॥६॥

tasya bhūmiṣu viniyogaḥ ॥ 6 ॥

In different contexts and circumstances, the application of that [samyama] differs.

SUTRA 3:7

त्रयमन्तरङ्गं पूर्वेभ्यः ।।७।।

trayamantaraṅgaṁ pūrvebhyaḥ ॥ 7 ॥

In relation to the preceding [limbs], the triad [of dharana, dhyana, and samadhi] is an internal limb.

SUTRA 3:8

तदपि बहिरङ्गं निर्बीजस्य ।।८।।

tadapi bahiraṅgaṁ nirbījasya ॥ 8 ॥

Even that [samyama] is an external limb of nirbija samadhi.

SUTRA 3:9

व्युत्थाननिरोधसंस्कारयोरभिभवप्रादुर्भावौ
निरोधक्षणचित्तान्वयो निरोधपरिणामः ।।९।।

vyutthānanirodhasaṁskārayorabhibhavaprādurbhāvau
nirodhakṣaṇacittānvayo nirodhapariṇāmaḥ ॥ 9 ॥

The decline of samskaras that cause mental agitation and the rise of samskaras that impel the mind to confine itself to the object of concentration introduce a brief moment of time filled with the essence of self-restraint. Yoking the mind to that moment results in mastery over its roaming tendencies.

SUTRA 3:10

तस्य प्रशान्तवाहिता संस्कारात् ॥१०॥

tasya praśāntavāhitā saṁskārāt ॥ 10 ॥

The peaceful flow of that [the result engendered by nirodha] is due to the samskaras.

SUTRA 3:11

सर्वार्थतैकाग्रतयोः क्षयोदयौ चित्तस्य समाधिपरिणामः ॥११॥

sarvārthataikāgratayoḥ kṣayodayau cittasya samādhipariṇāmaḥ ॥ 11 ॥

The elimination of all cognitions and the rise of one-pointedness lead to the transformation characterized by a completely still, pristine state of mind.

SUTRA 3:12

ततः पुनः शान्तोदितौ तुल्यप्रत्ययौ चित्तस्यैकाग्रतापरिणामः ॥१२॥

tataḥ punaḥ śāntoditau tulyapratyayau cittasyaikāgratāpariṇāmaḥ ॥ 12 ॥

Thereafter, the cognitions that have passed and those that are arising become identical. This results in a transformation characterized by one-pointedness of mind.

SUTRA 3:13

एतेन भूतेन्द्रियेषु धर्मलक्षणावस्थापरिणामा व्याख्याताः ॥१३॥

etena bhūtendriyeṣu dharmalakṣaṇāvasthāpariṇāmā vyākhyātāḥ ॥ 13 ॥

With this [degree of mental concentration], transformation of defining qualities, symptoms, and conditions occurring in individuals [or elements] and in tools of cognition can be scrutinized and comprehended.

SUTRA 3:14

शान्तोदिताव्यपदेश्यधर्मानुपाती धर्मी ॥१४॥

śāntoditāvyapadeśyadharmānupātī dharmī ॥ 14 ॥

The substratum conforms to [the changes occurring in its] past, present, and future attributes.

SUTRA 3:15

क्रमान्यत्वं परिणामान्यत्वे हेतुः ॥१५॥

kramānyatvam pariṇāmānyatve hetuḥ ॥ 15 ॥

Change in the sequence alters the result.

SUTRA 3:16

परिणामत्रयसंयमाद् अतीतानागतज्ञानम् ।।१६।।

pariṇāmatrayasaṁyamād atītānāgatajñānam ॥ 16 ॥

From samyama on the threefold transformation, knowledge of the past and future.

SUTRA 3:17

शब्दार्थप्रत्ययानामितरेतराध्यासात्
सङ्करस्तत्प्रविभागसंयमात्सर्वभूतरुतज्ञानम् ।।१७।।

śabdārthapratyayānāmitaretarādhyāsāt
saṅkarastatpravibhāgasaṁyamātsarvabhūtarutajñānam ॥ 17 ॥

The superimposition of word, meaning, and cognition engenders a fully conflated perception of them. From samyama on their distinct parts, comprehension of what creatures are saying.

SUTRA 3:18

संस्कारसाक्षात्करणात्पूर्वजातिज्ञानम् ।।१८।।

saṁskārasākṣātkaraṇātpūrvajātijñānam ॥ 18 ॥

From direct realization of samskaras, knowledge of previous births.

SUTRA 3:19

प्रत्ययस्य परचित्तज्ञानम् ॥१९॥

pratyayasya paracittajñānam ॥ 19 ॥

Understanding another person's cognition leads to an understanding of that person's mind.

SUTRA 3:20

न च तत्सालम्बनं तस्याविषयीभूतत्वात् ॥२०॥

na ca tatsālambanaṁ tasyāviṣayībhūtatvāt ॥ 20 ॥

That knowledge, however, does not include the object of cognition, because that [object] is not in the domain of samyama.

SUTRA 3:21

कायरूपसंयमात्तद्ग्राह्यशक्तिस्तम्भे
चक्षुःप्रकाशासम्प्रयोगेऽन्तर्धानम् ॥२१॥

kāyarūpasaṁyamāttadgrāhyaśaktistambhe
cakṣuḥprakāśāsaṁprayoge'ntardhānam ॥ 21 ॥

From samyama on the form of the body, immobilization of its power to be perceived. [In addition to accomplishing that,] upon blocking the light of the eyes, the experience of the disappearance [of the yogi's body].

SUTRA 3:22

सोपक्रमं निरुपक्रमं च कर्म
तत्संयमादपरान्तज्ञानमरिष्टेभ्यो वा
॥२२॥

sopakramaṁ nirupakramaṁ ca karma
tatsaṁyamādaparāntajñānamariṣṭebhyo vā ॥ 22 ॥

Karmas are of two kinds: accompanied by consequential factors and lacking consequential factors. From samyama on them, or from omens, knowledge regarding the latter part [of life].

SUTRA 3:23

मैत्र्यादिषु बलानि ॥२३॥

maitryādiṣu balāni ॥ 23 ॥

[From samyama] on friendliness and so on, capacities.

SUTRA 3:24

बलेषु हस्तिबलादीनि ॥२४॥

baleṣu hastibalādīni ॥ 24 ॥

[From samyama] on powers, the powers of an elephant, and so on.

SUTRA 3:25

प्रवृत्त्यालोकन्यासात् सूक्ष्मव्यवहितविप्रकृष्टज्ञानम् ॥२५॥

pravṛttyālokanyāsāt sūkṣmavyavahitaviprakṛṣṭajñānam ॥ 25 ॥

By directing the light born of extrasensory cognition, knowledge of subtle, obstructed, and distant objects.

SUTRA 3:26

भुवनज्ञानं सूर्ये संयमात् ॥२६॥

bhuvanajñānaṁ sūrye saṁyamāt ॥ 26 ॥

From samyama on the sun, knowledge of the spheres of existence.

SUTRA 3:27

चन्द्रे ताराव्यूहज्ञानम् ॥२७॥

candre tārāvyūhajñānam ॥ 27 ॥

[From samyama] on the moon, knowledge pertaining to the arrangement of the stars.

SUTRA 3:28

ध्रुवे तद्गतिज्ञानम् ॥२८॥

dhruve tadgatijñānam ॥ 28 ॥

[From samyama] on the pole star, knowledge of their [the stars'] movement.

SUTRA 3:29

नाभिचक्रे कायव्यूहज्ञानम् ॥२९॥

nābhicakre kāyavyūhajñānam ॥ 29 ॥

[From samyama] on the navel plexus, knowledge of the systems of the body.

SUTRA 3:30

कण्ठकूपे क्षुत्पिपासानिवृत्तिः ॥३०॥

kaṇṭhakūpe kṣutpipāsānivṛttiḥ ॥ 30 ॥

[From samyama] on the well of the throat, relief from hunger and thirst.

SUTRA 3:31

कूर्मनाड्यां स्थैर्यम् ॥३१॥

kūrmanāḍyāṁ sthairyam ॥ 31 ॥

[From samyama] on the kurma nadi, stability.

SUTRA 3:32

मूर्धज्योतिषि सिद्धदर्शनम् ॥३२॥

mūrdhajyotiṣi siddhadarśanam ॥ 32 ॥

[From samyama] on the light of the crown, a vision of the siddhas.

SUTRA 3:33

प्रातिभाद्वा सर्वम् ।।३३।।

prātibhādvā sarvam ॥ 33 ॥

Or from intuitive knowledge, everything is known.

SUTRA 3:34

हृदये चित्तसंवित् ।।३४।।

hṛdaye cittasaṁvit ॥ 34 ॥

[From samyama] on the heart, the knowing power of chitta.

SUTRA 3:35

सत्त्वपुरुषयोरत्यन्तासंकीर्णयोः प्रत्ययाविशेषो भोगः
परार्थत्वात्स्वार्थसंयमात्पुरुषज्ञानम् ।।३५।।

sattvapuruṣayoratyantāsaṁkīrṇayoḥ pratyayāviśeṣo bhogaḥ
parārthatvātsvārthasaṁyamātpuruṣajñānam ॥ 35 ॥

The mind and consciousness are so intensely fused that there is no difference between their cognitions. [This conflated cognition is] experience. An aspect of experience is smeared with the sense of being an object. [Withdrawing the mind from that and] practicing samyama on the other, which is accompanied by the sense of I-am-ness, engenders the knowledge of pure consciousness.

SUTRA 3:36

ततः प्रातिभश्रावणवेदनादर्शास्वादवार्ता जायन्ते ॥३६॥

tataḥ prātibhaśrāvaṇavedanādarśāsvādavārtā jāyante ॥ 36 ॥

From that arises [the power of] intuitive hearing, touching, seeing, tasting, and smelling.

SUTRA 3:37

ते समाधावुपसर्गा व्युत्थाने सिद्धयः ॥३७॥

te samādhāvupasargā vyutthāne siddhayaḥ ॥ 37 ॥

For one with an outwardly running mind, these are extraordinary accomplishments, but for one aspiring to samadhi, they are obstacles.

SUTRA 3:38

बन्धकारणशैथिल्यात्प्रचारसंवेदनाच् च चित्तस्य परशरीरावेशः ॥३८॥

bandhakāraṇaśaithilyātpracārasaṁvedanāc ca cittasya paraśarīrāveśaḥ ॥ 38 ॥

From the loosening of the cause of bondage and from sensitivity to pranic flow, the mind is able to enter and infuse another body.

SUTRA 3:39

उदानजयाज्जलपङ्ककण्टकादिष्वसङ्ग उत्क्रान्तिश्च ॥३९॥

udānajayājjalapaṅkakaṇṭakādiṣvasaṅga utkrāntiśca ॥ 39 ॥

From the conquest of udana, [a yogi is able to remain] unaffected by water, mud, thorns, and so on, and leave the body while transcending death.

SUTRA 3:40

समानजयाज्ज्वलनम् ॥४०॥

samānajayājjvalanam ॥ 40 ॥

From the conquest of samana, [a yogi is able to] ignite.

SUTRA 3:41

श्रोत्राकाशयोः सम्बन्धसंयमाद्दिव्यं श्रोत्रम् ॥४१॥

śrotrākāśayoḥ sambandhasaṁyamāddivyaṁ śrotram ॥ 41 ॥

From samyama on the relationship between the sense of hearing and space, the extraordinary power of hearing.

SUTRA 3:42

कायाकाशयोः सम्बन्धसंयमात्
लघुतूलसमापत्तेश्चाकाशगमनम् ॥४२॥

kāyākāśayoḥ sambandhasaṁyamāt
laghutūlasamāpatteścākāśagamanam ॥ 42 ॥

From samyama on the relationship between the body and space or from mental absorption in light cotton fiber, [the power of] moving through space.

SUTRA 3:43

बहिरकल्पिता वृत्तिर्महाविदेहा ततः प्रकाशावरणक्षयः ॥४३॥

bahirakalpitā vṛttirmahāvidehā tataḥ prakāśāvaraṇakṣayaḥ ॥ 43 ॥

Non-imaginary [fully palpable] cognition outside [the body] is *mahavideha*. From that [comes] the destruction of the veil that hides the light.

SUTRA 3:44

स्थूलस्वरूपसूक्ष्मान्वयार्थवत्त्वसंयमाद्भूतजयः ॥४४॥

sthūlasvarūpasūkṣmānvayārthavattvasaṁyamādbhūtajayaḥ ॥ 44 ॥

From samyama on the tangible form, essential nature, and subtle form [of the elements, as well as on their comingled nature and their purposefulness], victory over the elements.

SUTRA 3:45

ततोऽणिमादिप्रादुर्भावः कायसम्पत्तद्धर्मानभिघातश्च ॥४५॥

tato'ṇimādiprādurbhāvaḥ
kāyasampattaddharmānabhighātaśca ॥ 45 ॥

From that [victory over the elements] arise [siddhis of] anima, and so on, the wealth of bodily perfection, and [the siddhi of] being unhampered by the properties and functions of the elements.

SUTRA 3:46

रूपलावण्यबलवज्रसंहननत्वानि कायसम्पत् ॥४६॥

rūpalāvaṇyabalavajrasaṁhananatvāni kāyasampat ॥ 46 ॥

Beauty, charm, vitality, and healing power are bodily wealth.

SUTRA 3:47

ग्रहणस्वरूपास्मितान्वयार्थवत्त्वसंयमाद्
न्द्रियजयः ॥४७॥

grahaṇasvarūpāsmitānvayārthavattvasaṁyamād indriyajayaḥ
॥ 47 ॥

From samyama on the perceiving power, essential nature, self-identification, comingled nature, and purposefulness [of the senses], victory over the senses.

SUTRA 3:48

ततो मनोजवित्वं विकरणभावः प्रधानजयश्च ॥४८॥

tato manojavitvaṁ vikaraṇabhāvaḥ pradhānajayaśca ‖ 48 ‖

From that [victory over the senses], the ability to move at the speed of mind, the ability to comprehend without relying on sense organs, and the ability to enter and explore primordial prakriti.

SUTRA 3:49

सत्त्वपुरुषान्यताख्यातिमात्रस्य सर्वभावाधिष्ठातृत्वं सर्वज्ञातृत्वं च ॥४९॥

sattvapuruṣānyatākhyātimātrasya sarvabhāvādhiṣṭhātṛtvaṁ sarvajñātṛtvaṁ ca ‖ 49 ‖

One who has gained direct realization of the distinction between buddhi and purusha is capable of presiding over all samskaras and is endowed with omniscience.

SUTRA 3:50

तद्वैराग्यादपि दोषबीजक्षये कैवल्यम् ॥५०॥

tadvairāgyādapi doṣabījakṣaye kaivalyam ‖ 50 ‖

By renouncing attachment even to that attainment, destruction of the seed of impurities; that [leads to] kaivalya.

SUTRA 3:51

स्थान्युपनिमन्त्रणे सङ्गस्मयाकरणं पुनरनिष्टप्रसङ्गात्
॥५१॥

sthānyupanimantraṇe saṅgasmayākaraṇaṁ
punaraniṣṭaprasaṅgāt ॥ 51 ॥

When honored or rewarded by the extraordinary powers unique to siddhis, [a yogi] must avoid succumbing to attachment and pride lest unintended consequences ensue.

SUTRA 3:52

क्षणतत्क्रमयोः संयमाद्विवेकजं ज्ञानम् ॥५२॥

kṣaṇatatkramayoḥ saṁyamādvivekajaṁ jñānaṁ ॥ 52 ॥

From samyama on instants and their sequence, distinctive knowledge.

SUTRA 3:53

जातिलक्षणदेशैरन्यतानवच्छेदात् तुल्ययोस्ततः
प्रतिपत्तिः ॥५३॥

jātilakṣaṇadeśairanyatānavacchedāt tulyayostataḥ pratipattiḥ
॥ 53 ॥

[An experience is cognized on three grounds:] common denominator, distinctive denominator, and location. Due to the lack of interference by dissimilar [common denominator, distinctive denominator, or location, there arises the cognition of] sameness of the experience. [From samyama on the instant that exists between two] seemingly identical cognitions, [distinctive knowledge] concludes.

SUTRA 3:54

तारकं सर्वविषयं सर्वथाविषयम अक्रमं चेति
विवेकजज्ञानम् ।।५४।।

tārakaṁ sarvaviṣayaṁ sarvathāviṣayam akramaṁ ceti
vivekaja-jñānaṁ ॥ 54 ॥

Distinctive knowledge is liberating, has everything as its object, is not the object of anything, and is beyond sequence.

SUTRA 3:55

सत्त्वपुरुषयोः शुद्धिसाम्ये कैवल्यमिति ।।५५।।

sattvapuruṣayoḥ śuddhisāmye kaivalyamiti ॥ 55 ॥

When the purity of the mind becomes equal to the purity of purusha, absoluteness arises.

APPENDIX B

Detailed Translation (Word by Word)

SUTRA 3:1

देशबन्धश्चित्तस्य धारणा ॥१॥

deśabandhaścittasya dhāraṇā ॥ 1 ॥

Confining the mind to an [assigned] field is *dharana*, concentration.

deśa-bandha-cittasya

gen. sg. m. confining the mind to a field
deśa, field; place; domain; land; *bandha,* confinement; process of confining; *citta,* the mind

dhāraṇā *nom. sg. m.* concentration; holding

SUTRA 3:2

तत्र प्रत्ययैकतानता ध्यानम् ॥२॥

tatra pratyayaikatānatā dhyānam ॥ 2 ॥

There the continuous flow of a single cognition is *dhyana*, meditation.

tatra *loc. sg. n.* of *tat,* there; in that; in that defined space; in the space assigned for *dhāraṇā*, concentration

pratyaya-eka-tānatā

nom. sg. f. continuous flow of a single cognition; uninterrupted flow of single awareness; uninterrupted awareness of the object of concentration

pratyaya, cognition; objective awareness; thought construct; *eka,* single; one*; tānatā,* process of flowing, stretching, or weaving

dhyānam *nom. sg. n.* meditation

SUTRA 3:3

तदेवार्थमात्रनिर्भासं स्वरूपशून्यमिव समाधिः ॥३॥

tadevārthamātranirbhāsaṁ svarūpaśūnyamiva samādhiḥ ॥ 3 ॥

When that [object of dharana and dhyana] seems to have lost its defining features and is expressive only of its meaning, it is *samadhi.*

tat that, referring to the object of *dhāraṇā* and *dhyāna*

eva only

artha-mātra-nirbhāsaṁ

nom. sg. n. expressive of just its meaning

artha, meaning; object; content; *mātra,* just that, nothing else; *nirbhāsaṁ,* complete illumination; manifesting in every respect

svarūpa-śūnyam

nom. sg. n. devoid of one's defining feature; devoid of self-defining attributes; lacking an identifiable characteristic

svarūpa, defining feature; one's own form; essential nature; *śūnyam,* devoid; empty, non-existent

iva as if; like

samādhiḥ *nom. sg. m* completely established state of mind; complete mental absorption; the eighth limb of yoga; the state of highest yogic experience

SUTRA 3:4

त्रयमेकत्र संयमः ॥४॥

trayamekatra saṁyamaḥ ॥ 4 ॥

Together [these] three are called *samyama.*

trayam *nom. sg. n.* group of three [referring to *dhāraṇā*, *dhyāna*, and *samādhi*]

ekatra together; in one place and in one time

saṁyamaḥ *nom. sg. m.* literally, well-rounded discipline; a technical term that subsumes the practice and experience of *dhāraṇā*, *dhyāna*, and *samādhi*

SUTRA 3:5

तज्जयात्प्रज्ञालोकः ॥५॥

tajjayātprajñālokaḥ ॥ 5 ॥

From mastery over that [samyama], the light of intuitive wisdom [arises].

tat-jayāt *abl. sg. m.* from mastery over that; from victory over that

tat, that; following the rule of *samasa, tat* is a derivative of *tasya,* of that; *jaya,* mastery; victory; accomplishment

prajñā *nom. sg. f.* intuitive knowledge; revealed knowledge; inner illumination; the state of experience immediately preceded by *nirbīja samādhi*

ālokaḥ *nom. sg. m.* light; illumination

SUTRA 3:6

तस्य भूमिषु विनियोगः ॥६॥

tasya bhūmiṣu viniyogaḥ ॥ 6 ॥

In different contexts and circumstances, the application of that [samyama] differs.

tasya *gen. sg .m.* of *tat,* that

bhūmiṣu *loc. pl. f.* of *bhūmi,* context; circumstance; ground; domain

viniyogaḥ *n. sg. m.* application

SUTRA 3:7

त्रयमन्तरङ्गं पूर्वेभ्यः ॥७॥

trayamantaraṅgaṁ pūrvebhyaḥ ॥ 7 ॥

In relation to the preceding [limbs], the triad [of dharana, dhyana, and samadhi] is an internal limb.

trayam *nom. sg. n.* group of three [referring to the last three limbs]

antar internal

aṅgaṁ *nom. sg. n.* limb

pūrvebhyaḥ *abl. pl. n.* of *pūrva*, preceding

SUTRA 3:8

तदपि बहिरङ्गं निर्बीजस्य ॥८॥

tadapi bahiraṅgaṁ nirbījasya ॥ 8 ॥

Even that [samyama] is an external limb of nirbija samadhi.

tat that

api even

bahir-aṅgaṁ
nom. sg. n. external limb
bahiḥ, external; *aṅgaṁ*, limb

nirbījasya *gen. sg. m.* of *nirbija*, seedless; seedless *samādhi*; highest state of *samādhi*

SUTRA 3:9

व्युत्थाननिरोधसंस्कारयोरभिभवप्रादुर्भावौ
निरोधक्षणचित्तान्वयो निरोधपरिणामः ॥९॥

vyutthānanirodhasaṁskārayorabhibhavaprādurbhāvau
nirodhakṣaṇacittānvayo nirodhapariṇāmaḥ ॥ 9 ॥

The decline of samskaras that cause mental agitation and the rise of samskaras that impel the mind to confine itself to the object of concentration introduce a brief moment of time filled with the essence of self-restraint. Yoking the mind to that moment results in mastery over its roaming tendencies.

vyutthāna-nirodha-saṁskārayor

gen. du. m. of the subtle impressions of an agitated mind and of a well-contained mind

vyutthāna, state of agitation; rapidly outward-moving mind; restless mind; *nirodha,* confinement; well-controlled; cessation of mental operations; *saṁskāra,* subtle impressions; deep-rooted habits

abhibhava-prādurbhāvau

nom. d. m. decline and rise

abhibhava, decline; deceleration; diminution; *prādurbhāva,* rise; birth; manifestation; evolution

nirodha-kṣaṇa-citta-anvayaḥ

nom. sg. m. yoking of the mind with the segment of time filled with self- restraint

nirodha, confinement; well-controlled; cessation of mental operations; *kṣaṇa,* brief moment; instant; segment of time;

citta, mind, particularly the deeper dimension of mind; the storehouse of *saṁskāras*; *anvaya,* yoking; combining; placing properly

nirodha-pariṇāmaḥ

nom. sg. m. resultant confinement of mind

nirodha, confinement; well-controlled; cessation of mental operations; *pariṇāmaḥ,* result; transformation

SUTRA 3:10

तस्य प्रशान्तवाहिता संस्कारात् ॥१०॥

tasya praśāntavāhitā saṁskārāt ॥ 10 ॥

The peaceful flow of that [the result engendered by nirodha] is due to the samskaras.

tasya *gen. sg .m.* of *tat,* that; it refers to the result engendered by *nirodha,* as described in the previous sutra

praśānta-vāhitā

nom. sg. f. peaceful flow; the quality of carrying peacefulness

praśānta, peaceful; *vāhitā,* the quality of flowing; the process of flowing; the ability of the current to carry itself forward

saṁskārāt *abl. sg. m.* due to the subtle impression; from the subtle impression; because of the subtle impression

SUTRA 3:11

सर्वार्थतैकाग्रतयोः क्षयोदयौ चित्तस्य समाधिपरिणामः ॥११॥

sarvārthataikāgratayoḥ kṣayodayau cittasya samādhipariṇāmaḥ ॥ 11 ॥

The elimination of all cognitions and the rise of one-pointedness lead to the transformation characterized by a completely still, pristine state of mind.

sarvārthatā *nom. sg. f.* all cognitions; a state where the mind roams among various objects

ekāgratayoḥ *gen. du. f.* one-pointedness; pertaining to a state where the mind is focused on one object

kṣaya-udayau
nom. du. m. elimination and rise of
kṣaya, elimination; decline; destruction; *udaya,* rise; manifestation

cittasya *gen. sg. n.* of mind

samādhi-pariṇāmaḥ
nom. sg. m. transformation characterized by all-consuming focus
samādhi, all-consuming focus; completely still, pristine state of mind; *pariṇāmaḥ,* change; transformation; effect

SUTRA 3:12

ततः पुनः शान्तोदितौ तुल्यप्रत्ययौ
चित्तस्यैकाग्रतापरिणामः ॥१२॥

tataḥ punaḥ śāntoditau tulyapratyayau
cittasyaikāgratāpariṇāmaḥ ॥ 12 ॥

Thereafter, the cognitions that have passed and those that are arising become identical. This results in a transformation characterized by one-pointedness of mind.

tataḥ *abl. sg. n.* of *tat,* from that; due to that; from there

punaḥ again

śānta-uditau

nom. du. m. of *śāntodita,* that which has disappeared and that which is appearing; that which has slipped into the past and that which is emerging in the present

śānta, quiet; peaceful; that which has vanished; that which has become dormant; *udita,* that which has arisen; that which is in view; that which is in its manifest state

tulya-pratyayau

nom. du. m. of *tulyapratyaya,* two identical cognitions

tulya, identical; similar; *pratyaya,* cognition; distinct awareness

cittasya *gen. sg. n.* of mind

ekāgrata-pariṇāmaḥ

nom. sg. m. of *ekāgrataparіṇāma*, transformation emerging as one pointedness

ekāgrata, a state of one-pointedness; *pariṇāma,* transformation; change; evolution

SUTRA 3:13

एतेन भूतेन्द्रियेषु धर्मलक्षणावस्थापरिणामा व्याख्याताः ॥१३॥

etena bhūtendriyeṣu dharmalakṣaṇāvasthāpariṇāmā vyākhyātāḥ ॥ 13 ॥

With this [degree of mental concentration], transformation of defining qualities, symptoms, and conditions occurring in individuals [or elements] and in tools of cognition can be scrutinized and comprehended.

etena *ins. sg. n.* of *etat,* with this [referring to *ekāgrata pariṇāma*]

bhūta-indriyeṣu

loc. pl. m. of *bhūtendriya,* individuals and senses; individual beings or elements, such as earth, water, and so on, and tools of cognition, such as the mind and senses

bhūta, individual beings; entities; living or non-living matter; *indriya,* senses; instruments of perception; tools of comprehension

dharma-lakṣaṇa-avasthā-pariṇāmāḥ

nom. pl. m. of *dharmalakṣaṇāvasthāpariṇāma,* the transformation of defining qualities, symptoms, and conditions. [Note: due to grammatical structure, the last word, *pariṇāma,* is shared by the first three words; thus, *dharma, lakṣaṇ*a, and *avasthā* are read as *dharma pariṇāma, lakṣaṇa pariṇāma*, and *avasthā pariṇāma.*]

dharma pariṇāma, transformation of defining qualities; transformation of inner constituents; transformation of inherent and/or acquired properties; *lakṣaṇa pariṇāma,* transformation of symptoms, signs, or indications; *avasthā pariṇāma,* transformation of conditions, states, or stages; *pariṇāma,* transformation; change; result

vyākhyātāḥ *nom. pl. m.* scrutinized and comprehended; precisely and completely understood

SUTRA 3:14

शान्तोदिताव्यपदेश्यधर्मानुपाती धर्मी ॥१४॥

śāntoditāvyapadeśyadharmānupātī dharmī ॥ 14 ॥

The substratum conforms to [the changes occurring in its] past, present, and future attributes.

śānta-udita-avyapadeśya-dharma-ānupātī

nom. sg. m. that which conforms to past, present, and future attributes

śānta, past; quiet; dormant; *udita,* present; arisen; that which has come into view; currently active; *avyapadeśya,* future; *dharma,* attribute; defining characteristic; property without which the substratum cannot be what it is; *ānupātī,* that which conforms to; proportionate

dharmi *nom. sg. m.* substratum; embodiment of attributes; the locus of attributes

SUTRA 3:15

क्रमान्यत्वं परिणामान्यत्वे हेतुः ॥१५॥

kramānyatvam pariṇāmānyatve hetuḥ ॥ 15 ॥

Change in the sequence alters the result.

krama-anyatvam
nom. sg. n. difference in sequence
krama, sequence; *anyatvam,* difference; of different nature

pariṇāma-anyatve
loc. sg. n. difference in result
pariṇāma, result; transformation; change; consequence; *anyatvam,* difference; otherness

hetuḥ *nom. sg. m.* cause

SUTRA 3:16

परिणामत्रयसंयमाद् अतीतानागतज्ञानम् ॥१६॥

pariṇāmatrayasaṁyamād atītānāgatajñānam ॥ 16 ॥

From samyama on the threefold transformation, knowledge of the past and future.

pariṇāma-traya-saṁyamāt

abl. sg. m. from *saṁyama* on the threefold transformation

pariṇāma, transformation; change; effect; *traya,* group of three; triad; *saṁyama,* a technical term for *dhāraṇā, dhyāna,* and *samādhi*

atīta-anāgata-jñānam

nom. sg. n. knowledge of past and future

atīta, past; that which has expired; ancient; *anāgata,* future; that which has not yet commenced; *jñānam,* knowledge

SUTRA 3:17

शब्दार्थप्रत्ययानामितरेतराध्यासात्
सङ्करस्तत्प्रविभागसंयमात्सर्वभूतरुतज्ञानम् ॥१७॥

śabdārthapratyayānāmitaretarādhyāsāt
saṅkarastatpravibhāgasaṁyamātsarvabhūtarutajñānam ॥ 17 ॥

The superimposition of word, meaning, and cognition engenders a fully conflated perception of them. From samyama on their distinct parts, comprehension of what creatures are saying.

śabda-artha-pratyayānām

gen. pl. m. of word, meaning, and cognition

śabda, word; *artha,* meaning; *pratyaya,* cognition

itaretara one or the other

adhyāsāt *abl. sg. m.* from superimposition

saṅkaraḥ *nom. sg. m.* fully conflated; completely mingled

tat-pravibhāga-saṁyamāt

abl. sg. m. from *saṁyama* on their distinct parts

tat, their; *pravibhāga,* distinct parts; *saṁyamāt,* from *saṁyama*

sarva-bhūta-ruta-jñānam

nom. sg. n. the understanding of the sounds [produced by] all creatures

sarva, all; *bhūta,* creatures; *ruta,* sound; *jñānam,* understanding; knowledge

SUTRA 3:18

संस्कारसाक्षात्करणात्पूर्वजातिज्ञानम् ॥१८॥

saṁskārasākṣātkaraṇātpūrvajātijñānam ॥ 18 ॥

From direct realization of samskaras, knowledge of previous births.

saṁskāra-sākṣātkaraṇāt

abl. sg. n. from direct realization of *saṁskāras*

saṁskāra, karmic impressions; deep-rooted impressions of past actions; outstanding memories deposited in the mind; *sākṣātkaraṇa,* direct realization; experiencing directly, as opposed to knowing through inference or testimony

pūrva-jāti-jñānam

nom. sg. n. knowledge of birth[s]

pūrva, previous; *jāti,* birth; species; *jñānam,* knowledge; experience; understanding

SUTRA 3:19

प्रत्ययस्य परचित्तज्ञानम् ।।१९।।

pratyayasya paracittajñānam ॥ 19 ॥

Understanding another person's cognition leads to an understanding of that person's mind.

pratyayasya

gen. sg. m. of cognition, thought, feeling

para-citta-jñānam

nom. sg. n. knowledge of the mind of others
para, other; *citta,* mind; *jñānam,* knowledge; understanding; comprehension

SUTRA 3:20

न च तत्सालम्बनं तस्याविषयीभूतत्वात् ।।२०।।

na ca tatsālambanaṁ tasyāviṣayībhūtatvāt ॥ 20 ॥

That knowledge, however, does not include the object of cognition, because that [object] is not in the domain of samyama.

na not

ca and; furthermore; however; in addition to

tat *nom. sg. n.* that

sālambanaṁ

nom. sg. n. accompanied by an object; accompanied by that on which it rests; accompanied by that in which it rests; accompanied by the locus *tasya* *gen. sg. n.* of that

aviṣayībhūtatvāt

abl. sg. n. because of not being in the domain [of *saṁyama*]; because of lack of having the quality of being an object; because of not being an object; because of being outside the domain of the object

SUTRA 3:21

कायरूपसंयमात्तद्ग्राह्यशक्तिस्तम्भे
चक्षुःप्रकाशासम्प्रयोगेऽन्तर्धानम् ॥२१॥

kāyarūpasaṁyamāttadgrāhyaśaktistambhe
cakṣuḥprakāśāsaṁprayoge'ntardhānam ॥ 21 ॥

From samyama on the form of the body, immobilization of its power to be perceived. [In addition to accomplishing that,] upon blocking the light of the eyes, the experience of the disappearance [of the yogi's body].

kaya-rūpa-saṁyamāt

gen. sg. n. from *saṁyama* on the form of the body

kaya, body; *rūpa,* form; *saṁyama,* triad of *dhāraṇā*, *dhyāna*, and *samādhi*

tat here *tat* is used in place of *tasya*, *gen. sg. n.* of *tat*. Thus, in this context, *tat* means "its; of that; pertaining to that."

grāhya-śakti-stambhe

loc. sg. n. upon immobilization of the power to be perceived

grāhya, perceivable; *śakti,* power; ability; capacity; *stambha,* immobilization

cakṣuḥ-prakāśa-asaṁprayoge

loc. sg. m. upon blocking the light of the eyes; precise and complete disconnection of the light of the eyes

cakṣuḥ, eyes; *prakāśa,* light; *asaṁprayoga,* disconnection; disunion; complete and precise disunion; the process of separating completely and precisely

antardhānam

nom. sg. n. disappearance

SUTRA 3:22

सोपक्रमं निरुपक्रमं च कर्म
तत्संयमादपरान्तज्ञानमरिष्टेभ्यो वा ॥२२॥

sopakramaṁ nirupakramaṁ ca karma
tatsaṁyamādaparāntajñānamariṣṭebhyo vā ॥ 22 ॥

Karmas are of two kinds: accompanied by consequential factors and lacking consequential factors. From samyama on them, or from omens, knowledge regarding the latter part [of life].

sa-upakramaṁ

nom. sg. n. accompanied by consequential factors; state or condition where factors leading to the completion of a process are arranged in order; sequence of cause and effect actively moving toward fruition

sa, with; *upakrama,* sequence of cause and effect accompanied by supporting factors; orderly execution of action

nir-upakramaṁ

nom. sg. n. without consequential factors; sequence of cause and effect lacking supporting factors

nir, without; devoid of; *upakrama,* sequence of cause and effect accompanied by supporting factors; orderly execution of action

ca and

karma *nom. sg. n.* action

tat-saṁyamād

abl. sg. m. from *saṁyama* on them; from *saṁyama* on *sopakrama* and *nirupakrama* karmas

tat, originally *tayoḥ*, *gen. du.* of *tat,* that; *saṁyama,* triad of *dhāraṇā*, *dhyāna*, and *samādhi*

apara-anta-jñānam

nom. sg. n. knowledge pertaining to the end of the latter part

apara, latter; lower; remaining; *anta,* end; *jñānam,* knowledge

ariṣṭebhyaḥ *abl. pl. n.* from omens

vā or

SUTRA 3:23

मैत्र्यादिषु बलानि ।।२३।।

maitryādiṣu balāni ॥ 23 ॥

[From samyama] on friendliness and so on, capacities.

maitrī-ādiṣu *loc. pl. m.* on friendliness and so on
maitrī, friendliness; the essential property of friendly relationships; the essence of friendship; *ādiṣu,* on many others

balāni *nom. pl. n.* capacities

SUTRA 3:24

बलेषु हस्तिबलादीनि ।।२४।।

baleṣu hastibalādīni ॥ 24 ॥

[From samyama] on powers, the powers of an elephant, and so on.

baleṣu *loc. pl. n.* on powers; on strengths; on capacities

hasti-bala-ādīni
loc. pl n. powers of an elephant, and so on
hasti, elephant; *bala,* power; strength; capacity; *ādīni,* and; and so on; also

SUTRA 3:25

प्रवृत्त्यालोकन्यासात् सूक्ष्मव्यवहितविप्रकृष्टज्ञानम् ॥२५॥

pravṛttyālokanyāsāt sūkṣmavyavahitaviprakṛṣṭajñānam ॥ 25 ॥

By directing the light born of extrasensory cognition, knowledge of subtle, obstructed, and distant objects.

pravṛtti-āloka-nyāsāt

abl. sg. m. by directing the light of extrasensory cognition; from application of the light of extrasensory cognition

pravṛtti, extrasensory cognition; extraordinary cognition; cognition of the power that enables the senses to perceive; perceiving power of the perceiver; *āloka,* light; illumination; *nyāsa,* the process of directing, focusing, or anchoring

sūkṣma-vyavahita-viprakṛṣṭa-jñānam

nom. sg. n. knowledge of subtle, obstructed, and distant; gaining the knowledge of an object too subtle to be perceived by the senses, or an object blocked by other objects, or an object beyond the reach of the senses

sūkṣma, subtle, such as an atom; *vyavahita,* an object obstructed by another object impenetrable by the senses; *viprakṛṣṭa,* an object too distant and thus beyond the reach of the senses; *jñāna,* knowledge

SUTRA 3:26

भुवनज्ञानं सूर्ये संयमात् ।।२६।।

bhuvanajñānaṁ sūrye saṁyamāt ॥ 26 ॥

From samyama on the sun, knowledge of the spheres of existence.

bhuvana-jñānaṁ

nom. sg. n. knowledge of the spheres of existence; knowledge of the tiers of existence

bhuvana, that which is in existence; *jñānaṁ,* knowledge

sūrye *loc. sg. m.* on the sun; in the sun; upon the sun

saṁyamāt *abl. sg. m.* from *saṁyama*

SUTRA 3:27

चन्द्रे ताराव्यूहज्ञानम् ।।२७।।

candre tārāvyūhajñānam ॥ 27 ॥

[From samyama] on the moon, knowledge pertaining to the arrangement of the stars.

candre *loc. sg. m.* on the moon

tārā-vyūha-jñānam

nom. sg. n. knowledge of the arrangement of stars; knowledge pertaining to the order in which stars are arranged in space

tārā, star; shining entity; the entity which, due to its intrinsic luminosity, guides us to the other shore of life; self-luminous entity that grants moksha; *vyūha,* an organized formation; proper arrangement of things or people; *jñāna,* knowledge

SUTRA 3:28

ध्रुवे तद्गतिज्ञानम् ॥२८॥

dhruve tadgatijñānam ॥ 28 ॥

[From samyama] on the pole star, knowledge of their [the stars'] movement.

dhruve *loc. sg. m.* on the pole star; that which is unmoving; that which is immutable; the principle of constancy; unchanging, unmoving, undecaying state of reality

tat-gati-jñānam
nom. sg. n. knowledge pertaining to their movement, speed, status, or condition
tat derived from *tesham,* their; *gati,* movement; speed; status; condition; *jñāna,* knowledge

SUTRA 3:29

नाभिचक्रे कायव्यूहज्ञानम् ॥२९॥

nābhicakre kāyavyūhajñānam ॥ 29 ॥

[From samyama] on the navel plexus, knowledge of the systems of the body.

nābhicakre *loc. sg. n.* on the navel plexus; on the wheel of the navel; on the navel center; on the abdominal cavity, with the navel at its center
nābhi, navel; *chakra,* wheel; plexus; center

kāya-vyūha-jñānam

nom. sg. n. knowledge of the systems of the body; knowledge pertaining to the complex structure of bodily systems

kāya, body; *vyūha,* arrangement; formation; system; *jñāna,* knowledge

SUTRA 3:30

कण्ठकूपे क्षुत्पिपासानिवृत्तिः ॥३०॥

kaṇṭhakūpe kṣutpipāsānivṛttiḥ ॥ 30 ॥

[From samyama] **on the well of the throat, relief from hunger and thirst.**

kaṇṭha-kūpe *loc. sg. m.* on the well of the throat

kaṇṭha, throat; *kūpa,* well; pit

kṣut-pipāsā-nivṛttiḥ

nom. sg. f. relief from hunger and thirst; freedom from hunger and thirst

kṣut, hunger; *pipāsā,* thirst; *nivṛtti,* relief; freedom

SUTRA 3:31

कूर्मनाड्यां स्थैर्यम् ॥३१॥

kūrmanāḍyāṁ sthairyam ॥ 31 ॥

[From samyama] **on the kurma nadi, stability.**

kūrma-nāḍyāṁ

loc. sg. f. on the kurma nadi

kūrma, tortoise; name of one of the fourteen major *nāḍis; nāḍi,* pranic current; energy channel

sthairyam *nom. sg. n.* stability; the state of being stable

SUTRA 3:32

मूर्धज्योतिषि सिद्धदर्शनम् ॥३२॥

mūrdhajyotiṣi siddhadarśanam ॥ 32 ॥

[From samyama] **on the light of the crown, a vision of the siddhas.**

murdha-jyotiṣi

loc. sg. n. on the light of *mūrdha*

mūrdha, crown; *jyotiṣ,* light

siddha-darśanam

nom. sg. n. vision of *siddha*

siddha, an accomplished being; a yogi embodying extraordinary powers; an accomplished yogi who continues living after death; a yogi whose self-identity remains intact after death; a yogi who maintains his awareness without having a body as its locus; *darśana,* a vision; ability to see and comprehend

SUTRA 3:33

प्रातिभाद्वा सर्वम् ॥३३॥

prātibhādvā sarvam ॥ 33 ॥

Or from intuitive knowledge, everything is known.

prātibhāt *abl. sg. n.* from that which is rooted in intuition

vā or

sarvam *nom. sg. n.* all; everything

SUTRA 3:34

हृदये चित्तसंवित् ॥३४॥

hṛdaye cittasaṁvit ॥ 34 ॥

[From samyama] **on the heart, the knowing power of chitta.**

hṛdaye *loc. sg. n.* on the heart; on the space in the city of *brahman*; on the space of consciousness in the city of *brahman*; on the lotus in the space of consciousness; on the lotus shrine in the space of consciousness

citta-saṁvit *nom. sg. n.* the knowing power of *citta*, the locus of consciousness vested with the power of understanding the mind's complete range; the power that enables the mind to know itself

citta, all faculties of the mind, including that which serves as the substratum for all *saṁskāras*; *saṁvit,* the knowing power that knows everything there [in the mind]; the locus of self-understanding

SUTRA 3:35

सत्त्वपुरुषयोरत्यन्तासंकीर्णयोः प्रत्ययाविशेषो भोगः परार्थत्वात्स्वार्थसंयमात्पुरुषज्ञानम् ॥३५॥

sattvapuruṣayoratyantāsaṁkīrṇayoḥ pratyayāviśeṣo bhogaḥ parārthatvātsvārthasaṁyamātpuruṣajñānam ॥ 35 ॥

The mind and consciousness are so intensely fused that there is no difference between their cognitions. [This conflated cognition is] experience. An aspect of experience is smeared with the sense of being an object. [Withdrawing the mind from that and] practicing samyama on the other, which is accompanied by the sense of I-am-ness, engenders the knowledge of pure consciousness.

sattva-puruṣayoḥ

gen. du. m. of mind and consciousness

sattva, mind; the essence of mind; self-luminous mind; mind whose purity is identical to that of pure consciousness; *puruṣa,* pure consciousness

atyanta-asaṁkīrṇayoḥ

gen. du. m. of two totally fused entities

atyanta, intensely; totally; completely; *asaṁkīrṇa,* lack of difference between individual parts

pratyaya-aviśeṣaḥ

nom. sg. m. lack of difference between cognitions

pratyaya, cognition; *aviśeṣa,* lacking difference; devoid of distinct characteristics

bhogaḥ *nom. sg. m.* experience

parārthatvāt

abl. sg. n. owing to fulfilling the purpose of someone or something other than itself; the object that explicitly or implicitly serves the purpose of the subject; an aspect of experience accompanied by, dominated by, or smeared with the sense of being an object

svārtha-saṁyamāt

abl. sg. m. from *saṁyama* on self-awareness

svārtha, self-awareness; the content of a cognition referring to oneself; *saṁyama,* the trio of *dhāraṇā*, *dhyāna*, and *samādhi*

puruṣa-jñānam

gen. sg. n. knowledge pertaining to pure consciousness

puruṣa, pure consciousness; core being; *jñāna*, knowledge

SUTRA 3:36

ततः प्रातिभश्रावणवेदनादर्शास्वादवार्ता जायन्ते ।।३६।।

tataḥ prātibhaśrāvaṇavedanādarśāsvādavārtā jāyante ॥ 36 ॥

From that arises [the power of] intuitive hearing, touching, seeing, tasting, and smelling.

tataḥ *abl. sg. n.* from that

prātibha-śrāvaṇa-vedanā-ādarśā-āsvāda-vārtāḥ

nom. pl. f. intuitive hearing, touching, seeing, tasting, and smelling

prātibha, associated with or derived from intuition; *śrāvaṇa,* hearing; *vedanā,* touching; *ādarśā,* seeing; *āsvāda,* tasting; *vārtā,* smelling

jāyante	verb *jani,* to be born; *present tense, 3rd person pl.,* arise; are born; are induced; come forward

SUTRA 3:37

ते समाधावुपसर्गा व्युत्थाने सिद्धयः ।।३७।।

te samādhāvupasargā vyutthāne siddhayaḥ ॥ 37 ॥

For one with an outwardly running mind, these are extraordinary accomplishments, but for one aspiring to samadhi, they are obstacles.

te	*nom. pl. m.* of *tat,* they; these
samādhau	*loc. sg. m.* in *samādhi*
upasargāḥ	*nom. pl. m.* obstacles
vyutthāne	*loc. sg. m.* in an outwardly running mind; in regard to one with an unsettled mind; in relation to one lacking a concentrated mind
siddhayaḥ	*nom. pl. m.* accomplishments; extraordinary yogic powers

SUTRA 3:38

बन्धकारणशैथिल्यात्प्रचारसंवेदनाच् च चित्तस्य परशरीरावेशः ।।३८।।

bandhakāraṇaśaithilyātpracārasaṁvedanāc ca cittasya paraśarīrāveśaḥ ॥ 38 ॥

From the loosening of the cause of bondage and from sensitivity to pranic flow, the mind is able to enter and infuse another body.

bandha-kāraṇa-śaithilyāt

abl. sg. *n.* from the loosening of the cause of bondage

bandha, bondage; *kāraṇa,* cause; *śaithilya,* the state of loosening

pracāra-saṁvedanāt

abl. sg. n. from sensitivity to pranic flow

pracāra, prana; pranic force; life force; *saṁvedana,* sensitivity; feeling

ca and

cittasya *gen. sg. n.* of the mind

para-śarīra-āveśaḥ

nom. sg. m. entry into and infusion of another body

para, another; different; *śarīra,* body; *āveśa,* entry and infusion; taking possession; process and phenomenon of occupying

SUTRA 3:39

उदानजयाज्जलपङ्ककण्टकादिष्वसङ्ग उत्क्रान्तिश्च ॥३९॥

udānajayājjalapaṅkakaṇṭakādiṣvasaṅga utkrāntiśca ॥ 39 ॥

From the conquest of udana, [a yogi is able to remain] unaffected by water, mud, thorns, and so on, and leave the body while transcending death.

udānajayāt

abl. sg. m. from victory over *udāna*

udāna, prana shakti that moves upward;
jaya, the process or event of conquering

jala-paṅka-kaṇṭaka-ādiṣu

loc. pl. m. in regard to water, mud, thorns, and so on

jala, water; *paṅka,* mud; *kaṇṭaka,* thorn;
ādi, and so on

asaṅgaḥ *nom. sg. m.* state of unaffectedness; non-attachment; state of being unsmeared

utkrāntiḥ *nom. sg. m.* transitioning by rising above body consciousness; leaving the body consciously through the tenth gate, the *sahasrāra cakra*

ca and

SUTRA 3:40

समानजयाज्ज्वलनम् ॥४०॥

samānajayājjvalanam ॥ 40 ॥

From the conquest of samana, [a yogi is able to] ignite.

samāna-jayāt

abl. sg. m. from the conquest of *samāna*

samāna, prana shakti that brings about and maintains a harmonious balance;
jaya, the process or event of conquering

jvalanam *nom. sg. n.* ignition; lighting the fire

SUTRA 3:41

श्रोत्राकाशयोः सम्बन्धसंयमाद्दिव्यं श्रोत्रम् ॥४१॥

śrotrākāśayoḥ sambandhasaṁyamāddivyaṁ śrotram ॥ 41 ॥

From samyama on the relationship between the sense of hearing and space, the extraordinary power of hearing.

śrotra-ākāśayoḥ

gen. du. n. of the sense of hearing and space
śrotra, sense of hearing; organ of hearing; ear; *ākāśa,* space

sambandha-saṁyamāt

abl. sg. m. from *saṁyama* on the relationship
sambandha, relationship; *saṁyama,* triad of *dhāraṇā*, *dhyāna*, and *samādhi*

divyaṁ *nom. sg. n.* derived from or associated with the divine; celestial; extraordinary; not physical

śrotram *nom. sg. n.* sense of hearing; organ of hearing; ear

SUTRA 3:42

कायाकाशयोः सम्बन्धसंयमात्
लघुतूलसमापत्तेश्चाकाशगमनम् ॥४२॥

kāyākāśayoḥ sambandhasaṁyamāt
laghutūlasamāpatteścākāśagamanam ॥ 42 ॥

From samyama on the relationship between the body and space or from mental absorption in light cotton fiber, [the power of] moving through space.

kāya-ākāśayoḥ
gen. du. n. of body and space
kāya; body; *ākāśa,* space

sambandha-saṁyamāt
abl. sg. n. from *saṁyama* on the relationship
sambandha, relationship; *saṁyama;* the triad of *dhāraṇā, dhyāna,* and *samādhi*

laghu-tūla-samāpatteḥ
abl. sg. f. from mental absorption in light cotton fiber
laghu, light; *tūla,* cotton; cotton fiber; *samāpatti,* mental absorption

ca and

ākāśa-gamanam
nom. sg. n. moving through space; walking in space
ākāśa, space; *gamana,* the process of moving

SUTRA 3:43

बहिरकल्पिता वृत्तिर्महाविदेहा ततः प्रकाशावरणक्षयः ॥४३॥

bahirakalpitā vṛttirmahāvidehā tataḥ prakāśāvaraṇakṣayaḥ ॥ 43 ॥

Non-imaginary [fully palpable] cognition outside [the body] is *mahavideha*. From that [comes] the destruction of the veil that hides the light.

bahiḥ outside; outside the body

akalpitā — *nom. sg. f.* unimagined; not imaginary; palpable

vṛttiḥ — *nom. sg. f.* cognition; mental experience

mahāvidehā — *nom. sg. f.* the great experience that transcends the notion of being in the body; rising above the experience of embodiment

mahā, great; *videhā,* beyond the body

tataḥ — *abl. sg. n.* of *tat,* that

prakāśa-āvaraṇa-kṣayaḥ

nom. sg. m. the destruction of the veil that hides the light

prakāśa, light; *āvaraṇa,* veil; *kṣayaḥ,* destruction

SUTRA 3:44

स्थूलस्वरूपसूक्ष्मान्वयार्थवत्त्वसंयमाद्भूतजयः ॥४४॥

sthūlasvarūpasūkṣmānvayārthavattvasaṁyamādbhūtajayaḥ ॥ 44 ॥

From samyama on the tangible form, essential nature, and subtle form [of the elements, as well as on their comingled nature and their purposefulness], victory over the elements.

sthūla-svarūpa-sūkṣmānvayārthavattva-saṁyamād

abl. sg. m. from *saṁyama* on the tangible form, essential nature, and subtle form [of the elements, their comingled nature, and their purposefulness]

sthūla, tangible; physical; concrete; gross; *svarūpa,* essential nature; defining attribute; one's own form; *sūkṣma,* subtle; non-physical counterpart of the tangible form of elements; sheer that-ness; purely abstract source of elements; *anvaya,* the capacity or condition of pervading each constituent of elements; attributes present in all elements; *arthavattva,* purposefulness; quality of serving a purpose; *saṁyama,* the triad of *dhāraṇā, dhyāna,* and *samādhi*

bhūta-jayaḥ *nom. sg. m.* victory over elements
bhūta, elements; constituents of the material world: earth, water, fire, air, and space; *jaya,* victory; conquest

SUTRA 3:45

ततोऽणिमादिप्रादुर्भावः कायसम्पत्तद्धर्मानभिघातश्च ॥४५॥

tato'ṇimādiprādurbhāvaḥ
kāyasampattaddharmānabhighātaśca ॥ 45 ॥

From that [victory over the elements] arise [siddhis of] anima, and so on, the wealth of bodily perfection, and [the siddhi of] being unhampered by the properties and functions of the elements.

tataḥ *abl. sg. n.* of *tat,* from that

aṇimā-ādi-prādurbhāvaḥ
nom. sg. m. the rise of *aṇimā,* and so on
aṇimā, state of matter characterized by its atomic size; essence of an atom; quality of an atom; as small as an atom; *ādi,* and so on; *prādurbhāva,* the rise of; manifestation of; evolution of; birth of

kāya-sampat *nom. sg. n.* wealth of bodily perfection; bodily wealth

kāya, body; *sampat;* wealth

tat-dharma-anabhighātaḥ

nom. sg. m. not being hampered by the natural properties and functions of the elements

tat, that; *dharma,* quality; property; attribute; *anabhighāta,* the process or event of not being hampered; unscathed; unharmed

ca and

SUTRA 3:46

रूपलावण्यबलवज्रसंहननत्वानि कायसम्पत् ॥४६॥

rūpalāvaṇyabalavajrasaṁhananatvāni kāyasampat ॥ 46 ॥

Beauty, charm, vitality, and healing power are bodily wealth.

rūpa-lāvaṇya-bala-vajrasaṁhananatvāni

nom. pl. n. beauty, charm, vitality, and healing power

rūpa, beauty; form with distinctive features; the element of beauty that makes the body stand out; *lāvaṇya,* charm; attractiveness; the quality of enticement; *bala,* vitality; the qualities of strength, stamina, endurance, and agility; *vajrasaṁhananatva,* healing power; the quality of being unhampered and unaffected by foreign elements; unbreakable, impregnable, and impenetrable; adamantine

kāya-sampat *nom. sg. n.* wealth of bodily perfection; bodily wealth

kāya, body; *sampat;* wealth

SUTRA 3:47

ग्रहणस्वरूपास्मितान्वयार्थवत्त्वसंयमाद्
िन्द्रियजयः ॥४७॥

grahaṇasvarūpāsmitānvayārthavattvasaṁyamād indriyajayaḥ ॥ 47 ॥

From samyama on the perceiving power, essential nature, self-identification, comingled nature, and purposefulness [of the senses], victory over the senses.

grahaṇa-svarūpa-asmita-anvaya-arthavattva-saṁyamāt

abl. sg. m. from *saṁyama* on perceiving power, essential nature, self-identification, comingled nature, and purposefulness

grahaṇa, perceiving power; the power that enables the senses to perceive; process of perceiving; *svarūpa,* essential nature; defining attribute; one's own form; *asmitā,* self-identification; sense of I-amness; the power that enables the senses to identify with the objects they contact and become immersed in them; *anvaya,* the capacity or condition of pervading each other; attributes present in all the senses; *arthavattva,* purposefulness; quality of serving a purpose; *saṁyama,* the triad of *dhāraṇā*, *dhyāna*, and *samādhi*

indriya-jayaḥ

nom. sg. m. victory over the senses; mastery of the senses; complete control over the functions of the senses

indriya; sense; *jaya,* victory; mastery

SUTRA 3:48

ततो मनोजवित्वं विकरणभावः प्रधानजयश्च ॥४८॥

tato manojavitvaṁ vikaraṇabhāvaḥ pradhānajayaśca ॥ 48 ॥

From that [victory over the senses], the ability to move at the speed of mind, the ability to comprehend without relying on sense organs, and the ability to enter and explore primordial prakriti.

tataḥ *abl. sg. n.* from that

manojavitvaṁ

nom. sg. n. ability to move at the speed of mind

vikaraṇa-bhāvaḥ

nom. sg. m. ability to comprehend without relying on the sense organs

vikaraṇa, without relying on sense organs; beyond the senses; bereft of the senses; splitting into pieces; decentralization; process of scattering; *bhava,* the state; the condition

pradhāna-jayaḥ

nom. sg. m. ability to enter and explore primordial *prakṛti*; victory over primordial *prakṛti*; ability to identify and acquire all that exists in primordial *prakṛti*

pradhāna, prakṛti; primordial nature; the subtlest and absolute cause of all that exists; *jaya,* mastery; victory; ability to acquire and command

ca and

SUTRA 3:49

सत्त्वपुरुषान्यताख्यातिमात्रस्य सर्वभावाधिष्ठातृत्वं सर्वज्ञातृत्वं च ॥४९॥

sattvapuruṣānyatākhyātimātrasya sarvabhāvādhiṣṭhātṛtvaṁ sarvajñātṛtvaṁ ca ॥ 49 ॥

One who has gained direct realization of the distinction between buddhi and purusha is capable of presiding over all samskaras and is endowed with omniscience.

sattva-puruṣa-anyatā-khyati-mātrasya

gen. sg. m. to one who has gained direct realization of the distinction between *buddhi* and *puruṣa*

sattva, essence; pure and pristine buddhi; highly purified faculty of discernment; the very first evolute of *prakṛti*; the most subtle among all evolutes of manifest *prakṛti*; *puruṣa,* pure consciousness; pure awareness; sheer power of intelligence; *citi shakti*; *anyatā,* the state of being different; distinctive state; distinction; *khyāti,* realization; direct experience; *mātra,* only

sarva-bhāva-adhiṣṭhātṛtvaṁ

nom. sg. n. capable of presiding over all *saṁskāras*

sarva, all; *bhāva,* subtle impression; *saṁskāra*; karmic impression; abstract of actions; *adhiṣṭhātṛtva,* the capacity to preside over; state or quality to preside over, control, and rule

sarvajñātṛtvaṁ

nom. sg. n. the all-knowing power or quality

ca and

SUTRA 3:50

तद्वैराग्यादपि दोषबीजक्षये कैवल्यम् ॥५०॥

tadvairāgyādapi doṣabījakṣaye kaivalyam ॥ 50 ॥

By renouncing attachment even to that attainment, destruction of the seed of impurities; that [leads to] kaivalya.

tat-vairāgyāt *abl. sg. n.* by renouncing attachment to that

tat, that; following the rule of *samasa, tat* stands for *tasya*, of that; *vairāgya,* renouncing attachment; transcendence of attachment; non-attachment

api of; even; also

doṣa-bīja-kṣaye

loc. sg. m. at the destruction of the seed of impurities

doṣa, impurity; defect; *bīja,* seed; *kṣaya,* destruction *kaivalyam* *nom. sg. n.* absoluteness; the essence of the non-dual state; the state indicated by absolute independence

SUTRA 3:51

स्थान्युपनिमन्त्रणे सङ्गस्मयाकरणं पुनरनिष्टप्रसङ्गात् ॥५१॥

sthānyupanimantraṇe saṅgasmayākaraṇaṁ punaraniṣṭaprasaṅgāt ॥ 51 ॥

When honored or rewarded by the extraordinary powers unique to siddhis, [a yogi] must avoid succumbing to attachment and pride lest unintended consequences ensue.

sthāni-upanimantraṇe
loc. sg. n. when honored or rewarded by the extraordinary powers associated with siddhis
sthāni, one endowed with power to command; presiding force; office holder; *upanimantraṇa,* the process or event of inviting, greeting, and rewarding

saṅga-smaya-akaraṇaṁ
nom sg. n. the process of avoiding attachment and pride
saṅga, attachment; *smaya,* pride; ego; *akaraṇa,* not doing; avoiding doing; refraining from doing

punaḥ again

aniṣṭa-prasaṅgāt

abl. sg. n. because of the possibility of unintended consequence[s]

aniṣṭa, unintended; undesirable; *prasaṅga,* context; scenario; consequence

SUTRA 3:52

क्षणतत्क्रमयोः संयमाद्विवेकजं ज्ञानम् ।।५२।।

kṣaṇatatkramayoḥ saṁyamādvivekajaṁ jñānaṁ ॥ 52 ॥

From samyama on instants and their sequence, distinctive knowledge.

kṣaṇa-tat-kramayoḥ

gen. sg. m. of instants and their sequence

kṣaṇa, instant[s]; extremely brief measure of time; the thinnest slice of time; *tat,* that; their; *krama,* sequence; placement

saṁyamāt *abl. sg. m.* from *saṁyama*

vivekajaṁ *nom. sg. n.* distinctive; born of distinction; rising out of distinction

jñānaṁ *nom. sg. n.* knowledge

SUTRA 3:53

जातिलक्षणदेशैरन्यतानवच्छेदात् तुल्ययोस्ततः प्रतिपत्तिः ।।५३।।

jātilakṣaṇadeśairanyatānavacchedāt tulyayostataḥ pratipattiḥ ॥ 53 ॥

[An experience is cognized on three grounds:] common denominator, distinctive denominator, and location. Due to the lack of interference by dissimilar [common denominator, distinctive denominator, or location, there arises the cognition of] sameness of the experience. [From samyama on the instant that exists between two] seemingly identical cognitions, [distinctive knowledge] concludes.

jāti-lakṣaṇa-deśaiḥ

ins. pl. n. through common denominator, distinctive denominator, and location

jāti, common denominator; a quality or characteristic common to all members of a group; *lakṣaṇa,* distinctive denominator; a unique quality or characteristic of an individual member that distinguishes it from other members of the group; *deśa,* location; space

anyatā-anavacchedāt

abl. sg. m. due to lack of interference by dissimilar

anyatā, otherness; dissimilarity; *anavaccheda,* not penetrated by; not interfered by

tulyayoḥ *loc. du. n.* in or within two identicals

tataḥ *abl. sg. n.* from that

pratipattiḥ *nom. sg. f.* conclusion

SUTRA 3:54

तारकं सर्वविषयं सर्वथाविषयम अक्रमं चेति
विवेकजज्ञानम् ।।५४।।

tārakaṁ sarvaviṣayaṁ sarvathāviṣayam akramaṁ ceti
vivekaja-jñānaṁ ॥ 54 ॥

Distinctive knowledge is liberating, has everything as its object, is not the object of anything, and is beyond sequence.

tārakaṁ — *nom. sg. n.* liberating; that which enables one to cross the streams of cognitions and objects associated with them; that which infuses *citta samvit* with the ability to transcend the world of cognitions

sarvaviṣayaṁ — *nom. sg. n.* having everything as its object; that which subsumes the entire realm of objective awareness

sarvathāviṣayam — *nom. sg. n.* that which is not the object of anything; that which transcends the entire realm of objective awareness

akramaṁ — *nom. sg. n.* that which is beyond sequence; that which transcends the linearity of time consisting of instants

ca — and

iti — thus

vivekaja-jñānaṁ

nom. sg. n. born of distinctive knowledge; distinctive knowledge arising from distinguishing one instant from another

SUTRA 3:55

सत्त्वपुरुषयोः शुद्धिसाम्ये कैवल्यमिति ॥५५॥

sattvapuruṣayoḥ śuddhisāmye kaivalyamiti ॥55॥

When the purity of the mind becomes equal to the purity of purusha, absoluteness arises.

sattva-puruṣayoḥ

gen. du. m. of mind and *puruṣa*

sattva, mind, more precisely the faculty of discernment; attribute of *prakṛti* characterized by pure illumination; the most subtle essence of the manifest aspect of *prakṛti*; *puruṣa,* pure being; pure consciousness

śuddhi-sāmye

loc. sg. n. upon having equality in purity

śuddhi, purity; *sāmya,* state of equality or equanimity; quality of sameness

kaivalyam *nom. sg. n.* absoluteness; the finest spiritual experience that arises in the state of *nirbīja samādhi*

iti thus it concludes

APPENDIX C

Pronunciation and Transliteration Guide

Sanskrit letters form an organized arrangement of sounds, beginning with vowels and concluding with consonants. Each letter corresponds to only one sound. The following pronunciations are approximate, and it is helpful to listen to a recording of the alphabet for accuracy.

Vowels in Sanskrit are either short or long. In transliteration, a horizontal line placed over the short vowels (a, i, u, and ṛ) indicates lengthening. Diphthongs (e, ai, o, and au) are long and do not require a diacritical mark. When spoken, long vowels sound about twice as long as short vowels.

a	**a**bout
ā	f**a**ther
i	p**i**t
ī	k**ee**p

u suture
ū f**oo**d
ṛ **ri**d
ṝ **ree**d
e t**a**ble
ai **ai**sle
o t**o**te
au l**ou**d
aṁ nasalization of the preceding vowel (s**ung**)
aḥ a slight aspiration of the preceding vowel (**aha**)

Consonants fall into five classes, starting at the back of the throat and working forward to the lips. Each class is, in turn, divided into categories: unaspirated or aspirated, and a nasal sound.

1. The guttural consonants are pronounced from the back of the throat:
   k **k**id
   kh pac**kh**orse
   g **g**ive
   gh bi**gh**orn
   ṅ ri**ng**

2. The palatal consonants are pronounced from the soft palate:
   c **ch**ip
   ch pin**chh**it
   j **j**ump
   jh lod**geh**ouse
   ñ pi**ñ**ata

3. The cerebral (or retroflex) consonants are pronounced with the tip of the tongue contacting the roof of the mouth (a retroflex placement signified by a dot under the letter):

    ṭ **t**ar
    ṭh can'**t h**andle
    ḍ **d**art
    ḍh lan**dh**unter
    ṇ u**n**der

4. The dental consonants are pronounced with the tip of the tongue behind the upper row of teeth:

    t **t**ell
    th po**th**andle
    d **d**ot
    dh hea**dh**unter
    n **n**od

5. The labial consonants are pronounced with the lips:

    p **p**utt
    ph mo**ph**ead
    b **b**ut
    bh a**bh**or
    m **m**op

Semi-vowels narrow the stream of air, creating friction as the air passes through the mouth:

y **y**es
r **r**apid
l **l**ap
v halfway between w (**w**ow) and v (**v**ow)

Sibilants include two variants of sh. In practice, they sound about the same:

ś	**sh**ove
ṣ	**sh**allow
s	**s**unny
h	**h**ot

Glossary

abhinivesha Fear of death; the fifth and final affliction.

abhyasa The ardent effort to retain the peaceful flow of mind, free of roaming tendencies.

Aghora Marga A mystical path of tantra leading to the union of Shakti and Shiva. This path is popularly associated with Kaula tantra, and normally aspirants on this path appear unkempt. However, scriptural sources tell us that this is the most exalted path, one trodden by great adepts.

ahamkara The faculty of identification; the aspect of the mind that identifies itself with the objects of cognition.

ajna chakra The center of consciousness corresponding to the region in the center of the forehead; the command center; the center of thought and cognitive activities.

anahata chakra The heart center; the center of consciousness characterized by the experience of *anahata,* "unstruck" sound.

apavarga Ultimate freedom; the highest goal of life.

asmita Self-identity; the power of identification; the second of the five afflictions.

avastha Condition or state.

avastha parinama Transformation in condition.

avidya Ignorance; lack of awareness, or partial awareness, of our pure being; the first of the five afflictions and the mother of all afflictions.

bandha A yogic technique to restrain the mind and breath in a particular location in the body; the combined application of asana and pranayama to restrain the mind and breath in the selected location in the body.

bhoga Fulfillment; worldly experiences; sensory satisfaction.

bindu The central point of reference; in tantra and kundalini yoga, it refers to the concentrated field of energy in different chakras; the central point of reference in the most interior space of Sri Chakra.

bindu bhedana The process of penetrating bindu, the most concentrated energy field at the ajna chakra, anahata chakra, or manipura chakra.

brahma nadi The subtlest energy channel, which connects the ajna chakra to the sahasrara.

brahma rishi The highest-caliber enlightened master.

buddhi The faculty of discernment; the faculty of comprehension and inner illumination.

buddhi samvit The knowing power of buddhi, the faculty of discernment.

buddhi sattva The pure and pristine essence of buddhi; the essence of self-revealing power.

chakra Wheel of energy; center of consciousness in the body; space in the body characterized by highly concentrated prana.

chaturtha pranayama Literally, the "fourth pranayama"; a breathing practice characterized by the subtle flow of prana; the subject of sutra 2:51.

chiti shakti The knowing power of consciousness.

chitta The totality of the mind, particularly the aspect of the mind that serves as the locus for the entire range of our past experiences.

chitta dharana The concentration of the mind on the mind itself.

chitta samvit The knowing power of chitta.

deva Bright being; siddha master.

dharana Concentration; the sixth limb of ashtanga yoga.

dharma Defining qualities of a substance; quality; characteristic; intrinsic property.

dharma megha samadhi The transitional state between sabija and nirbija samadhi.

dharma parinama Transformation in defining attributes.

dharmi Substratum serving as a locus for its attributes.

Dhruva The pole star; the immutable space of consciousness.

dhyana Meditation; the seventh limb of ashtanga yoga.

divyakarana mudra A technique yogis apply to restrain the mind and prana in the region of the soft palate and channel the combined forces of mind and prana toward the sahasrara chakra. This mudra is accomplished mainly by placing the tip of the tongue on the hard palate and mentally becoming aware of the space in the region of the soft palate.

dvadashanta The space of consciousness twelve finger-widths above the fontanelle.

dvesha Aversion, the fourth of the five afflictions.

Ishvara The primordial divine being; the guru, guide, protector, and nurturer of all living beings.

Ishvara pranidhana Trustful surrender to Ishvara; the fifth of the five niyamas.

ishta mantra A mantra with which we have a personal affinity.

jiva The individual self or soul.

jyotishmati Inner luminosity; filled with light; endowed with light; accompanied by light; self-luminous meditative state; pranic luminosity.

kaivalya State characteritzed by the absence of everything other than the experience of consciousness; the highest goal of yoga.

kaya kalpa A system of rejuvenation.

kurma nadi The energy channel that originates at the perineum and travels all the way to the hollow of the throat.

lakshana Symptom; sign; indication.

lakshana parinama Transformation in symptom.

maha vyapti anusandhana The step-by-step practice of tracing prana from one location to another, ultimately becoming aware of prana pervading the entire body.

mahat The collective faculty of comprehension; the first step in the evolution of the phenomenal world.

manas The thinking mind.

manipura chakra The navel center; the center of the fire element.

marmasthana Vital point in the human body.

mudra A yogic and tantric technique to unleash prana shakti.

muladhara chakra The root center; the center of the earth element.

nadi Energy channel; pranic current.

nirbija samadhi Seedless samadhi; supreme spiritual absorption; the highest state of samadhi and the final goal of yoga.

nirodha samskaras Subtle impressions that impel the mind to remain confined to its object of focus; subtle impressions imbued with the power to restrain the mind in a well-defined time and space.

nivritti kala The pranic stream that releases our mind and consciousness from the fivefold affliction.

niyama Literally, "restraint"; the second of the eight limbs of yoga.

nyasa Bringing awareness to an identifiable spot and anchoring it there.

parakaya pravesha The process or act of entering another body.

pracchardana vidharana An advanced pranayama practice that burns deeply buried layers of contaminants while infusing the mind with vitality, clarity, and one-pointedness; the subject of sutra 1:34.

prajna Intuition; the self-luminous field of consciousness; the intrinsic property of a pure and pristine mind.

prakritilaya Dissolved in prakriti; a special category of yogi who dies while established in *asmita anugata samadhi* and thus reincarnates with her wisdom and experience intact.

pranava anusandhana A technqiue of making the mind follow the flow of the sound *om* in the body.

pranayama Expansion of prana; a practice for attaining mastery over prana shakti; the fourth limb of ashtanga yoga.

prapancha vyapti A yogic technique for training the mind to become aware of all the constituents of the body.

pratishtha kala The pranic stream that enables our mind and consciousness to become established in their own essence; the pranic stream that brings stability to our body, mind, and senses.

pratyahara Withdrawing the mind from the sensory realm and restraining it in an assigned space; the fifth limb of ashtanga yoga.

purashcharana Literally, "the first step." In mantra sadhana, a purashcharana consists of a time- and number-bound mantra practice.

purusha Pure consciousness; the knower.

raga Attachment; the third of the five afflictions.

rajas One of the three intrinsic attributes of primordial nature; the principle of pulsation.

sabija samadhi Samadhi with seeds.

sadhana A well-defined, structured method of spiritual practice.

sahasrara chakra The crown center; the center of consciousness transcending the physicality of the body.

samadhi A perfectly still, pristine state of mind; a state of mind free from all karmic impressions; a state in which no other cognition stands between the mind and the object of meditation; the eighth limb of ashtanga yoga.

samapatti Mental absorption; a mental state in which the mind is fully absorbed in the object of meditation.

samskara Subtle karmic impression

samvit The knowing power.

samyama Well-rounded discipline; term for the triad of dhyana, dharana, and samadhi.

sandhi Juncture.

sankalpa The power of intention.

sattva One of the three intrinsic attributes of primordial nature; the principle of illumination.

shanta kala The pranic stream that infuses the mind with patience and fortitude.

shuddha samvit The knowing power of pure consciousness; the pure and pristine knowing power of Ishvara's prakriti.

siddha A yogi of extraordinary accomplishment.

siddhi Extraordinary accomplishment.

Sri Chakra A geometrical design yogis employ for their ritualistic or meditative practices.

Sri Vidya A subset of tantra sadhana leading to experiencing the oneness of Shakti and Shiva.

sthana anusandhana Experiencing the presence of prana in different locations in the body and observing pranic movement from one location to another.

shuddha samvit The knowing power of pure consciousness.

svadhishthana chakra The pelvic center; the center of the water element.

svadhyaya Self-study; study of scriptures; contemplating on the meaning of mantra; the fourth of the five niyamas.

talu chakra The center of consciousness corresponding to the region of the soft palate.

taraka The liberator; the final destination of the meditative journey that begins with the state of vishoka.

tamas One of the three intrinsic attributes of primordial nature; the principle of inertia and darkness.

tanmatra Subtle element; literally, "that alone"; the subtlest state of evolution, which contains the potential for the world made of matter and energy.

vairagya Non-attachment; the intrinsic property of unsmearability.

vashikara Mastery; a fully controlled state of mind.

videha Beyond the body or transcendence of the body; a special category of yogi who dies firmly established in the experience of self-luminous joy and thus reincarnates with his knowledge and experience intact.

vidya kala The pranic stream that infuses the mind with intuitive knowledge.

vishoka Sorrowless joy; a blissful state untouched by anguish and remorse.

vishuddhi chakra The throat center; the center of the space element.

viveka khyati Unshakable discerning knowledge.

vritti samskara chakra The cycle of mental action to samskara and samskara to mental action.

yama The first of the eight limbs of ashtanga yoga.

Citation Index

Subject Index

unaffected by (udana), 219–221, 222
Brahma, 269, 270
brahma nadi, 163
brahma rishis, 80
brahmacharya (continence), 169
brahman (consciousness), 170
brahmanda, 174
brahmapura (city of brahman), body as, 170, 171
breathing techniques. *See also* pranayama
dharana, uniting mind and breath in, 88–89
exhalation and inhalation, 146–147
in meditation on ajna chakra/lotus of the heart, 178–179, 181–184, 188–190
opening of the nostrils, as doorway of the sun, 143, 144
pranic pulsation, breath as subtle counterpart of, 70
training mind to follow flow of, 116–117
Buddha, 128–129, 132, 133
Buddha gayatri, 132
buddhi (faculty of discernment), xiv
attributes of, 177
development of siddhis and, xvii
identification, power of, 82
meditation on the lotus of the heart and, 174, 176–177, 186
perceptual power and, 114–115, 116
prakriti, developing from, 81
samskaras affecting, 105
senses, effects of victory over, 250
buddhi samvit, xiv–xv, 176, 186
buddhi sattva, xv, 79–80, 114, 135, 177–178, 252

celestial beings and realms, 140–141, 149, 151
chakras
ajna chakra, 18, 20, 24, 25, 142, 159, 176–187, 189, 191–193
anahata chakra, 142
dharana/dhyana/samadhi and, 3, 25, 35, 60
knowledge and, 152–153, 155
manipura chakra, 148, 222–223
muladhara chakra, 142, 146, 147, 148
nabhi chakra, 158
pranic pulsation at, 173
sahasrara chakra, 124, 143, 147, 151, 152, 154, 162, 173–174, 192–193, 215, 220, 223, 234
svadhishthana chakra, 148
talu chakra, 24, 145, 186–190, 192, 194
vishuddhi chakra, 162
vritti samskara chakra, 74, 100
chakshusmati vidya, 119
chandra kala, 151
chasm of maya, crossing, 255–273. *See also* viveka jnana
absoluteness, 271–273
attachment and pride, avoidance of, 258–259
kaivalya, 255–257
taraka (liberation), 270
chaturtha pranayama, 12, 15–16, 18, 19
chesta (volition), 45
chhaya purusha (concentrating on one's own shadow), vii
chidakasha, 172
chit (consciousness), 171
chiti shakti (power of consciousness), 170, 255
chitta (totality of the mind), 10, 12, 82, 167–169, 200–201, 250
chitta dharana (concentration of mind on mind itself), 18–19
chitta prasadanam (purification of mind), 127

samyama on divinities and development of extraordinary power, 132–133
demonic beings, 140
descending pranic force (avaroha), 124
desirelessness (vashikara), 58, 229
devas, 80, 227
dharana (concentration), xii, xiii, 1–21
animal sounds, interpretation of, 99
bindu bhedana, practice of, 19–20
chaturtha pranayama, intensifying practice of, 12, 15–16, 18
chitta (totality of the mind), focused on, 10–12
chitta dharana, practice of, 18–19
dhyana as advanced stage of, 22–23, 117
etymology and definition, 1, 10
exterior limbs of ashtanga yoga leading to, 12–15, 17
grandeur of the mind, realizing power of, 2–8, 15, 20–21
as internal limb of ashtanga yoga, 8–10, 46
meditation on the lotus of the heart and, 194
one-pointedness of mind, path to, 14, 15, 69–70
parakaya pravesha and, 209–210
prajna and, 38
prana dharana, practice of, 16–17
pranic pulsation and, 17–19, 117
on precisely defined space, 14, 15, 17–18, 69–70, 117
pure consciousness, knowledge of, 198–199
purpose of, 14
samadhi beginning with, 88
samyama, as part of continuum of, 33–36 (*See also* samyama)
as sixth limb of ashtanga yoga, 6–8
transitioning to dhyana from, 23–24
uniting mind and breath in, 88–89
dharma, 45, 70, 77, 78–81, 87, 91–93, 101, 132, 177, 212
dharma megha (cloud of virtues), 52, 53
dharma megha samadhi, 52–54
dharma parinama, 74, 75–76, 77, 87
dharmi, 78–81, 101
Dhruva (pole star)
inability to see and nearness of death, 125
realm of siddha masters above, 163
samyama on pole star, knowledge of stars' movements from, 154–156
symbolism of, 155
dhyana (meditation), xii, 8, 22–27
as advanced stage of dharana, 22–23, 117
as internal limb of ashtanga yoga, 8–10, 46
meditation on the lotus of the heart and, 194
parakaya pravesha and, 209
pracchardana vidharana pranayama, 24–25
prajna and, 52
pranic pulsation and, 22–26, 117
pure consciousness, knowledge of, 199–200
samadhi, transitioning to, 26–32
samyama, as part of continuum of, 33–36 (*See also* samyama)
transitioning from dharana to, 23–24
dhyana mantras, 133
dhyata, 52
dhyeya, 52
dirghayutvan, 51
discernment
faculty of (*See* buddhi)
power of (viveka khyati), 7, 267
dispassion, absolute (para vairagya), 53, 256
distinctive denominator, 263, 264–265

distinctive knowledge. *See* viveka jnana
divine providence, viii–ix, 5
divyakarana mudra, 145–146, 188–189, 199
doorway of the sun and moon (surya dvara), 142–147, 150, 152, 154, 189, 193, 212, 259
dvadashanta. *See* twelve-finger-width space
dvesha (aversion), 6

effortlessness (prayatna shaithilya), 159
eight limbs of yoga (ashtanga yoga), xii–xiii, 6–10. *See also* dharana; dhyana; pranayama; samadhi
asana, xii, 7, 15, 33, 35, 44, 46, 48
internal and external limbs of, 8–10, 44–47
niyama, xii, 7, 14, 33, 44, 46, 48
pratyahara, xii–xiii, 7–8, 13, 15, 17–19, 33, 38, 44, 48
yama, xii, 7, 14, 33, 44, 46, 48
ekagrata parinama, 69
ekendriya, 58
elements, victory over (bhuta jaya)
bodily wealth arising from, 241, 243, 244–246
freedom from properties and functions of elements, leading to, 237–240
samyama on elements leading to, 237–240
elephant, strength of, 131–133
emotion and intellect, 107–109
enlightenment
as essence of Buddahood, 129
state of, 252–254
ethical issues
parakaya pravesha involving complex bodies, 214
sight of another, blocking, 118–119
experience, cognizance of, 263–265
extraordinary accomplishments. *See* siddhis
extrasensory powers
death, foretelling or predicting, vii, 120–126, 209
friendliness and related capacities, samyama on, 127–130
invisibility, 113–119
knowledge of subtle, obstructed, and distant objects (jyotishmati), 134–138
limitations of samyama on cognitions, 110–112
meditation on the lotus of the heart, intuitive senses arising from, 202–204
past, present, and future, knowledge of, xv, 21, 90–93, 106, 110, 194
prolonging or terminating life, 124
purpose of, 165, 205–206
realization of another person's cognition and mind, xi, xv, 107–112
strength and stamina, from samyama on powers, 131–133
eyebrow center (bhru-madhya), 16, 25, 89, 117, 118, 144, 178, 182, 183, 186, 198, 220
eyes
inner corners of, 16, 25, 89, 117, 144, 179, 182, 186, 198, 220
sensation of pressure on, in ajna chakra meditation, 184, 185
eyesight
blocking, 113–119
darshana shakti (seeing power), 173
freeing mind from dependence on, 187
intuitive, from meditation on the lotus of the heart, 202–204
limitations in/deformities of, as

prana manthana, 17, 158–159
prana samapatti, 71, 73–74, 192
prana samvedana, 17, 182
prana samyama, 17
prana sanchara, 182
prana sanchaya, 17, 182
prana shakti (life force)
  dharana/dhyana/samadhi and, viii, 25, 73
  extrasensory power and, 124
  four streams of, 146–147, 152, 192–194, 214–216
  knowledge and, 143–147, 152, 155, 159, 162
  meditation on the lotus of the heart and, 174, 192–194
  parakaya pravesha and eluding death, 211–216, 218, 219, 220, 226
  sadhana propelled by, 259
  udana and, 219–221
pranava, 19
pranava anusandhana, 19, 47
pranayama, xii–xiii, 7
  aharana pranayama, 16
  chaturtha pranayama, 12, 15–16, 18, 19
  dharana and, 12–13, 15–16, 19
  as external limb of ashtanga yoga, 44, 56
  meditation on the lotus of the heart and, 177
  navel plexus, samyama on, 158–159
  one-pointed mind, achieving, 33
  pracchardana vidharana pranayama, 24–25
  prajna and, 38
  samadhi and, 48
  samikarana pranayama, 16
  in tantric tradition, 35
  vision of siddhas, 163
pranic field, 12, 24, 25, 29–32, 34, 38, 41, 42, 179, 187
pranic flow, 47, 116, 146, 161, 193, 204, 207
pranic force, 17, 50, 73, 117, 123, 124, 158, 185, 193–194
pranic pulsation
  breath as subtle counterpart of, 70
  chitta samvit's absorption in, 238
  dharana and, 17–19, 117
  dhyana and, 22–26, 117
  as direct manifestation of divine will, 49, 53
  importance of sensitivity to, 71
  intuitive light, emergence of, 164
  jyotishmati and, 135
  mahavideha and, 233, 234
  meditation on the lotus of the heart and, 173, 178–185, 187, 192, 194, 199–201
  mental quietude and, 143
  parakaya pravesha and, 209, 217
  prajna (intuitive wisdom), emergence of, 38
  prana samapatti and, 73, 74
  prapancha vyapti anusandhana and, 117–118
  pure consciousness, knowledge of, 199–201
  samadhi and, 28–31, 117
  samyama and, 34, 42, 49, 50, 52, 53, 135
  shantyatita and, 147
  sthana anusandhana and, 118
pranic thrust (vayu-vikshepa), 154
prapancha vyapti anusandhana, 47, 117–118, 137
prapti, 242
prashanta vahita (peaceful flow of mind), 62–64
pratibha. *See* intuition
pratibha-jnana (intuitive light/intu-

shayanam, 52
Shiva, 4, 269
Shiva Sankalpa Sukta, 2, 126
shoka, 17
Shrestha, 251
shuddha samvit, 174, 175, 180, 250, 256
shuddhi-samya, 273
siddha medicine, 244
Siddha tradition, 35, 152
siddhas
  dharma and dharmi, relationship between, 80
  Ishvara, compared to, 269
  space, power of moving through, 227
  svadhyaya (self-study) and, 169
  vision of, from samyama on light of the crown, 160–163
siddhis (extraordinary accomplishments), vii–ix, xi–xvii. *See also* elements, victory over; extrasensory powers; immortality; parakaya pravesha
  buddhi sharpened by development of, xvii
  defined, xi–xii
  hearing, extraordinary power of, 224–226
  internal limbs of ashtanga yoga and, 45
  invisibility, 113–119
  kaya kalpa and, 245
  meditation on the lotus of the heart and awakening of, xiv–xvi
  moving through space, extraordinary power of, 227–231
  non-attachment to, 255–259
  purpose of, 165, 205–206, 272
sight. *See* eyesight
smell (gandha)
  elements, samyama on/victory over, 240
  gandha samvit, 204
  intuitive, 202–204
smoke hanging above head, sense of, 125
soft palate. *See* talu
soma (indivisible moon), 151–152
sopakrama, 121–124
space
  ananta samapatti (absorption in the inner space), 159
  body and, samyama on relationship between, 227–231
  defined, 228
  hearing and, samyama on relationship between, 224–226
  mahavideha (cognition of space outside the body), 212–213, 232–236
  power of moving in, 227–231
sparsha dharana, 229
sparsha samvit, 204
spheres of existence, samyama on sun and knowledge of, 139–150, 189
spinal cord, 142, 154
spiritual transparency (adhyatma-prasada), 200
spontaneous combustion, 222–223
Sri Chakra, 151
Sri Krama tradition, 89
Sri Vidya, ix, 152
Sri Vidya mantra, 136
Sri Vidya tradition
  bindu in, 151
  doorway of the sun in, 142–143
  inner moon in, 152
  kaya kalpa in, 244
  meditation on the lotus of the heart in, 170
  navel plexus, samyama on, 158
  obstacles to curbing undesirable samskaras, techniques for overcoming, 59–60
  samyama and, 36
  samyama on sun and knowledge of

PANDIT RAJMANI TIGUNAIT, PHD, is a modern-day master and living link in the unbroken Himalayan Tradition. He embodies the yogic and tantric wisdom which the Himalayan Tradition has safeguarded for thousands of years. Pandit Tigunait is the successor of Sri Swami Rama of the Himalayas and the spiritual head of the Himalayan Institute. As a young man he committed himself to arduous spiritual practice and studied with renowned adepts of India before being initiated into the lineage of the Himalayan Tradition by his master, Sri Swami Rama, in 1976.

Pandit Tigunait is fluent in Vedic and Classical Sanskrit and holds two doctorates, one from the University of Allahabad (India), and another from the University of Pennsylvania. As a leading voice of YogaInternational.com and the author of 18 books, his teachings span a wide range, from scholarly analysis and scripture translation to practical guidance on applying yogic wisdom to modern life. Over the past 35 years, Pandit Tigunait has touched innumerable lives around the world as a teacher, guide, author, humanitarian, and visionary spiritual leader.

HIMALAYAN INSTITUTE®

The main building of the Himalayan Institute headquarters near Honesdale, Pennsylvania

The Himalayan Institute

A leader in the field of yoga, meditation, spirituality, and holistic health, the Himalayan Institute is a nonprofit international organization dedicated to serving humanity through educational, spiritual, and humanitarian programs. The mission of the Himalayan Institute is to inspire, educate, and empower all those who seek to experience their full potential.

Founded in 1971 by Swami Rama of the Himalayas, the Himalayan Institute and its varied activities and programs exemplify the spiritual heritage of mankind that unites East and West, spirituality and science, ancient wisdom and modern technology.

Our international headquarters is located on a beautiful 400-acre campus in the rolling hills of the Pocono Mountains of northeastern Pennsylvania. Our spiritually vibrant community and peaceful setting provide the perfect atmosphere for seminars and retreats, residential programs, and holistic health services. Students from all over the world join us to attend diverse programs on subjects such as hatha yoga, meditation, stress reduction, ayurveda, and yoga and tantra philosophy.

In addition, the Himalayan Institute draws on roots in the yoga tradition to serve our members and community through the following programs, services, and products.

Mission Programs

The essence of the Himalayan Institute's teaching mission flows from the timeless message of the Himalayan Masters, including its founder, Swami Rama, and is echoed in our on-site and online mission programming: first we need to become aware of the reality within ourselves, and then we need to build a bridge between our inner and outer worlds. We seek to bring you the best of an authentic tradition, distilled for the modern seeker.

Our mission programs express a rich body of experiential wisdom, focused on yoga and meditation practice and philosophy, including our flagship Vishoka Meditation offerings. In-person mission programs are offered year-round at our campus in Honesdale, Pennsylvania, and include seminars, retreats, and teacher training certification programs.

The Institute is also a leader in hybrid in-person/online education. It offers a wide range of live online courses and certification programs, as well as on-demand digital courses. Join us in person or online to find wisdom from the heart of the yoga tradition, guidance for authentic practice, and a vibrant global community of like-minded seekers.

Wisdom Library and Mission Membership

The Himalayan Institute's online Wisdom Library curates the essential teachings of the living Himalayan Tradition. This offering is a unique counterpart to our in-person Mission Programs, empowering students by providing online learning resources to enrich their study and practice outside the classroom.

Our online Wisdom Library features multimedia blog content, livestreams, podcasts, yoga classes, meditation and relaxation practices, wellness content, and downloadable practice resources. These teachings capture our Mission Faculty's decades of study, practice, and teaching experience, featuring new content as well as the timeless teachings of Swami Rama and Pandit Rajmani Tigunait.

We invite seekers and students of the Himalayan Tradition to become a Himalayan Institute Mission Member, which grants unlimited access to the Wisdom Library. Mission Membership supports the Institute's global humanitarian efforts, while helping you deepen your study and practice in the living Himalayan Tradition.

Spiritual Excursions

Since 1972, the Himalayan Institute has been organizing pilgrimages throughout India and Nepal. Our spiritual excursions follow the traditional pilgrimage routes where adepts of the Himalayas lived and practiced. For thousands of years, pilgrimage has been an essential part of yoga sadhana, offering spiritual seekers the opportunity to experience the transformative power of living shrines of the Himalayan Tradition. Join us on pilgrimage in the Himalayas, or for retreat offerings at the Himalayan Institute Khajuraho campus in central India.

Global Humanitarian Projects

The Himalayan Institute's humanitarian mission is yoga in action—offering spiritually grounded healing and transformation to the world. Our humanitarian projects serve rural communities in India and Cameroon through education and literacy initiatives, health services, and vocational training. By putting yoga philosophy into practice, our programs are empowering communities globally with the knowledge and tools needed for a lasting social transformation at the grassroots level.

Publications

The Himalayan Institute publishes over 60 titles on yoga, philosophy, spirituality, science, ayurveda, and holistic health. These include the best-selling books Living with the Himalayan Masters and The Science of Breath by Swami Rama; Vishoka Meditation, Sri Sukta, and two commentaries on the Yoga Sutra: The Secret of the Yoga Sutra: Samadhi Pada and The Practice of the Yoga Sutra: Sadhana Pada by Pandit Rajmani Tigunait, PhD; and the award-winning Yoga: Mastering the Basics by Sandra Anderson and Rolf Sovik, PsyD. These books are for everyone: the interested reader, the spiritual novice, and the experienced practitioner.

PureRejuv Wellness Center

For over 40 years, the PureRejuv Wellness Center has fulfilled part of the Institute's mission to promote healthy and sustainable lifestyles. PureRejuv combines Eastern philosophy and Western medicine in an integrated approach to holistic health—nurturing balance and healing at home and at work. We offer the opportunity to find healing and renewal through on-site and online wellness retreats and individual wellness services, including therapeutic massage and bodywork, yoga therapy, ayurveda, biofeedback, natural medicine, and one-on-one consultations with our integrative medical staff.

Total Health Products

The Himalayan Institute, the developer of the original Neti Pot, manufactures a health line specializing in traditional and modern ayurvedic supplements and body care. We are dedicated to a holistic and sustainable lifestyle by providing products that use natural, non-GMO ingredients and eco-friendly packaging. Part of every purchase supports our global humanitarian projects, further developing and reinforcing our core mission of spirituality in action.

Residential Service Programs

Karma yoga (selfless service) is at the heart of the Institute's mission, and is embodied by the Himalayan Institute Residential Program and the SEVA Work-Study Program offered at our Honesdale campus. Learn more about residential service opportunities on our website, and join a vibrant community of practitioners dedicated to service.

For further information about our programs, humanitarian projects, and products:

call:	800-822-4547
email:	info@HimalayanInstitute.org
write:	Himalayan Institute 952 Bethany Turnpike Honesdale, PA 18431
or visit:	HimalayanInstitute.org

The Secret of the Yoga Sutra
Samadhi Pada

Pandit Rajmani Tigunait, PHD

The *Yoga Sutra* is the living source wisdom of the yoga tradition, and is as relevant today as it was 2,200 years ago when it was codified by the sage Patanjali. Using this ancient yogic text as a guide, we can unlock the hidden power of yoga, and experience the promise of yoga in our lives. By applying its living wisdom in our practice, we can achieve the purpose of life: lasting fulfillment and ultimate freedom.

Paperback, 6" x 9", 331 pages
$24.95, ISBN 978-0-89389-277-7

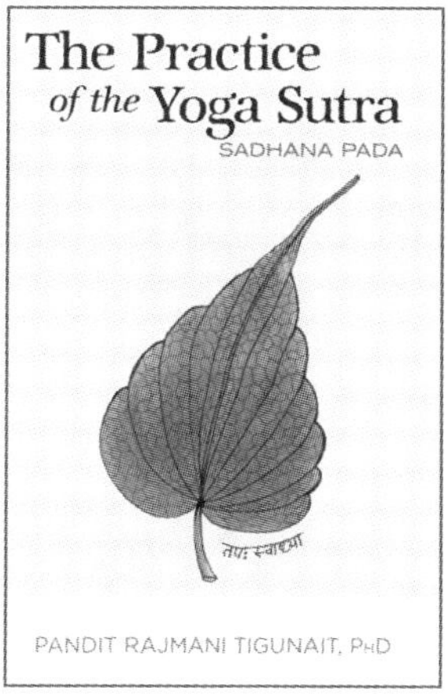

The Practice of the Yoga Sutra
Sadhana Pada

Pandit Rajmani Tigunait, PHD

In Pandit Tigunait's practitioner-oriented commentary series, we see this ancient text through the filter of scholarly understanding and experiential knowledge gained through decades of advanced yogic practices. Through *The Secret of the Yoga Sutra* and *The Practice of the Yoga Sutra*, we receive the gift of living wisdom he received from the masters of the Himalayan Tradition, leading us to lasting happiness.

Paperback, 6" x 9", 389 Pages
$24.95, ISBN 978-0-89389-279-1

800-822-4547
shop@HimalayanInstitute.org
HimalayanInstitute.org

HIMALAYAN INSTITUTE®

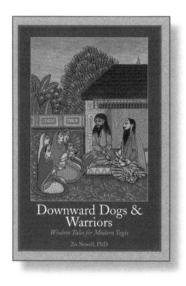

Flying Monkeys, Floating Stones

Wisdom Tales from the Ramayana for Modern Yogis

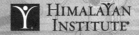

Through the lenses of art and asana, this book presents stories and images from the *Ramayana,* the epic narrative of the life of Rama, one of the most beloved aspects of the divine in all of Indian history. As a parable of the spiritual journey, the *Ramanayana* is a story about the division between distracted consciousness and the Self, and a guide to what we must do to reunite with our own inner Self. Each of us has our individual path to the divine, and an inner *Ramayana* unfolds in each of us.

In the hands of Zo Newell, an accomplished practitioner and religious scholar, the story of Rama and his abducted wife, Sita, reveals elements of the human psyche; and with images and selected asanas, we are invited to experience the age-old journey to wholeness.

"It is my hope that the stories and practices in this book will speak to you through your body and your senses as well as your mind, and allow you a glimpse of their reality."